The Department Chair
As Academic Leader

The Department Chair As Academic Leader

by
Irene W.D. Hecht
Mary Lou Higgerson
Walter H. Gmelch
Allan Tucker

AMERICAN COUNCIL ON EDUCATION ★
ORYX PRESS ★
Series on Higher Education
1999

The rare Arabian Oryx is believed to have inspired the myth of the unicorn. This desert antelope became virtually extinct in the early 1960s. At that time several groups of international conservationists arranged to have 9 animals sent to the Phoenix Zoo to be the nucleus of a captive breeding herd. Today the Oryx population is over 1,000 and over 500 have been returned to the Middle East.

© 1999 by The American Council on Education and The Oryx Press
Published by The Oryx Press
4041 North Central at Indian School Road
Phoenix, Arizona 85012-3397

Published simultaneously in Canada
Printed and Bound in the United States of America

∞ The paper used in this publication meets the minimum requirements of American National Standard for Information Science—Permanence of Paper for Printed Library Materials, ANSI Z39.48, 1984.

Library of Congress Cataloging-in-Publication Data

The department chair as academic leader / by Irene W.D. Hecht ... [et al.].
    p. cm. — (American Council on Education/Oryx Press series on higher education)
    Includes bibliographical references and index.
    ISBN 1-57356-134-7 (alk. paper)
    1. Departmental chairmen (Universities)—United States.
    2. Universities and colleges—United States—Departments.
    3. Educational leadership—United States. 4. Universities and colleges—United States—Administration. I. Hecht, Irene W. D., 1932– . II. Series.
    LB2341.D414 1999
    378.1'11—dc21   98-36050
                                                                          CIP

CONTENTS

FOREWORD

A friend of mine called recently to say that she had been tapped to chair her department. "I guess it was my turn," she told me. "I was released from two courses and have a nice letter from the dean. 'Good luck,' it says. 'My door is always open.'"

The Department Chair as Academic Leader, I told my friend, is the book you need. It covers just about every topic that will land on your desk, gives good advice on how to approach each one, and then provides lists of articles for further reading. Read it through, I advised; use it first to understand better the role you are assuming, then to set your agenda.

My own sense of the department chair's role has changed over time. I used to think there was such a thing as "institutional morale," for example. Hundreds of campus visits later I've come to see that—just as "all politics is local"—on most campuses there are in fact dozens of microenvironments with sharply divergent cultures: good-spirited, productive departments coexist alongside dysfunctional ones. As a faculty member once explained to me, "When we go to work in the morning, we go to our department." And more often than not, the morale—the tone of life in a department—is a mirror of its chair.

Therefore, my friend as chair should cultivate, above all, the department's quality of life and tend to its culture and morale, while taking special notice of her abilities to convene, reward, and celebrate.

This book goes to some length to make a case for the importance of chairs in institutional life. I suspect many readers—chairs in place—already knew that. What strikes me most, however, is the sheer range of responsibilities chairs take on today. When I first taught, a generation ago, my department chair seemed to take care of schedules, student problems, library ordering, letters of recommendation, and meeting with the dean once or twice a semester. But look through the chapters of this book; now the chair is supposed to be a strategic planner, master of budgets, personnel whiz, shrewd marketer, and external diplomat. Chairs in the 1960s didn't deal with assessment, computers, diversity, distance learning, union contracts, and book-length employment regulations.

As chair you will never be able to do all these new things alone. If the department lacks capabilities in assessment, for example, find two or three members willing to take that on as a professional endeavor and invest in this training. It also pays to cultivate special relationships with key administrative specialists—with a smart personnel officer and a savvy budget expert, for example, and with indispensable colleagues in student affairs, information technology, and the library. Get to know especially well any person who assigns space: classrooms, offices, and parking assignments can be fighting issues!

At the same time, take advantage of professional development opportunities to study two or three of these issues in depth yourself. Of all the topics you could possibly learn more about, probably none is so crucial to shaping the department now and for the long run as the personnel function. Half or more of this book—all of the material on faculty and staff hiring, promotion and tenure decisions, faculty development, and so on—has to do with your role in attracting, coaching, motivating, reviewing, and rewarding people. What do you do with an alcoholic staff member? A balky search committee? A faculty member who won't retire? On all these fronts you will want to be as surefooted as possible.

Today's reality, underscored by this book, is that there are so many things to which a chair needs to pay attention, and that prompts the next observation: Good chairs have an agenda. Every topic raised in this book at one time or another will demand your attention, but you can't master them all. Time is finite, so choices have to be made. Granted, part of your agenda goes with the job (seeing students); some of it is situational (addressing problems as they arise); some of it will come from above or outside (responding to directives by senior administrators or accreditors). But effective chairs set aside time for issues of their own. They have ideas about what the department needs and what impact they want to make, and they organize to achieve their goals.

I've seen chairs, then, devote extraordinary efforts over time to improving teaching and advising within their department, or to advancing curricular issues, diversity, or faculty development. They came to know those topics in depth. They marshaled a critical mass of colleagues' support for the issues, used the influence they had in personnel and budgeting to advance them, and in time changed the character of the department in intended ways.

What is the right agenda for you? As a new chair you should look to your own abilities and dispositions for an agenda that is authentic to you, one that will inspire genuine effort and bring professional satisfaction.

The agenda you set might well have elements both large and small. On the small side, keep in mind the many smart things Hecht, Higgerson, Gmelch, and Tucker say about keeping the departmental wheels greased: Get schedules out on time, distribute agendas before meetings, make sure the photocopier works. It's the "Mayor Daley" rule of governance: First and above all, people want their garbage picked up, the snow plowed, and their streetlights to work. Deftness in small things breeds confidence about larger agendas.

Whatever larger agendas you choose to pursue, a relevant if seldom discussed power you hold is the influence you can exert over departmental conversation. You exercise that power, for example, by calling faculty meetings at which you can raise topics, introduce evidence, and bring in guest presenters; chairs can also sponsor day-long symposia, hold retreats, convene brown-bag lunches, support faculty travel to meetings, and so on. To whatever extent these convenings can have a consistency of theme and a positive, scholarly tone, a stage is set for the change you want to bring about.

One of the best devices for the care and feeding of departmental conversation turns out to be assessment—an activity your department will have to carry out in any case, either for accreditors or a state board. The power of assessment lies in its ability to put evidence on the table that compels discussion: How do our majors perform on certification exams? What level of writing and thought shows up in senior exams? Are we happy with the amount of time and effort our students devote to their courses? Practitioners say that some of the most powerful assessment is that done by departmental faculty themselves, through focus groups of majors, senior interviews, or team readings of student portfolios, for example.

A good way to keep departmental conversations "honest" is to include students in them. It is worth noting that whatever the limits of a chair's powers over faculty, that influence is far less ambiguous when it comes to students, who often see the chair as an authority figure and will respond to the chair's invitations. Further, a characteristic of a learning-oriented department is that its students are actively involved in its life and join in creating learning opportunities for themselves—an impulse that you as chair might want to nurture.

Finally, let me mention again the endnotes to each chapter in this book, which are brief but suggestive. In some instances, you may need to read more deeply, and a good reference librarian will be able to direct you to additional sources quickly. Many new chairs have had little reason before coming to the role to pay much heed to the formal literature on higher education. But there are indeed resources that can prove invaluable when you need help, including research literature (on the effectiveness of certain pedagogies or the validity of course evaluations, for example), practitioner literature (the do's and don'ts of searches or how to conduct post-tenure reviews), and periodical literature concentrated on current developments (*The Chronicle of Higher Education* and *Change*, for example).

Such resources can deepen and extend the rationale that brought you to this book: to learn from those who have gone before and to build knowledge for the choices you'll make. To the dean's "good luck," let me add a sincere "thank you" for the commitment you have made to the people you serve.

Ted Marchese, vice president, American Association
for Higher Education, and executive editor, Change

INTRODUCTION

I n 1981 the American Council on Education published the first edition of
Chairing the Academic Department: Leadership among Peers, by Allan Tucker,
a volume that has stood alone as the only comprehensive text on the
important issue of leading the academic department. While there has been
intense interest in the subject of leadership in American society, the bulk of
that interest as manifested within higher education has focused on the roles of
presidents and chief academic officers. Writing 18 years ago, Tucker had the
foresight and insight to perceive that department chairs were, indeed, academic leaders. He was also well aware that the leadership function of chairs
was unusual. Lodged in hierarchical institutions, chairs exercised leadership
among colleagues who perceived themselves as every bit as important, intelligent, and capable as their presumed leaders. Tucker also had a thorough grasp
of the complexity of chairs' responsibilities. Other designated leaders in higher
education are assigned particular, defined responsibilities. Department chairs
play all functions from the menial to the managerial to the inspirational, and
most of them do all that while still maintaining a presence in the classroom.
Tucker ably described all those duties. For nearly 18 years Tucker's text has
continued to hold a unique position for both its perceptivity and the comprehensive sweep of its content.

Allan Tucker supervised a reissue with revisions in 1984. However, he died
in 1992 before the third edition appeared in that same year. During his lifetime
Tucker may have been something of a voice in the wilderness in proclaiming
department chairs to be leaders. However, the intensity and the nature of the
challenges now facing higher education have sharpened and narrowed the

cone of vision to focus on what transpires within the principal unit of the university, namely, the disciplinary program or department. It should be no surprise then that our conceptions regarding the position of department chair are in a process of rapid evolution. The fact that in the 1990s we have seen a growing number of volumes devoted specifically to the responsibilities of chairs is a good indication of changes in perspective regarding the roles and importance of chairs. However, the new volumes that began to appear in the 1990s did not attempt the broad focus of *Chairing the Academic Department.* Instead, these authors were interested in more specific questions, or they pursued particular interpretations. For example, John W. Cresswell's *The Academic Chairperson's Handbook* (1990) spoke specifically to the prospective chair, beginning with a self-assessment instrument to help determine his or her readiness for this challenging position. From there the volume examined a variety of leadership issues that are important to chairs, including improving teaching and encouraging scholarship. Much of the content is presented through notes elicited from experienced chairs in response to questions posed by Cresswell and his colleagues. As implied in the word "handbook," the volume is designed to perform as a personal tool kit, helping chairs assess their capabilities and furnishing a practical, conceptual, and spiritual guide to the issues of chairing a department.

Two years later, in 1992, Mark Hickson's and Don W. Stacks's volume, *Effective Communication for Academic Chairs,* appeared. These authors were looking for the core talent that any chair must possess to be optimally effective. Their answer was that deft communication constituted the make-or-break skill. Regardless of the task, it is the relative proficiency in communicating that will separate the ept from the inept chair.

In 1993 Gmelch's and Miskin's *Leadership Skills for Department Chairs* was added to the chair bookshelf.[1] This volume sought to explore the essence of the chair's responsibilities, which the authors defined in terms of four major roles: faculty developer, manager, leader, and scholar. In calling attention to the chair's responsibility for faculty career development, Gmelch and Miskin (1993, 10–11) highlighted the faculty as the department's major resource and emphasized the chair's responsibility for enhancing the human talent of the department. In envisioning the chair as a leader, Gmelch and Miskin further emphasized the chair's responsibility to people, but this time in a collective sense. They also stated that the concept of leader implied the importance of fostering a sense of mission within the department. It is not sufficient to complete ministerial tasks. The chair must also nurture a mutual understanding of purpose within the department. By including the role of manager, the authors acknowledged that one part of a chair's role is, indeed, to keep order in the administrative life of the department. In retaining the role of scholar as another aspect of the chair's life, Gmelch and Miskin reminded us that chairs continue to be faculty members and that they must purposefully nurture that segment of their lives.

The emphasis on humanistic personal skills is picked up from a different angle in Ann Lucas's *Strengthening Leadership: A Team-Building Guide for Chairs in Colleges and Universities* (1994). Lucas focused on the human challenge of being a department chair, defined as that of finding the means to motivate faculty, whether to enhance productivity, improve teaching, increase scholarship, or augment service. A major component of the chair's role, according to Lucas, is the ability to create a favorable department atmosphere, whether by creating a supportive communication climate or by managing conflict.

The appearance of these volumes from different presses, virtually simultaneously, is a good indication that publishers are seeing the subject of chairing departments as currently marketable. But the modest increase in quantity is not the only discernible change. More intriguing is the change in focus that is taking place. While the works of Creswell and colleagues, Gmelch and Miskin, and Lucas looked at the world of the chair within the department, other volumes have begun to look at the role of the chair as part of a larger institutional nexus. The shift in direction may have been heralded by Green's and McDade's *Investing in Higher Education: A Handbook of Leadership Development* (1992). This volume, which looked at leadership comprehensively within universities, is noteworthy for including department chairs in that discussion. This is perhaps our earliest indication of a perspective that saw the department chair as a component in the leadership structure of American colleges and universities.

Two volumes authored in part or in whole by Mary Lou Higgerson explored the work of chairs through case studies, all of which portray dilemmas that require chairs to struggle with interests beyond the confines of the department. The first of these, Higgerson's and Rehwaldt's *Complexities of Higher Education Administration* (1993), created a case book with materials that, while they involve chairs, cannot be handled without working with constituencies beyond the department. Higgerson's later volume, *Communication Skills for Department Chairs* (1996), on the other hand, uses chairs as the principal protagonists. The cases illustrate the importance of deft communication in solving problems. The audience, however, reaches beyond the department. What is special to both these volumes is that chairs appear within complex— and very realistic—cases involving the gamut of institutional actors. Readers coming from different institutional positions can find the cases challenging. The important point is that chairs are seen as part of an institution-wide leadership nexus.

What is happening is that the department chair, whom we once saw as a minor figure lodged at the bottom of the organizational pyramid, is now perceived to be a member of the institutional leadership team. The defining description of this phenomenon has been provided by the Pew Charitable Trusts' *Policy Perspectives* (1996). Here we find the department described as "the principal agent for the purposeful recasting of American higher education." Although this provocative, seminal article never mentions the chair, speaking only of the importance of the collective entity, the department, its assertions inevitably imply that the work of the chair is different in importance and dimension from anything we have contemplated previously.

Another step in this process of redefinition is John B. Bennett's *Collegial Professionalism* (1998). Bennett's contribution is his analysis of the sources of collegial disintegration—which others have deplored and even tried to map, and for which he seeks some cures. Bennett proffers two models for campus life: one is characterized by what he describes as "insistent individualism," the other by what he terms "relationality." While all participants in college or university life can make a positive contribution to "relationality," if this transformation is to occur within an institution, most of the work will have to take place at the department level. That clearly makes the fostering of "relationality" a task for chairs.

In readdressing the topic of chairing the academic department, this volume has two purposes. First, it seeks to retain and build upon the comprehensive approach developed by Allan Tucker in 1981, and, second, it seeks to include new content and perspectives. A straight reissue of Tucker's text would not serve current needs. The context of higher education has undergone such a profound metamorphosis that it is imperative to bring in new content and perspectives. Even in so doing, change continues at such a pace that in attempting to write a comprehensive book on this subject we are aiming at a moving target. So in retaining Tucker's broad vision while bringing in both new content and perspectives, we do so in the full realization that the wisdom of today will be revised and augmented in the future.

Tucker was ahead of his time in seeing department chairs as leaders. However, chairs today are not just leaders among their peers, which is how Tucker described their role. Their responsibilities have multiplied in number and expanded in compass. Chairs are not only leaders within their departments; they are also academic leaders within and, at times, even beyond their institutions. Our institutions are now catching up with this insight, and there is growing appreciation for the importance of the chair's leadership function. A major goal of *The Department Chair as Academic Leader* is to examine the leadership functions of department chairs in the light of the new issues, perspectives, and practices affecting higher education.

In the past the chair's focus was primarily internal. Emphasis was on the governance of the department, the interests and needs of faculty predominantly as individuals, and the general task of advocacy *vis-a-vis* "the administration." Tucker's discussion was affected by that time and vision and emphasized the chair's relations with faculty and dean. The realities of higher education in the 1990s is causing us to place greater weight on the collective work of the department and interdisciplinarity, if not as a substitute, at least as a counterweight to the earlier emphasis on accomplishments of faculty as individuals. Concurrently, departments are being pushed to be aware of their existence within an institution. Again, this is not an either-or situation. Departments are not expected to look exclusively externally, but they are expected to understand better how they fit into a larger picture.

Chairs' responsibilities are more complex than they were when the last edition of *Chairing the Academic Department* was published. Even a decade ago, when we spoke of faculty we had in mind full-time tenured or tenure track individuals. The work environment now includes an army of part-time adjunct and non-tenurable, full-time faculty. Chairs' budget responsibilities are being expanded with the advent of responsibility center budgeting or the process of decentralizing budgets. Chairs are expected to evidence some expertise in planning and even in fund-raising.

Even the familiar world of the classroom is undergoing change. Curriculum and pedagogy demand leadership attention. The content of the curriculum in some institutions has become a battleground. For any institution curriculum is an ongoing concern as knowledge expands exponentially and students create new demands for instruction. As for pedagogy, one of the creative areas of American higher education has been the proliferation of new teaching methods, a situation that is now being profoundly affected by the possibilities of applying technology to teaching.

Were Allan Tucker still alive, he would undoubtedly have carried out a fourth revision of his defining work. His name is associated with this text not only as a tribute to his seminal contribution to the study of department chairs, but also in view of the fact that portions of the text from his third edition appear in *The Department Chair as Academic Leader*. However, the organization and orientation of this new volume has changed markedly. While Tucker's third edition was divided into 13 parts, this volume is divided into four functional topics reflecting the major components of any chair's work. Part I sets the stage by describing the new geography chairs face, followed by a general discussion of their responsibilities.

Part II is concerned with department chairs' work with people. The educational enterprise is a human-focused endeavor. However, there are particular responsibilities that go with this segment of any chair's job. Chairs must be prepared to be comprehensive in their view of who their constituents are. These include all the members of the department: faculty, both full-time and part-time; students of varying ages and races; and the department staff. All these human beings need to be the chair's concern. The chair must give attention to renewing these constituencies through recruitment. S/he needs to manage the workload of the faculty, a task that has become much more complicated than it was 10 or 20 years ago. As ever, chairs must evaluate faculty and staff, but evaluating does not end with summative judgment. It must also include interest in the professional development of those individuals.

All chairs also have operational responsibilities for the department, which is the focus of part III. The operational changes are significant. Emerging in importance is the chair's ability to knit together all the members of the department to function effectively on a collective basis. This emphasis on building the work of the group is a new phenomenon for many departments and their chairs. It is an emphasis that impacts the way chairs manage curriculum development. Just as the chair needs to knit together the people of the department, s/he must lead those individuals in creating a viable, coordinated curriculum as opposed to a collection of interesting courses. Operationally, chairs are facing some of their most daunting new responsibilities in both budgeting and planning.

Part IV explores the chair's roles and responsibilities in connecting with audiences beyond the department. The most important external person for the chair is the dean, with whom it is important to develop a sound collaborative relationship. Here we seek to suggest some ways of bridging the chasm that exists too often in higher education between the administration and the faculty. Avoiding problems is also part of the chair's job, which is treated in the chapter on legal issues. While assessing the department may seem like an internal issue, the shape of assessment is largely being set externally today. Hence that topic is treated in part IV. Finally, we look at a variety of external audiences with whom chairs may be either required or compelled to interact.

Another change we have introduced is in the voicing of the text. Much of the time we seek to speak directly to chairs about their work in the most immediate manner possible. Our desire is to connect as closely as possible with the concerns and responsibilities of today's chairs. In so doing we recognize the difficulty presented by the diversity of institutional types that make up the American postsecondary system. Procedures vary among community colleges and baccalaureate institutions. Size impacts the organizational systems of institutions even when they fall into similar categories. The American idiosyncrasy of private and public universities, which has greatly enriched our postsecondary system, adds yet another variation. Research universities have special concerns, such as in the area of the ethics of research—which may not affect institutions focused on teaching of undergraduates. Yet another institutional type is the proprietary school, a sector that is in a period of rapid expansion. Therefore, while speaking as directly as possible to chairs, we also seek to frame our comments as generically as possible, with the understanding that chairs will need to adjust our observations to make them applicable to the variations in their individual settings.

The new realities of departmental life have also led to a shift in emphasis from the concerns of faculty as individuals to a focus on collective accomplishment. That reorientation is perhaps most pronounced when we look at the issue of assessing the department in chapter 13. However, it is an underlying theme throughout the volume. This shift in vision has largely been propelled by outside constituencies that are clamoring for institutional accountability in ways that can be met only by looking at group results. But we think the change is also reflective of a general change in perspective that has made us much more aware of the connections between individuals and the dynamics of their interactions.

We should also say a word about the references. It has not been our purpose to create a scholarly bibliography. Aside from documenting references used in the chapter text, our purpose has been to provide suggestions to chairs who may wish to pursue a particular subject in further detail. With rare exceptions, we have not cited any work earlier than 1990, the goal being to pick up recent thinking.

Despite significant changes in organization and emphasis, this work owes much to Allan Tucker's leadership. Like many insightful people, Tucker saw early what others failed to see. In his case, he comprehended the importance of the role of the department chair long before it was generally recognized within higher education. What we believe we have added is an extension of the horizon to encompass a world Tucker was not privileged to see. Our best hope is that, like the preceding volumes, this one will prove itself helpful to the work of higher education's unacknowledged leaders—the 80,000 department chairs who help keep the enterprise humming.

NOTES

1. Gmelch and Miskin also published *Chairing an Academic Department* in 1995, in which they add further detail on carrying out the obligations of the four roles of chair described in their earlier volume.

REFERENCES

Bennett, John B. 1998. *Collegial Professionalism: The Academy, Individualism, and the Common Good.* Phoenix: American Council on Education/Oryx.
   A number of observers have commented on the disintegration of collegiality on campuses. Bennett provides an analytic framework for those observations from which he builds two models; one of "insistent individualism," the other of "relationality." In his conclusion, Bennett suggests how academic leaders, including department chairs, can foster "relationality."

Creswell, John W., Daniel W. Wheeler, Alan T. Seagren, Nancy J. Egly, and Kirk D. Beyer. 1990. *The academic chairperson's handbook*. Lincoln: University of Nebraska Press.
As suggested by the title, this is presented as a personal handbook for use by prospective and working chairs. Much of the advice is culled from observations by experienced chairs.

Gmelch, Walter H., and Val D. Miskin. 1993. *Leadership skills for department chairs*. Bolton, Mass.: Anker.
This is one of the more recent texts on department leadership.

————. 1995. *Chairing an academic department*. Thousand Oaks, Calif.: Sage.
In this volume the authors add further detail on carrying out the obligations of the four roles of chair described in their earlier volume.

Green, Madeleine F., and Sharon McDade. 1992. *Investing in higher education: A handbook of leadership development*. Washington: American Council on Education.
This continues to be a useful compendium of the many opportunities for leadership training that exist in American higher education. The limitation for chairs is that the references pertaining to that audience are few and far between, a reflection of current reality.

Hickson, Mark II, and Don W. Stacks. 1992. *Effective communication for academic chairs*. New York: State University of New York Press.
The topics treated by a spectrum of authors are the familiar responsibilities of the department chair, i.e., leading the department, faculty assessment, budgeting, motivating faculty, etc. It is the approach that is different. The premise of this volume is that being an effective chair requires "the ability to create shared understandings with others...." (xiv). Rather than seeing the position as one devoted to completing tasks, this volume stresses that the role of chairs is principally an interactive one whose purpose should be to bring people together to work effectively.

Higgerson, Mary Lou. 1996. *Communication skills for department chairs*. Bolton, Mass.: Anker.
This volume discusses the problems and issues that face chairs, addressing them in a hands-on manner through case studies. The detailed case index makes it easy to find the case that will permit the reader to explore a hypothetical solution in dialog with the author in preparation for facing a real-life issue in the department.

Higgerson, Mary Lou, and Susan R. Rehwaldt. 1993. *Complexities of higher education administration*. Bolton, Mass.: Anker.
An excellent compendium of case studies that reflect the new challenges in education administration.

Lucas, Ann F. 1994. *Strengthening leadership: A team-building guide for chairs in colleges and universities*. San Francisco: Jossey-Bass.
    A recent volume on the challenges of chairing, emphasizing the necessary humanistic skills.

The Pew Higher Education Roundtable, The Pew Charitable Trusts. Double agent. *Policy Perspectives* 6, no. 3 (February).
    This Pew policy paper offers one of the most succinct and insightful views on the pivotal importance of the department in the process of effecting meaningful change in higher education. Although the paper does not consider the role of chairs, implicit in its argument is a need for a new vision of chair leadership.

Tucker, Allan. 1981. *Chairing the Academic Department: Leadership among Peers*, 1st ed. New York: American Council on Education/Macmillan.

ACKNOWLEDGMENTS

Many individuals helped shape this work. They include the many chairs who attended the American Council on Education national workshop for chairs since 1992. It is with and through them that we have seen the evolving world of department chairs. In addition, each of us has worked with chairs on individual campuses either solo or as combinations of working partners.

Generous colleagues who have read portions of the manuscript include:

Thomas A. Angelo, Associate Professor and Director, The Assessment Center, De Paul University School for New Learning

Leland Blank, Assistant Provost for Continuous Improvement and Professor of Industrial Engineering, Texas A&M University

Jill Bogard, Director, Library and Information Service, American Council on Education

Debra L. Brum, Associate Vice President for Faculty Affairs, California State Polytechnic University

Gilbert Brum, Associate Dean, School of Hotel and Restaurant Management, California State Polytechnic University

Richard G. Higgerson, University Legal Counsel, Southern Illinois University at Carbondale

Raymond N. Johnson, Professor of Accounting, School of Business Administration, Portland State University

James R. (Dick) Pratt, Professor and Director, Environmental Sciences and Resources, Portland State University

Mary Kay Tetreault, California State University

The project would never have been initiated without the urging of James (Jim) Murray, Vice President and Director of External Affairs, American Council on Education. And it would not have been brought to a successful conclusion without the guidance of Susan Slesinger and Christine Davis of Oryx Press.

Last and far from least, my husband Ron Saroff has patiently endured the process of creation and through his past professional experience in the field of planning proffered wise advice and counsel.

To all these individuals we owe appreciation and recognition. We gladly acknowledge their contribution to the positive aspects of this project, while its limitations remain the authors' and particularly the designer's and general impresario's responsibility.

Irene W.D. Hecht
Senior Associate, American Council on Education
Portland, Oregon
April 16, 1998

PART ONE

· · · · · · · · · · · ·

Roles and Responsibilities:
Past, Present, and Future

CHAPTER 1

The Academic Department

A New Geography

A merican higher education has been undergoing an extensive re-definition since the end of World War II. For nearly 50 years these changes have been led largely from what we fondly call "the administration." If we are to digest what has happened to postsecondary education we must now immerse ourselves in the life of academic departments. Departments and their chairs are now the key locus of institutional change, and chairs must become leaders of that change. As leaders, chairs will need to refocus their attention and rethink their roles. Chairs cannot leave their departments to pursue exclusively disciplinary desires. No longer will they have the luxury of presenting themselves as either partisan advocates of department preferences or the dutiful mouthpieces of the dean. In this chapter we attempt to trace the process by which higher education has traveled to this new landscape, outline the new geography of chairing, and offer some reflections on the type of leadership now required. In the subsequent chapters we will look at the responsibilities of chairs, discussing them within the changed geography of higher education.

THE JOURNEY TO A NEW GEOGRAPHY

The Advent of the Department

Universities have not always been organized into discipline departments. In fact, if one looks back over the 600 years that universities have existed, departmentalization is a relatively recent phenomenon. While scholars point to an exception here and there, equivalents of academic departments do not show up until the second half of the 1700s, and even then such a pattern was an exception. Prior to and shortly after the Civil War, American colleges were administered by presidents who personally served as scholars, leaders, teachers, chief disciplinarians, librarians, admissions officers, keepers of student records, business managers, secretaries of the faculty, and secretaries of the boards of governors.

As enrollments began to grow, presidents found it necessary to appoint individuals with special expertise to assume some of these presidential functions. The first appointment was that of librarian and the second was that of registrar. The need to establish a registrar's office became apparent in the 1880s, according to some historians, when elective curricula began to appear at some colleges and the task of keeping academic records became more complicated. As enrollments and curricula continued to expand, there were increased numbers of disciplinary and academic problems that could not be solved with routine answers. In the 1890s the first deans were appointed, to whom curricular and disciplinary authority was gradually delegated. Academic deans became chief personnel officers for the faculty, and deans of men and deans of women assumed responsibilities for student services. The addition of new administrative positions such as director of admissions, business manager, and public relations officer continued well into the twentieth century. In the beginning, librarians, registrars, deans, and other appointed officials considered their administrative responsibilities as part-time jobs and continued to serve in faculty capacities as scholars, teachers, and student advisors. As the number of students increased, it was necessary for presidents to employ full-time tutors and professors. In the middle 1800s faculty members at both Harvard and the University of Virginia began to group themselves into separate departments of instruction.

The rise of departments grew out of a need to improve the organization and management of the academic process as knowledge expanded at an ever accelerating pace. The day of the "tiered clergyman" teaching everything from rhetoric to natural philosophy was over. The influence of the German universities and their search for scientific truth led to the era of disciplinary specialization. Kerr (1994) and others point to this influence, especially at the graduate level, as the driving force behind undergraduate departmentalization of American colleges and universities. In retrospect, it appears inevitable that the increase in specialization and departmentalization would have changed the perspective of the faculty. Critics charged, and still charge, that publishing, research, and concern for tenure have pushed teaching into a subordinate position. Allegiance to the discipline has become more important than loyalty to, and concern for, the college or university. Can students learn interdisciplinary approaches to living in a complex, sophisticated world at universities divided into departments?

In the 1950s some of the larger American universities began to establish institutes, centers, and bureaus for specialized teaching and research. These new units frequently cut across departments and were intended to encourage interdisciplinary studies and activities. Although there are many such units in institutions of higher learning throughout the country, the discipline department remains the mainspring in the organization of academic work at our colleges and universities.

Organization of Departments

Departments often are designated as either pure or mixed. A pure discipline department is one in which all its faculty members are trained, have common backgrounds, and teach in the same discipline. "Pure" departments such as history, chemistry, English, and mathematics are more apt to be found in large colleges and universities. In smaller colleges, where a discipline has too few faculty members to justify departmental status, several discipline programs may be housed in one "mixed" department for administrative and economic efficiency. We are also seeing more "mixed" departments as we reconfigure our disciplinary categories and, in some cases, as institutions seek to foster interdisciplinary teaching and research. Not infrequently, such "mixed" departments end up with the designation of "division" with a division director or division chair who reports to a dean or a vice president, depending on the size of the division and the institution. In some institutions the disciplines within a division may be departmentalized, with each department having a chair responsible to the division director or chair. It is sometimes the case that within the same institution, some divisions are departmentalized and some are not. Divisional structure is found at some small- to mid-sized baccalaureate granting colleges, and it is a common organizational feature of community colleges. In large community colleges, divisions are sometimes subdivided into departments according to discipline, depending on the size of the program offered in that discipline.

In terms of department size, there is wide variability across and within institutions. In small colleges one may find departments with four or fewer faculty. Looking at the attendees at the American Council on Education national workshops for chairs, the majority of chairs are working in departments with between 10 and 19 faculty. Departments with between 20 and 35 members are also common. In large universities one may find departments of 75 or more faculty. Such mega-departments may have as many faculty members as a small college, making the functions of the chair resemble those of a dean. The importance of size is its impact on the organization of the department. Suggestions for managing a department of 15 may be impractical for a department of three and irrelevant to a department of 50. Chairs will need to assess the validity of any suggested guidelines in terms of the number of faculty in their departments.

Some Idiosyncrasies of Chair Authority

Chairs exist in a gray area between delegated and elected authority. Some chairs are appointed by the dean and serve at the dean's pleasure, others are appointed by the dean from a list of candidates recommended by a faculty search committee, and still others are elected by their colleagues to serve for one or more terms. In some departments, the position of chair rotates among its members. In the latter case the position is regarded as a necessary chore that good citizenship obliges one to shoulder periodically. However, at some point in the procedure, appointment does need to come formally from the chief academic officer. This is a necessary step because the chair's institutional position is derived through a chain of delegated authority that runs to dean, president, and board. The appointive power of the chief academic officer, whether exercised directly or through consultation with the department, is clearest in larger departments where the practice of "taking turns" is irrelevant. Less characteristic is the chair who is recruited from outside the institution. In those cases the chief academic officer is the key player. External appointments are more likely to occur when a department has been in disarray and someone is wanted to restore order; in cases where retirements have left a once-strong department without experienced leadership; with high-prestige departments that need a nationally (or even internationally) recognized leader; or when a new disciplinary area is launched, and a chair is recruited to build that new department.

Regardless of the source of appointive authority, chairs cannot lead effectively without the support of the department faculty. Since chairs live literally in the midst of their "citizenry," they are acutely aware of the fragile nature of their authority. Formal position endows chairs with very limited power or authority. Their ability to lead effectively, therefore, must derive from sources other than that of positional authority. As we look in more detail at the varied responsibilities of chairs, we will be probing for these sources of leadership power. Much of that power emerges from the ability of chairs to shape the culture in which they and their colleagues work; on their ability to focus the energy of their faculty; on the ways in which they determine how their colleagues both individually and collectively use their time—the one absolutely irreplaceable commodity we each possess; and on their perseverance in seeing that actions agreed to are actually carried forward.

Whatever the provenance of their positions, chairs are apt to share several characteristics. First is the fact that they are drawn from the faculty ranks, which means that while they have distinguished themselves as teachers, scholars, and researchers, their administrative skills have not been tested. For example, surveys administered to chairs attending American Council on Education national workshops for chairs have found that more than two-thirds of chairs had no prior administrative experience. The lack of administrative background is a source of frustration for both chairs and deans. On the chair side of the equation are individuals who feel overwhelmed by the extent of detail for which they are responsible. The first complaint is that they had no idea of the number of tasks they would have to carry out and that they were unprepared in their first year for the institutional rhythms of that work. Any chair who has a good department secretary learns quickly that such a person can be the incomparable lifeline, especially in the first year of administrative immersion. At the dean's end of the equation are complaints that chairs just "don't understand" their administrative responsibilities; that they leave the dean hanging out with key tasks incomplete, tardy, or neglected. Worst of all, say deans, chairs have no concept of "institutional vision," preferring instead to push limited departmental agendas to the detriment of the greater community. This state of mutual frustration helps build a destructive climate of faculty versus administration under which many institutions now labor.

A second shared characteristic is the lack of preparation afforded new chairs for what is a major change in professional roles. It would be difficult to say whether this cavalier system of appointment for key administrative leaders, without the benefit of any preparation, is a reflection either of higher education's lack of appreciation for the managerial aspects of leadership or of an idealistic faith in the intelligence and ingenuity of faculty anointed as chairs. Fortunately, the latter seems to be the case frequently enough to keep our institutions from sinking into anarchy.

While specially designed national and regional workshops are conducted for new presidents, vice presidents, and deans to help prepare them for their new responsibilities, relatively little has been done for department chairs, who outnumber all other types of university administrators combined. However, there are indications that this situation is gradually changing. The American Council on Education has been a notable exception with its Department Chair Leadership Program, which it has operated since the 1970s. In 1994 that program assumed its current form of an annual set of three national workshops.[1] More recently the Council of Colleges and Arts and Sciences (CCAS) has begun to offer training for chairs. Some discipline organizations such as the American Association of Colleges and Schools of Business (AACSB) and the Modern Language Association have begun offering workshops for chairs in their disciplines. In addition, two professional meetings whose programming focuses on the work of chairs are sponsored by Kansas State University and Maricopa Community College. Both meetings also offer chair workshop sessions prior to the meetings.[2]

A third shared characteristic is that chairs enjoy, at best, limited financial rewards. Chairs may receive extra compensation and other perquisites, such as full-time summer appointments, course relief, and travel monies. Their primary compensation, however, is the psychological reward of making a difference to colleagues and the institution. Insofar as the commonest standard of success and importance in our society is dollars earned, we have not been accustomed to think of chairs as major campus leaders. However, wise deans know that the skill of the chairs that report to them has a significant impact on the success they experience as deans.

A fourth distinguishing characteristic of chairs is the generally short period of tenure. While individual examples of chairs serving 10 or more years can be found with little effort, the turnover rate for chairs is 15 to 20 percent per year, with the term of service usually running six years. Thus, one could call chairs transitory leaders. The temporary nature of the position may be one of the elements that raises doubts in many people's minds about the accuracy of the characterization of the position of chair as one embodying leadership. On the other hand, if we describe leadership as the art of focusing the energy of a group of people on particular problems and tasks, combined with the art of guiding collective implementation for achieving mutually-agreed upon goals, then we immediately see the position of chair as one embodying the most potent qualities of leadership. If the major public task of our institutions is educating future generations, then we have to acknowledge academic departments as the heart of the institutional enterprise, for that is where students are taught. For those universities who pursue a major research agenda as part of their public responsibility, the department is likewise the key organizational element, for it is within departmental laboratories that research is actually carried out. As the designated leaders of departments, chairs are, therefore, critical leaders in all our colleges and universities.

EVOLVING GEOGRAPHY

Creating a New Landscape

How is it that the department is being transformed from the lowliest player in the institutional pyramid to the most critical organizational unit? What has happened to make the chair such an important academic leader? The answer lies in the nature of the problems now faced by America's postsecondary institutions. The reality is that institutional organization has evolved in response to perceived need. In the earliest phases of development, the only leadership institutions appeared to need was a president. Ideally this would be a person of vision and charisma, but a good work-a-day president was quite satisfactory if he embodied adequate organizational skills and a strong constitution. There was no doubt this was a top-down model. As postsecondary institutions grew in size and complexity, the elaboration of administrative functions soon evolved well beyond the capacities of any single individual. Leadership, nonetheless, continued to be hierarchical. This model of institutional leadership functioned adequately through the many changes of the post-World War II years. Hierarchical leadership was highly functional as institutions changed structures from teachers' colleges into comprehensive universities and as agricultural and mechanical institutions became universities. When the community college model burst onto the educational stage in the 1960s, the basic outlines of the hierarchical structure were adopted and adapted to its needs.

The problems that need to be addressed today, however, are of a different dimension and the locus of solution can no longer be the exclusive concern of the traditional administrative hierarchy. And what are these new problems? Before we map them, it will be helpful to review briefly the dimensions of change that have taken place since World War II because it is these changes that have created the new geography of higher education. In 1900 a mere 0.3 percent of our population was pursuing postsecondary education. By 1990 the figure was 5 percent. The major impetus to change came at the end of World War II. Having achieved victory in a brutal war, the blessings of peace faced the nation with a potential crisis. The demobilization of millions of military personnel bore the threat of bringing home an army of unemployed. The length of the war, which had drawn on the country's youth, had effectively disrupted the educational and work patterns of a generation.

The GI Bill

The ingenious answer to the feared stresses of demobilization was what we have come to know as the GI Bill. Although this remarkable legislation was rooted in urgent, though temporary, problems, its effects on postsecondary education have been revolutionary and permanent. The GI Bill provided every demobilized veteran the guarantee of $500 a year for tuition plus a small cost-of-living allowance. Although the tuition was paid directly to institutions, it was the veteran who selected the school. The effects were spectacular and immediate. "During their peak enrollment year of 1947, veterans accounted for 49.2 percent of all college enrollments and 69.3 percent of male students" (Olson 1994, 24). This bulge, of course, dissipated as returning veterans moved from classroom to job market. But the footprint they left behind was permanent.

Massification and Democratization of Higher Education

One major effect was to change the role of higher education in American society. "Two years before World War II began, approximately 160,000 U.S. citizens graduated from college each year; by 1950 that figure had risen to

nearly 500,000" (M. Bennett 1994, 10). The rise in the proportion of our
population completing four years or more of college education has continued
to climb. By 1970, 11 percent of the population fell in that category. By 1989
the figure was 21 percent (ACE 1992, 3). Attending college has become a
"norm" rather than a rare exception. It was the World War II veterans who
effectively dissolved the prior sociological framework of American higher
education and initiated its massification, a phenomenon that is now developing rapidly in western Europe and is showing its head in Australia and Asia
(Daniel 1996).

The GI Bill can also lay claim as a contributor to the arrival of women and
African Americans on American campuses. To be sure, women's colleges had
appeared on the American scene before the Civil War and colleges for newly
freed slaves were founded soon after that war. However, in terms of numbers,
graduates in both categories were few in number and their presence, limited to
special institutions created for them, left largely unchanged their marginalized
status in American society. The impact of the GI Bill on women is difficult to
measure because, as June A. Willenz, executive director of the American
Veterans Committee, has pointed out, "...there are no records at all of how
women veterans used the different titles of the bill" (Willenz 1994, 44). The
echo of their presence, however, can be measured. In 1950, of the baccalaureates awarded, barely 25 percent were earned by women. In 1990 more than 50
percent of baccalaureates went to women. The impact on African-American
veterans was also significant. Separate statistics based on race were not
collected for them any more than for women. However, one indirect measure
is available by looking at enrollment in historically black colleges and universities where enrollments immediately after the war rose by 50 percent (Wilson
1994, 36). In 1990, African Americans constituted about 9 percent of total
fall enrollment (NCES 1997, 214).

Shifts in Program Content
Those same veterans impelled changes in the content of education. What they
sought was an education that would be effective in creating an immediate
bridge to work. As Clark Kerr (1994, 29) has put it, "Letters and sciences
became less dominant, and professional schools became more dominant."
Higher education has lived with the results ever since. The explosion of
business programs and business schools is one reflection of the career focus of
World War II veterans. While not a change impelled exclusively by war
veterans, the transformation of a war of guns and bullets into the less immediately destructive but chronically tense Cold War perpetuated a program focus
on disciplines and activities that helped support a new form of "war." Science
and engineering programs benefited from those preoccupations, and theoretical scientific study continued to be influenced by the prospect of military
applications.

Structural Change in Higher Education

The GIs even propelled structural adjustments in higher education. As Kerr (1994, 29) points out, teachers' colleges, which were important sites of veteran enrollment, "were transformed into comprehensive colleges and universities." Today the "normal" schools of the nineteenth century and the state teachers' colleges of the early twentieth century may live on, but their names have been transmuted, erasing all links to their founding purpose. Metamorphosed as state comprehensives, these institutions may still have departments or even schools of education, but these are now but one component in far more complex institutions with multifaceted missions. These changes have actually effected a kind of homogenization of American higher education. While institutions remain differentiated in terms of missions and student bodies, there is a much stronger tendency among all toward the same standards of performance, at least in terms of institutional aspiration. Thus, the students invited into the academic tent through the GI Bill brought profound programmatic and structural change to our institutions.

The Move to Adult Education

The veterans also forced institutions to rethink the definition of a student. The orderly predictability of the educational process was shattered. Undergraduates who had been uniformly between 18 and 22 years old were suddenly in their mid- to late twenties or even older, often married, and some with children. Today the adult student is a given on any college campus. In fact, as a national statistic, adults—defined as those over 25 years old—constitute 45 percent of higher education enrollments (Rose 1994, 48). It has been a logical evolution to move from the adult student to the part-time student. While returning veterans had the benefits of subventions that usually covered tuition plus a small living allowance, which saved them from the burden of having to work while going to school, such has not been the case for non-veteran adults. Adult students today typically must work to cover living and schooling expenses. In 1993 part-time students constituted 43 percent of fall enrollment in institutions of higher education (NCES 1997, 182). Today we are coping with rapid transformations of knowledge and work, a fact that is encouraging us to regard education as a lifetime process, perhaps intermittently renewed. The fact that we have come to take adult education as normal has made it much easier for us to adjust our concepts to the idea that education can (perhaps must) be a continually renewed process. Again, the returning veterans of World War II helped us make the necessary adjustments.

New Processes and Purposes

But the most profound changes lie in the realm of our concepts of what constitutes education and its processes, purposes, and roles in our society. For millennia, education has been the domain of the privileged, who, by definition, were small in number. It was reserved to those with power. It was a means of perpetuating a ruling group and enculturating its linked generations. It was a process of initiation into the ruling elite. The founding of the American Republic implied a new role for education. Thomas Jefferson could see education as a necessity for an informed citizenry, who were the ruling "elite" of the Republic. However, prior to the GI Bill, the nation had been able to preserve postsecondary educational practices with an elitist bias that marginalized women and minorities, while liberalizing the scope of primary and secondary education. Implicit in a democracy is the necessity of educating the citizenry. Implicit in American democracy is that the citizenry comes in two genders and many colors. *Ipso facto*, education must be available to all. Education must be a platform, not a barrier. Education is the foundation of citizenship and the springboard to personal success. It was the GI Bill that turned that potential into reality. Higher education has not been the same since.

Credit for Prior Learning
In responding to the needs of these returning veterans, institutions began to redefine learning. This new cadre of students were certainly not novices to life and had learned much that could be translated into categories of "formal" learning. Among the adjustments made by institutions to these new students was the granting of "credit for military training and experience" (Olson 1994, 24). Enter the acceptance of Credit for Prior Learning. This was an amazing step which profoundly changed the position of educational institutions. Perhaps it has been easier to take this step because of historical precedent. There was a time when people learned their professions through apprenticeships. Law is a good example of this method, and in fact even today it is theoretically possible in some states to prepare for bar exams solely through apprenticing and "reading" law in a law office. But as our colleges and universities evolved in the nineteenth and first half of the twentieth centuries, they became the recognized purveyors of higher knowledge. In acknowledging the legitimacy of "prior learning," colleges and universities gave up some of their monopoly power. To be sure, they demanded the right to examine that "prior learning" and establish standards for translating it into the vocabulary of academic credit. Nonetheless, this step is an important component in the redefinition of education.

Breaking the Age Barrier and Creating Lifelong Learning
The returning veterans also forced on institutions a new view of education's place within the human life cycle. It was the returning veterans who sowed the notion that education did not need to be narrowly age defined. To be sure, those adult veterans were still thought of as young people whose course in life had been thrown off schedule through no fault of their own. In accepting them into the nation's colleges and universities, society was giving them a one-time

opportunity to catch up. The social and institutional impact, however, was not temporary. Campuses suddenly realized what a remarkable learner the adult is. We all came to understand that education has no need to be an age-specific activity. That has been a fortunate insight since with the rapid evolution of technology, the reorganization of economic structure, and the extension of work life beyond age 65, we have been forced to "reeducate" ourselves. Learning as a lifelong process is becoming our normal expectation. The notion of multiple, serial careers is all but taken for granted. These changes have spurred an astonishing burst of demand for more education, a demand that provided the inspiration for the development of community colleges. It is this amazing sector that has been most adventurous in serving adult learners, offering three basic streams of education: preparation for transfer to baccalaureate college; vocational/technical training (which may even be pursued in collaboration with or as a service to industry); and enrichment education for the general citizenry. Nor is this revolution of educational structures at an end. The latest entrants are the proprietary institutions offering specific career-oriented training and education.[3] This sector is shaking up the education map in terms of concepts of employment and methods of teaching.

A Culture of Change and Innovation

It is even possible that the sudden arrival of veterans on campus may have given institutions of higher education practice in being flexible and innovative. The necessity of dealing with a massive influx of unusual students required immediate responses to everything from practical needs for married housing and classrooms, to transition services for students who had never been in a college classroom or had been absent for several years. Even earlier, institutions had responded to war needs by readjusting their schedules to run year-round, thus speeding the production of skilled personnel for the war effort. Perhaps it is those experiences that developed the flexibility and talent for innovation on American campuses that we now take for granted.

Ernest A. Lynton, commonwealth professor of the University of Massachusetts, Boston, delivered one of the most insightful statements on the changes wrought by the GI Bill.

> Inevitably, the far greater participation rate triggered [by the GI Bill] and subsequent legislation has changed the basic societal purpose of higher education from being primarily a screening device to becoming truly a preparation for lifetime development and achievement. (Greenberg 1994, 59)

That statement touches the core of the transformation in American higher education. Institutions that had been used to sift the nation's intellectual, social, and political leaders (its economic leaders often jumped the traces and amassed fortunes without benefit of educational baptism) now had the role of preparing *all* citizens, who so wished, to participate in that society.

Why take space to describe this new geography in a book devoted to chairing academic departments? Because, quite simply, we are still building the roads by which we will traverse this new territory, and the guides we need as we master this new terrain are the department chairs.

LIVING IN A NEW GEOGRAPHY

The New Chair

At one level, departments have been dealing with many of the consequences of the education revolution since it began. However, the responses were formulated *ad hoc*. The pressures higher education is now experiencing require that we move to more thoughtful, principled, long-term positions. Are these matters of concern to department chairs? Absolutely, because all the issues cited affect the workings of departments. Furthermore, in those instances where there are problems, none can be solved without the involvement of departments. Thus the education revolution has borne with it the seeds of a new job description for chairs. Many chairs have been working with these changes by sheer necessity. What is needed now is a clearer understanding of the scope and dimensions of the challenges and their implications for the role of department chair.

The demographic changes are the most obvious of the challenges that have transformed the work context of departments. Instead of meeting a basically homogeneous (mostly male) student body of adolescents, classroom professors now face a kaleidoscope of ages and colors of whom at least half are women. In many institutions the consequences of the GI revolution have made ease of access the institution's social goal. Insofar as this demographic revolution affects every instructor, it becomes a matter for collective concern for the department. As the leader of the departmental dialog, the chair must be concerned with how department faculty cope with these changes both at the individual and collective levels. There is a need to adjust the process of education to communicate effectively with new populations, adjustments that are best made through departmental dialog in which faculty learn from each other how to maximize their success as teachers and advisors.

As education shifts from a screening device to a life development, the relationship of teacher and student are being revolutionized. In the days of education-as-screening-device, the teacher's (Darwinian) role was to weed out the "unfit" and polish the "fit." It was the teacher who defined success and the student who struggled to meet the standard. When education becomes the foundation for "lifetime development and achievement," education becomes a social good to which each citizen has a right. Although colleges and universities continue to set standards for admission, this fact adds tension to the equation rather than negating the new definition of access as right. The effect on the instructor is a reorientation of the teaching role, which now needs to include supporting students' development and mastery rather than standing as a gatekeeper to the Holy Land of Degrees. A teacher's success becomes a derivative of student success. Again, this change in emphasis is a matter that must concern departments since it affects every faculty member. Stress is inevitable in balancing the maintenance of rigorous standards with the goal of supporting student development and mastery. Departments need to sort out these issues and chairs need to see that time is set aside for that purpose.

This change in role definition leads logically to a reexamination of pedagogy. With the burden shifting from the student, who heretofore needed to adjust to the professor's teaching methods, the responsibility is moving to the instructor, who needs to find the best means for supporting students' educational achievements. This is at the heart of the shift from teaching to learning as the measure of pedagogical success. Complicating or—in some instances—easing the pedagogical challenge is the advent of the computer, which is finally providing some important new resources. However, to use this new medium effectively means that teachers need to move beyond their own blackboard educations. Quite possibly, the most successful new teachers will be those best able to discard the learning methods of their own novitiate. This kind of transformational change can succeed only if departments participate in defining the standards they will uphold, the methods they will apply to their teaching, and the support they are prepared to give for individual efforts—which will include mistakes—as all learn to navigate a new topography.

Not only is pedagogy an issue but so, too, is the very content of the curriculum. Perhaps most indicative of the depth of the changed status of higher education is the fact that the curriculum debate is taking place not only within universities among faculty, but between students and faculty—with students demanding such things as ethnic studies, women's studies, and non-western courses. Even the general public has weighed in with loud cries for sticking to basics and protests against bending to the demands of the "politically correct." The curriculum debate is further complicated by the need, acknowledged by the professoriate, that many of the questions we believe are important to answer can be treated fully only in an interdisciplinary manner. To do so requires either creating purposefully interdisciplinary programs or finding ways to make collaborations among members of different disciplines feasible, normal, recognized, and rewarded. We can have noisy public debate over these pedagogical issues, but the only place where change can take place is in individual classrooms. However, the dimensions of the challenge are so broad that solutions need to be explored among department colleagues. Experimentation will survive to create new methodologies if that experimentation is carried on reflectively within departments and with the support of colleagues. Again, it is chairs who are critical to creating a climate in which such debate can take place and where successful innovation can be systematized and shared within departments.

The effects of fiscal crisis, added to the sociological changes of the GI revolution, have resulted in a change in the relationship between the public and higher education. Insofar as more than half our higher education sector is publicly funded by state legislatures, there has always been the implicit right to know, and hence interfere, in the internal affairs of many of our postsecondary institutions. However, it is only in the 1990s that legislatures have in fact made demands for information that was once regarded as a purely internal matter.

Now states are visiting institutions with demands for reports on faculty productivity and student completion rates. Not only are they asking for information, but legislatures are also speaking loudly in terms of tying funding to performance. The message is: deliver what we deem satisfactory and we will fund you. Defy us, and you will starve. Although these messages are addressed to university administrators, performance can take place only at the department or program level. Therefore, university administrations have urgent need to bring department chairs into the leadership circle of their institutions. And chairs need to expand their horizon of concern beyond the immediate daily concerns of their departments.

If the ivory tower has become a less secure edifice in the face of fiscal erosion, it has been painfully shaken by the ethical transgression of some faculty. The pain has been exacerbated by its appearance in the public media. It is one thing when institutions quietly conduct internal investigations of improper conduct. It is quite another when the *Wall Street Journal* publishes articles on professorial malfeasance. The public esteem for the professoriate is brought into question, complicating the relationship between the public and the academy. Departments have long been accustomed to functioning with tolerance toward colleagues. Academic freedom is something we rightly cherish. However, departments need to cultivate a countervailing regard for standards, particularly high ethical standards, if we are to retain public confidence and esteem. Once again, these are matters for chairs to bring to the attention of their departments.

CONCLUSION

The kind of leadership that chairs need to exert is that of building bridges, creating connections, and defusing tensions. This will include closing the gap between the democratic propensities of departments and the hierarchical structure of the traditional university. It will encompass reconnecting departmental disciplines with their institutions when they have become detached from the institutions in which they reside. The chair may also need to moderate one of the inherent tensions within higher education, namely, the struggle between tradition and innovation. Transmitting the intellectual heritage from the past is a key responsibility of institutions and their departments. At the same time, universities have been the frontier for exploring the unknown. In that sense they are champions of change. These tensions are played out at the detail level within departments. Thus, another linking function of chairs is to build bridges between tradition and innovation. The chronic tension between the individual interests of faculty and the mission of the collective faculty body, the department, is another concern. The individual cannot be sacrificed to the collective; yet neither can a chair permit individuals, however talented, to hold the collectivity hostage. Lastly, there is the need to connect the mission of the institution with the needs of society. The hard wiring of that connection can take place only from the departmental level. The chair, as critical front-line manager of institutional connections, must now function as part of the leadership nexus of the university.

In this evolving topography, the role of the chair is being transformed from a manager focused internally on the department; its faculty, staff, and students; and curriculum to a leader within the university, and even within the larger society. Rather than being an advocate for individual faculty or even the department as a whole, the chair has the more intricate challenge of connecting the basic organizational unit of the university to the larger institution. It is that new geography that we will explore.

NOTES

1. For information on the American Council on Education (ACE) chair workshops use their Web site, http://www.acenet.edu, or the ACE chairs information inquiry line at 202-939-9343.
2. Kansas State University holds its meeting in Orlando, Florida, in February. For information write: Dr. William Pallett, The Idea Center, Kansas State University, 1615 Anderson Avenue, Manhattan, KS 66502. For information on the Maricopa Community College chair meeting write: National Community College Chair Academy, 1833 West Southern Avenue, Mesa, AZ 85202.
3. As of 1998 we may be seeing the second revolution in the delivery of adult education with the emergence of proprietary institutions. Although far from being the only such institution, University of Phoenix has emerged as one of the most spectacular in its growth. Not until 1980 do we see any systematic effort to trace the growth of this sector. See, for example, table 48 in *1989-90 Fact Book on Higher Education* (ACE 1989), which records "Opening Fall Enrollment of All Students by Control of Institution, Selected Years 1950–1987.

REFERENCES

American Council on Education (ACE). 1989. *1989-90 Fact book on higher educa-tion.* New York: Macmillan.
This is a highly useful compilation of basic quantitative material on American higher education. All data are presented in historical context, most of it reaching back to the 1960s, and some extending to prior to World War II.

American Council on Education (ACE). 1992. Higher education and national affairs. (6 January): 3.

Bennett, John B. 1983. *Managing the academic department: Cases and notes.* New York: Macmillan.
Organized into seven chapters, this volume looks at conceptual and practical areas of chair responsibility.

Bennett, John B., and Elwood B. Ehrle. 1988. *Managing the academic enterprise: Case studies for deans and provosts.* New York: Macmillan.
Although the title suggests that these cases have been organized for chief academic officers, there is much that is directly relevant to chairs.

Bennett, Michael J. 1994. The law that worked. *Educational Record* (fall): 6–14.

Creswell, John W., Daniel W. Wheeler, Alan T. Seagren, Nancy J. Egly, and Kirk D. Beyer. 1990. *The academic chairperson's handbook.* Lincoln: University of Nebraska Press.
Based on data solicited from experienced chairs, this serves as an introduction to the life and work of chairs for those new to the position.

Daniel, John S. 1996. *Mega-universities and knowledge media: Technology strategies for higher education.* London: Kogan Page.
While this volume does not speak to the immediate concerns of department chairs, it does reveal the astonishing changes that technology is bringing to postsecondary education globally.

Educational Record. 1994. (fall).
This issue of *Educational Record* is devoted to a review of the GI Bill and its impact on American higher education. All the *Educational Record* articles cited in the chapter footnotes appeared in this issue. Individual authors are listed in the references.

Gmelch, Walter H., and Val D. Miskin. 1993. *Leadership skills for department chairs.* Bolton, Mass.: Anker.
This is one of the more recent texts on department leadership.

———. 1995. *Chairing an academic department.* Thousand Oaks, Calif.: Sage.
This volume adds further detail on carrying out the obligations of the four roles of chairs described in their earlier volume.

Green, Madeleine F., and Sharon McDade. 1992. *Investing in higher education: A handbook of leadership development.* Washington: American Council on Education.

This continues to be a useful compendium of the many opportunities for leadership training that exist in American higher education. The limitation for chairs is that the references pertaining to that audience are few and far between, a reflection of current reality.

Greenberg, Milton. 1994. The GI Bill, reflections on the past and visions of the future. *Educational Record* (fall): 57–61.

Heifetz, Ronald A. 1995. *Leadership without easy answers.* Cambridge, Mass.: Harvard University Press.

This intriguing volume suggests that, rather than being positional, leadership should be seen as a functional task. The function of a leader is in posing and pressing critical questions.

Hickson, Mark II, and Don W. Stacks. 1992. *Effective communication for academic chairs.* New York: State University of New York Press.

The topics treated by a spectrum of authors are the familiar responsibilities of the department chair, i.e., leading the department, faculty assessment, budgeting, motivating faculty, etc. It is the approach that is different. The premise of this volume is that being an effective chair requires "the ability to create shared understandings with others...." (xiv). Rather than seeing the position as one devoted to completing tasks, this volume stresses that the role of chairs is principally an interactive one whose purpose should be to bring people together to work effectively.

Higgerson, Mary Lou. 1996. *Communication skills for department chairs.* Bolton, Mass.: Anker.

This volume speaks to the problems and issues that face chairs, addressing them in a hands-on manner through case studies. The detailed case index makes it easy to find the case that will permit the reader to explore a hypothetical solution in dialog with the author in preparation for facing a real-life issue in the department.

Higgerson, Mary Lou, and Susan R. Rehwaldt. 1993. *Complexities of higher education administration* Bolton, Mass.: Anker.

An excellent compendium of case studies that reflect the new challenges in education administration.

Kerr, Clark. 1973. Administration in an era of change and conflict. *Educational Record* (winter): 38–46

———. 1994. Expanding access and changing missions: The federal role in U.S. higher education. *Educational Record* (fall): 27–31.

Lucas, Ann F. 1994. *Strengthening leadership: A team-building guide for chairs in colleges and universities.* San Francisco: Jossey-Bass.

A recent volume on the challenges of chairing, emphasizing the necessary humanistic skills.

National Center for Education Statistics (NCES). 1997. *Digest of education statistics, 1997.* U.S. Department of Education, Office of Educational Research and Improvement, Washington.

Olson, Keith W. 1994. The astonishing story: Veterans make good on the nation's promise. *Educational Record* (fall): 16–26.

The Pew Higher Education Roundtable, The Pew Charitable Trusts. 1996. Double agent. *Policy Perspectives* 6, no. 3 (February).
This Pew policy paper offers one of the most succinct and insightful views on the pivotal importance of the department in the process of effecting meaningful change in higher education. Although the paper does not consider the role of chairs, implicit in its argument is a need for a new vision of chair leadership.

Rose, Amy D. 1994. Significant and unintended consequences: The GI Bill and adult education. *Educational Record* (fall): 47–48.

Willenz, June A. 1994. Invisible veterans. *Educational Record* (fall): 4–46.

Wilson, Reginald. 1994. GI Bill expands access for African Americans. *Educational Record* (fall): 32–39.

CHAPTER 2

Roles and Responsibilities of Department Chairs

ROLES, CONTEXT, AND TRANSFORMATIONS

The Role of Department Chairs

The changing context of higher education described in the previous chapter sets the stage for our review of department chairs' roles and responsibilities. As front-line managers, department chairs serve more than one constituency, a fact that requires department chairs to assume multiple roles. Chairs are the primary spokespersons for department faculty, staff, and students. At the same time, institutions of higher education have an increasing reliance upon department chairs to implement and carry out campus policy and the mission of the institution for the central administration. Chairs represent the central administration to department members at the same time that they articulate the needs of the department members to the administration. Consequently, department chairs are the essential link between the administration and department members. When chairs fulfill their role effectively, there is good communication between the administration and faculty. When chairs do not succeed in this task, there is often a lack of trust between the administration and the faculty because neither constituency understands the needs or perspectives of the other. Department chairs must do more than forward information between the administration and department members. Chairs must interpret and present information and arguments that accurately reflect the intent of each constituency to the other for the overall the institutional mission by connecting department objectives with that broader mission.

At one time, the chair position was reserved for the most prestigious scholars within the discipline. These chairs presided over departments in an almost ceremonial manner, and did not wrestle with budget cuts, declining enrollments, productivity reports, accountability measures, fund-raising, or changing technology. While many institutions still stipulate that department chairs have a record of scholarship and publication, all institutions expect chairs to be more than a role model or figurehead. Department faculty seek a strong advocate, a consensus builder, a budget wizard, and a superb manager. Academic deans and provosts seek department chairs who have superb managerial and communication skills, and are able to implement university policies and directives.

One distinctive characteristic of chairs' role is its paradoxical nature. Department chairs are leaders, yet are seldom given the scepter of undisputed authority. Department chairs are first among equals, but any strong coalition of those equals can severely restrict the chairs' ability to lead. Deans and vice presidents look to chairs as those primarily responsible for shaping the department's future, yet faculty members regard themselves as the primary agents of change in department policies and procedures. Department chairs are both managers and faculty colleagues, advisers and advisees, soldiers and captains, drudges and bosses.

Department chairs are the only academic manager who must live with his or her decisions every day. The dean and the vice president make many important administrative decisions, such as which colleges or departments will get the lion's share of the year's operating budget. The dean and the vice president, however, do not have to say good morning—every morning—to their colleagues in the department; they do not have to teach several times a week alongside their colleagues; they do not have to maintain a family relationship with their faculty members. The department chair, on the other hand, must be acutely aware of the vital statistics of each family member including births, deaths, marriages, divorces, illnesses, and even private financial woes. This intimate relationship is not duplicated anywhere else on the campus because no other academic unit takes on the ambiance of a family, with its personal interaction, its daily sharing of common goals and interests, and its concern for each member. No matter how large the department, no matter how deeply divided over pedagogical and philosophical issues it may be, its members are bound together in many ways: they have all had the same general preparation in graduate school; their fortunes generally rise or fall with the fortunes of the discipline to which they all belong; and they share the same value system of their profession. Working alongside the members of this "family" is the chair, a manager who is sometimes managed, a leader who is sometimes led, a parent who continually strives to keep peace for the sake of mutual benefit and progress.

These conditions are not the only ones that make the department chair's role paradoxical. The chair must deal with the expectations and desires of the students in the department, the personal and professional hopes and fears of the faculty, the goals and priorities of the college dean, the often perplexing priorities of the central administration, the sometimes naive and sometimes jaundiced views of the alumni, and the bureaucratic procedures of accrediting agencies. Few administrators can, by themselves, face these conflicting constituencies and find solutions to all problems. Yet the department chair must induce these constituencies to work together to help solve the problems they themselves generate.

Today the internal paradox of the chair's role is further complicated by external pressures. The central administration, professional accrediting agencies, state boards of higher education, and granting agencies are just some of the external audiences that department chairs must understand and address. The demands of these multiple constitutencies impact individual departments as much as they do institutions. A state board of higher education, for example, may decide to review the relative merit and quality of programs within the same discipline offered at different institutions throughout the state. In such instances, a department finds itself virtually plucked from the security of the institution into the spotlight and placed under the magnifying glass of the state board of higher education. In dealing with some external audiences, department chairs serve as the representative for the institution as well as the department. In interacting with high school and community college counselors, regional businesses, or civic organizations, department chairs speak for both the department and the institution.

Accountability initiatives designed to monitor the quality and cost effectiveness of higher education have increased the importance of the department chair's role. Institutions cannot respond to externally imposed mandates for accountability of such things as student learning outcomes assessment without the support and leadership of department chairs. Department chairs are the primary interpreters of externally imposed mandates for department faculty, and the tone with which chairs present those initiatives influences faculty response. Today, the central administration needs cooperation and effective leadership at the department chair level more than ever to implement change and assure program quality. At the same time, department chairs are the primary source of information about specific programs and daily operations. This information is essential to the central administration as they champion requests for new resources or fend off attacks on institutional quality.

Department chairs, however, are more than agents of the central administration. They are also the primary spokespersons and advocates for the academic department. In this role, chairs are the guarantors of department quality. In fact, chairs are the only administrators with delegated responsibilities that allow for a direct influence on program quality. Further, department chairs are the only administrators with the requisite discipline training and vantage point needed to assess program quality and identify areas of needed change. As front-line managers, department chairs are both chief advocates for the department and primary agents of the central administration. Chairs need to champion the resource needs of the department and ensure the effective use of current resources. Chairs must promote the quality of the departments' programs while they remain alert to the need for curricular revision.

This dual role is more difficult because the various constituencies and external audiences with which the chair interacts tend to hold simple perceptions of the department chair's role. Faculty, for example, prefer to perceive the department chair as their primary spokesperson and advocate. Faculty are less inclined to perceive the chair's role as one that includes representing the central administration. Some faculty may even be outraged to think of their chair as an agent of the administration. At the same time, central administration may become irritated with a department chair who seems determined to argue the needs of the department in the face of an institutional crisis. The department chair, for example, who holds the line on increasing the enrollment in the general education course to protect instructional quality may be viewed by the administration as jeopardizing course enrollment, which, in turn, makes the institution less cost effective, an important datum for many state boards of higher education. Simultaneously, faculty may view a department chair who attempts to persuade them of the merit of designing a department assessment program as having "sold out" to the administration. The department chair often experiences stress as s/he walks the tightrope between serving the department and its faculty and students, and representing the central administration. This dual role, however, is apparent in all of the responsibilities typically assigned to the department chair.

Changing Roles from Faculty Member to Department Chair

In talking with several hundred department chairs each year, we find that many say they were not prepared for the role shift from faculty to chairs. Particularly, chairs being promoted from inside the department do not anticipate their life to be much different. While new chairs foresee having new responsibilities, they are not always prepared for the shift in how faculty colleagues and others treat them. Almost immediately, new chairs discover that long-time faculty colleagues (and friends) respond to them differently. Some faculty, for example, will assume that the new chair is "too busy" to join the informal lunch bunch now that s/he is an "administrator." Others will be less candid than previously in discussing issues affecting the department. Some may even avoid the chair. Yet, the same group of faculty colleagues are likely to hold high expectations for the performance of the new chair. Close acquaintances will expect the new chair to "fix" those policies and procedures about which he or she used to commiserate with faculty colleagues. Most faculty will expect the new chair to be able to "hold the line" with the administration on every issue because they trust the new chair to know the situation and have a full understanding of the department's needs. Walking the fine line between the role of colleague and department chair can be difficult.

John Bennett (1983, 2–6) identified three major transitions that new department chairs experience. The first shift comes in moving from being a specialist to functioning as a generalist. As a faculty member, an individual specializes in one academic area. However, when an individual becomes a department chair, he or she must have a thorough understanding of the full spectrum of department offerings. Moreover, faculty colleagues expect the new chair to represent all specializations within the department with equal enthusiasm. In addition to being held accountable for more content, the new chair is also responsible for a range of duties that faculty never perform. The new chair must acquire a substantive grasp of the total department as soon as possible, because other faculty will be suspicious and critical of any chair who can only advocate his or her teaching and research specialty.

The second transition the department chair experiences is the shift from functioning as an individual to running a collective. For the most part, faculty work independently at their own pace. Other than holding assigned classes or attending scheduled meetings, faculty determine when they work on course preparation, research, or other projects. On most campuses, faculty set their own office hours and determine when they come and go around class and meeting times. Department chairs, however, must orchestrate the work done by this group of individuals who work independently. Worse yet, some chair duties cause the new chair to interfere with the independence of faculty members. Chairs, for example assign courses and class times, schedule meetings, and solicit faculty attendance at special events such as recruitment or placement fairs and award programs. Chairs need to balance their respect for faculty autonomy with their responsibility for carrying out the department mission.

The third major transition described by Bennett is the shift from loyalty to one's discipline to loyalty to the institution. Chairs must represent the institution's perspective. There will be times when chairs may need to sacrifice a discipline need or a department preference for an institutional need. These tough decisions are likely to make chairs unpopular with faculty who recognize only the discipline perspective and may believe that the chair should place the department first in every situation. Whether or not the department implements a student learning outcomes assessment program may not be a matter for the department to decide. Similarly, campus policy on course enrollment and the need to involve faculty in student recruitment and retention activities are likely to be matters on which the chair cannot refuse the department's support and participation. Individuals who remain loyal to the discipline and fail to learn the institution's perspective and respond to campus needs become liabilities to the institution and undermine the standing of the department on the campus.

The Selection Process

One would expect that the increasing reliance upon chairs to carry out the heart of the institution's business would result in more thorough and competitive searches for skilled department leaders. Instead, institutions continue to fill department chair positions by hiring strong teachers and researchers who then must assume a role that requires very complex and challenging administrative skills. When chairs are sought externally, the position announcement typically lists demonstrated effectiveness in teaching and an established record of peer-reviewed research as essential qualifications. Seldom do chair ads include a listing of those skills and qualifications that would make an individual appropriate for a front-line managerial position. Chair applicants are not asked to demonstrate skill in managing conflict, effectiveness in designing marketing strategies for student recruitment, or propposls for enhancing alumni support.

Institutions are generally content to look internally when filling department chair positions. A national search may be conducted if an institution believes there is no acceptable internal candidate or in cases where it is felt that a person of national status is needed to lead the department. For searches limited to internal applicants, the candidates may not receive a detailed job description, a fact which confirms the lack of thought given to the complex responsibilities assigned to department chairs. There are two basic models for conducting a search for a department chair. The first model uses a full-scale search process with the stipulation that applicants must be tenured faculty within the particular academic department conducting the search. All tenured faculty may apply and applicants are subjected to the typical screening procedures, including interviews with all appropriate parties. The department forwards its recommendation to the college dean. If the dean agrees with the recommendation, a new chair is appointed. In the second model, chairs are elected from within the department. That election may need confirmation in the form of formal appointment by the dean. The rotational model of selection is a variation of the election model. This may occur in small departments where serving as chair becomes a civic duty that each department member undertakes in rotation.

The term of service is variable. In some institutions chair appointments are of indefinite duration, an arrangement more likely with chairs hired externally. Internally selected chairs usually serve for a fixed term, a procedure that may be specified in department operating manuals. Terms are commonly set at three or sometimes five years. Often, department guidelines stipulate limits for term renewal. An individual, for example, may be required to vacate the chair position after serving two terms. The term of office of department chairs influences the perceptions and expectations held by both incumbents and colleagues. Chairs appointed for an indefinite term of office see themselves as formally designated leaders. They assume that they have specific responsibilities, authority to carry those out and the power to support their decisions. Chairs elected to serve a three-year term are likely to perceive themselves as temporary managers. These chairs know that they will return to the ranks of the faculty on a prescribed date. Consequently, term chairs may make preserving their colleague relationships their top priority. They may be reluctant to tackle sensitive issues and reticent to engage in long-term activities. Their objective becomes not rocking the boat rather than leading the department through any significant change. As logical as this course of action may be, given the limitations of a three-year term, it may discourage the proactive planning required in academic departments today. This drawback may be overcome if it becomes common practice to have chairs serve two consecutive three-year terms. That length of time carries the chair past the learning-the-ropes phase to a point where s/he has confidence in her or his leadership abilities. Renewable five-year terms can have the same advantage, though there may be reluctance in departments to see the same chair remain in place for a decade. Perhaps that is why chairs attending ACE's workshops more frequently report that their departments function with renewable three-year terms.

One of the peculiar features of the position of department chair is that most individuals accepting the position have little, if any, previous administrative experience to match the nature and magnitude of their new roles and responsibilities. Furthermore, institutions rarely offer formal on-campus training for new chairs. When such training is offered, it is usually limited to instruction on campus policy and regulations. Department chairs learn how to complete various budget forms and read available campus printouts. Seldom does on-campus chair training include professional skills development in such important leadership tasks as managing conflict, team building, or implementing change. In chapter 1 of this text, we identified the available national training opportunities for department chairs. These seminars, workshops, and meetings focus on the professional and leadership skills needed by department chairs rather than any campus-specific policy or regulations. Still, these opportunities require institutions to make some initial investment in training chairs and, unfortunately, many institutions fail to do this. Where else in institutions of higher education do we hire individuals without appropriate previous experience and expect them to accept admittedly difficult and complex responsibilities without the benefit of relevant training? The special skill needs of today's department chairs can be understood if we examine chairs' role in greater detail.

THE WORK OF DEPARTMENT CHAIRS

The lengthy list of department chairs' responsibilities can be organized into the following categories: department governance and office management; curriculum and program development; faculty matters; student matters; communication with external audiences; financial and facilities management; data management; and institutional support.

Department Governance and Office Management

Department chairs are responsible for all tasks supporting shared governance from shaping the department mission and building consensus around department goals to conducting department meetings and implementing long-range department programs, plans, goals, and policies. For shared governance to work effectively, department chairs must encourage faculty members to invest in department planning. Chairs must lead faculty in determining what services the department should provide to the university, community, and state. Chairs keep department members mindful of the department mission and goals. They improve the university climate when they successfully manage these shared governance tasks within their departments. These tasks require chairs to be strong communicators, able managers of conflict, superb team builders, and sensitive facilitators of group discussions.

In their capacity as office managers, chairs supervise and evaluate the clerical and technical staff of departments, maintain essential department records, assign office space, and determine departments' equipment needs. Department chairs interview and hire new staff, manage conflict among staff members, and ensure that the support staff serves the instructional and administrative needs of the department. When necessary, chairs serve as liaisons between faculty and support staff to make certain that the goals of the department are met. These duties require daily attention because ineffective office management can jeopardize the instruction and research priorities of the department.

Curriculum and Program Development

Chair responsibilities for department curriculum and program dervelopment fall into three general categories: instruction, research, and service. Responsibility for the instructional program includes such specific tasks as scheduling classes, monitoring library acquisitions, initiating curricular review and program development, and managing the department assessment program. It is the chair's job to collect, interpret, and present to the department data relevant to discussions about curriculum and program effectiveness. It is also the chair's task to prepare the department for accreditation and program review. If the department offers graduate work, the chair must monitor dissertations, prospectuses, and programs of study for graduate students. These tasks require the department chair to be both coach and critic. S/he must uphold the standard for quality instruction and inspire continual improvement.

When departments have research missions, chairs are responsible for making certain that faculty understand and adhere to federal guidelines and campus policy on scientific standards. Chairs may help faculty secure the necessary resources to conduct research, including additional space, research assistants, equipment, and clerical support. The search for resources may even require chairs to be entrepreneurial in seeking assistance both within and outside the institution. In pursuing a research mission, chairs need to demonstrate their understanding of, and interest in, the research programs of individual faculty. They should also see that the department has a collective understanding of these endeavors and that, where possible, linkages are made between research projects that can multiply their results.

Most departments have some service programs, although the degree to which the service activity is centralized varies greatly from one department to another. Even when service commitments are left to individual faculty, department chairs should monitor outreach and service programs to see that they promote the goals of the department. Visible and effective service programs can net tangible benefits for both the department and the institution, including positive press, funding support, internship sites for students, job placements for graduates, and in-kind contributions. To carry out this responsibility, chairs need to be well versed in the activities of the department's faculty.

Faculty Matters

Department chairs are ultimately responsible for the quality of faculty activity even though most faculty work independently. Chairs recruit and select new faculty, assign faculty teaching loads and committee work, and evaluate faculty performance. Chairs, therefore, are accountable for managing faculty work assignments in a way that draws on individual strengths and maximizes collective success. Chairs make merit recommendations and initiate promotion and tenure recommendations. No administrator has more direct influence over the professional growth and development of individual faculty. Chairs are responsible for promoting professional development among both tenured and untenured faculty. On occasion, department chairs must deal with unsatisfactory faculty and staff performance and, when necessary, initiate termination of a faculty member. These tasks require sensitivity to individuals, support for university standards for excellence, and adherence to institutional procedures.

At the same time, department chairs must keep faculty members informed of department, college, and institutional plans, activities, and expectations. Chairs need to encourage faculty participation in department matters, but must also mediate conflict among faculty members. When done effectively, these tasks establish and maintain morale within the department.

Student Matters

Students are another important internal constituency that fall within the scope of department chairs' responsibilities. Chairs are ultimately responsible for the department's efforts to recruit and retain students. They have the power to make exceptions to department policy for students. For example, chairs can approve course substitutions, accept transfer credit, and waive program requirements for individual students. When departments have student organizations, the department chair must monitor the activities of these groups.

The chair's role as student advisor and counselor allows the chair to interact on an individual basis with numerous students. While these conversations may be the source of important anecdotal information about student learning and success, the department chair is also responsible for collecting aggregate data regarding student progress and success. Among the more frequently used measures of accountability are student learning outcomes assessment and graduation rates. It is the department chair who must know what data points are used by the central administration, the state board of higher education, and accrediting agencies to evaluate the productivity and effectiveness of the department. Sometimes chairs need to survey current students and alumni to gather information attesting to the quality of the department's instructional program. Chairs must know what information to collect, how to interpret the data for program improvement, and how to use it for program advocacy. When chairs are effective in performing these tasks they help the department better serve students.

Communication with External Audiences

The central administration, alumni, governing boards of higher education, accrediting agencies, area businesses, granting agencies, and state legislators are some of the external audiences department chairs may need to address. The manner in which chairs communicate with these external audiences can improve and maintain the department's image and reputation. The department chair is the primary spokesperson and advocate for the department with all external audiences. It is the chair who completes forms and surveys received by the department, processes department correspondence and requests for information, and serves as liaison with external agencies and institutions. It is the department chair who communicates department needs to the dean and central administration and keeps the administration informed of department achievements and activities. It is also the department chair who coordinates activities with outside groups and represents the department at special events. Chairs need to be adept at recognizing the perspectives held by the various external audiences and be able to structure the department communication with these groups in a way that enhances the department's relationship with them.

The task of communicating with external audiences is time consuming, but important to the long-term welfare of the department. Savvy department chairs go beyond responding to the requests of external audiences to initiating communication with them. Department chairs may issue department newsletters that keep key external audiences informed about departments' accomplishments and activities. They may survey alumni to encourage more significant relationships with graduates who may be able to contribute money, time, and talent to the department or institution. Department chairs may also solicit press coverage for department achievements and activities. These tasks utilize skills in public relations, persuasion, and marketing.

Financial and Facilities Management

Department chairs prepare and propose department budgets, seek outside funding, and administer the department budget. They set priorities for the purchase of new equipment and the use of travel funds. The department's expenditures for any fiscal year should correspond with the department's annual and long-term priorities. It is easier to fulfill this responsibility if faculty understand and accept the department mission and priorities. For this reason, chairs must educate department members about the finances of the department. Department members will be less critical of the chair's actions with regard to spending department funds if they understand the context for budget decisions. As a campus administrator, chairs must adhere to state and university guidelines for spending department monies. Chairs also have responsibility for managing the department's physical facilities. This responsibility encompasses the assignment of space and the maintenance of department equipment. Chairs have ultimate responsibility for the total department's inventory and must know when equipment is loaned out or in need of repair. They also must monitor department security and maintenance. Issues involving who gets keys to what rooms and storage closets become matters for the department chair to decide. Department chairs must inform central administration of needed safety renovations or repairs. In this regard, chairs are custodians of department space and equipment.

Data Management

Department chairs have responsibility for managing the department's record-keeping system. They decide how long various computer printouts are kept and what summaries to make of data received or collected by the department. They control what information is forwarded to department faculty and staff. Furthermore, they have considerable control over the form and substance of information shared within and outside the department. Because department chairs have virtually full responsibility for determining what data is collected and disseminated in support of the department, they need skills ranging from that of efficient data manager to that of analyst and expert advocate.

Institutional Support

Department chairs also have responsibility for promoting and advancing the welfare of the institution. In this role, chairs have an obligation to represent accurately state initiatives for higher education, the institutional mission, and mandates from central administration. Department chairs must represent and interpret campus policy accurately to department members and students. Chairs who attempt to befriend department members by bemoaning demands made by the administration shirk their responsibility to the institution. Chairs need very clear communication skills to fulfill their dual roles as primary spokesperson for the administration and chief advocate for the academic department.

THE POWER OF THE DEPARTMENT CHAIR

Department chairs who are aware of the long list of responsibilities assigned to them sometimes lament the fact that they lack the power to accomplish many of these delegated or assumed duties. This perception may, in part, be attributable to the tension inherent in the role itself. Chairs may experience discomfort in a role that places them in a position lying somewhere between the faculty and the administration. Chairs often experience conflict over whether they are primarily a faculty person with some administrative responsibilities or an administrator with some faculty responsibilities. Nonetheless, chairs are not without power and it is valuable to understand the sources of power at their command. Generally speaking, the power of higher education administrators can be categorized into three types, depending on how and from where it is acquired—namely, power from authority, position power, and personal power.

The Power of Authority

Authority granted officially from a higher level in the bureaucracy is called "formal authority." It gives an individual the right to command resources or to enforce policies or regulations. The ultimate power from this source exists when a person to whom the authority is granted is able to make final decisions and firm commitments for his or her department without requiring additional signatures of approval. In the case of a state college or university system, the board of regents or board of trustees is empowered by the state legislature to operate and control the system. The board, in turn, delegates authority and responsibility to the college and/or university presidents for the operation of the individual institutions. The presidents delegate authority to vice presidents and deans. Any official authority chairs may have has been delegated to them by their deans; deans cannot delegate more authority than has been delegated to them by their vice presidents. Faculty members will permit their behavior to be influenced or affected by the department chair if they believe that he or she has formal authority.

Position Power

Power that comes simply from having a title is called "position power." Recommendations made by people with certain types of "position power" are generally given more serious consideration than recommendations made by individuals who do not have it. Department chairs by virtue of holding the title may have influence not only with faculty members within their own departments, but with people in and outside the college over whom they have no authority or jurisdiction. Those who have such influence are perceived by some as having power. Chairs not only have the authority and responsibility to recommend salary raises, promotion, tenure, and teaching assignments, but they can often provide certain types of assistance to faculty members that faculty need but cannot provide for themselves, such as helping them develop professional acquaintances, recommending them for membership in select professional associations, nominating them for executive positions in their associations, helping them obtain sabbaticals or funds for travel to professional meetings, and helping them make contacts leading to paid consulting jobs.

Moreover, department chairs frequently are asked by their faculty members to write letters of reference to other institutions in support of applications for new positions.

Personal Power

Chairs also use whatever personal power they may have. Faculty members will permit themselves to be influenced or affected in some way by the chair if they respect the particular individual holding the position. Personal power derives from peers' respect for and commitment to the chair. It is informally granted to the chair by the faculty members and depends on how they perceive him or her as an individual and as a professional. A chair with a great amount of personal power is usually perceived by the faculty as possessing some of the following characteristics: fairness and even-handedness in dealing with people; good interpersonal skills; national or international reputation in the discipline; expertise in some area of knowledge; influence with the dean; respect in the academic community; ability and willingness to help faculty members develop professionally; ability to obtain resources for the department; highly regarded by upper-level administration; knowledgeable about how the college operates; privy to the aspirations, plans, and hidden agenda of the institution's decision makers; and ability to manage the department efficiently.

Personal power is not a power that can be delegated. Rather, it is a power that chairs must earn. The essence of personal power is credibility. It is, therefore, important that department chairs work to earn credibility with all relevant internal constituencies and external audiences. With credibility, department chairs have a personal power that inherently makes them more effective and able to manage the long list of responsibilities. When faculty perceive their chair as credible, they are more likely to give the chair full benefit of the doubt in every decision or action. When chairs have high credibility, others are less critical of their decisions and they experience less resistance to change. On the other hand, chairs with low credibility find that others (faculty and the dean) second guess all of their decisions. Without credibility, chairs face great resistance to their ideas and cannot be effective change agents.

The Power of Leadership

Chairs remain uneasy about the issue of power. Few believe they carry much weight by virtue of authority, though the fact is that chairs probably possess more authority than they think they do. As for positional power, the contra-dictions in the role of chair make it difficult to have much faith in the force of the title. Chairs do not have difficulty understanding that a major source of their power is personal. Their personal credibility is the most potent coin they have to put on the power table. However, there is a facet of that personal power that remains to be explored. If one defines leadership as the power to focus the energy of a group of people, the ability to guide the process of decision-making, and the presence to get others to act in concert with each other, then the chair has the potential of being one of the most powerful leaders in the institution. That leadership capacity derives from a firm base of personal power, which makes it so important to cultivate the credibility that underlies personal power. That power can be exerted to great effect in three areas: the department dialog; the department culture; and the department's actions.

The content of the departmental dialog says a great deal about the effectiveness of the department. If department meetings are clogged with long discussions of managerial matters or time is filled with hostile debate in which positions and proposed decisions are fruitlessly recyled, the result is a marginal or dysfunctional department. The chair, without being an autocrat, can have a great influence on the content of that dialog. It may take persistenc and patience, but the chair can shift the content of debate to issues that are truly important to the future health and prosperity of the department.

The chair also has great potential power over the culture of the department. A department riven with interpersonal rivalries and animosities has little hope of becoming collectively effective. Changing the dialog between people does not come easily. But if the chair is clear about what needs to change, s/he can transform unproductive dialog by intervening with new ideas, identifying destructive interchanges, and establishing standards of debate.

The chair possesses considerable personal power in guiding the department to take appropriate action. Academicians are often well practiced in debate. Depending on discipline, some find it difficult to move from debate to decision and from there to implementation. An important role for the chair is as monitor of action. The first step is to see that debate is brought to closure and that decisions are made. Obviously, one does not want to truncate debate. If one does that, expect the decision to be recycled. However, there is a propensity to let debate take the place of decisions. A chair can fend off that outcome. Once decisions are made, someone needs to follow up to see that action has been taken. If no one is interested in whether a decision has been implemented, chances are the action will be delayed, deferred, and ultimately forgotten.

CONCLUSION

The complex role of department chair requires a skilled individual who can both serve and coordinate multiple constituencies. Institutional reliance upon department chairs as primary change agents and managers will continue to increase as institutions respond to external pressures for productivity and accountability. The central administration is powerless in preserving program quality. In fact, the very reputation of the institution depends on the success of its department chairs in bridging institutional and departmental needs. Despite the anomalous quality of the position, chairs have immense potential to affect the future of their institutions and of higher education in general. The roles and responsibilities of chairs has changed in two major regards. The fulcrum has tipped their responsibilities from being concerned for the individual welfare of faculty to creating a successful working synergy among department faculty; and from being an advocate for department desires to linking the work of the department to the broader institution and external audiences. This does not mean that the older interests of developing individual faculty and advancing the interests of the department are discarded. It does mean that those interests must now be combined with new needs and interests. Chairs may be short on formal authority or positional authority. However, for those interested in affecting the future of his or her colleagues, there may be no more important leadership position than that of department chair.

REFERENCES

Bennett, J. B. 1988. Department chairs: Leadership in the trenches. In *Leaders for a new era: Strategies for higher education*, edited by M.F. Green, 57–73. New York: American Council on Education/Macmillan.
    Bennett contends that the "core academic success" of institutions of higher education rests upon the quality and capabilities of the chairs. Working from this premise, the author discusses the ambiguous but important role of the chair, the rewards and frustrations associated with the position, and the leadership opportunities for chairs.

————. 1983. *Managing the academic department: Cases and notes*. New York: American Council on Education/Macmillan.
    This text presents short case studies on the responsibilities usually assigned to department chairs. Chapter 1 contains a description of the department chair position.

Gmelch, W. H., and V. D. Miskin. 1993. *Leadership skills for department chairs*. Bolton, Mass.: Anker.
    The authors describe four roles of the department chair: faculty developer; manager; leader; and scholar. The text examines ways in which chairs can create productive department and enhance personal productivity.

Lucas, A. E. 1994. *Strengthening departmental leadership: A team-building guide for chairs in colleges and universities*. San Francisco: Jossey-Bass.

In chapter 2 of the text, the author discusses the roles and responsibilities of department chairs. The nine chair responsibilities described include leading the department, motivating faculty to enhance productivity, motivating to teach effectively, handling faculty evaluation and feedback, motivating faculty to increase scholarship, motivating faculty to increase service, creating a supportive communication climate, managing conflict, and developing chair survival skills.

Murray, J. 1996. Job dissatisfaction and turnover among two-year college department/ division chairpersons. ERIC Document Reproduction Service, no. ED 394 579. Proceedings of the 5th Annual International Conference of the National Community College Chair Academy, February, Phoenix.

The authors discuss the cost associated with turnover in managerial positions and describe the relationship between role conflict or ambiguity and employee dissatisfaction. Drawing up relevant literature, the authors point out that the chair's position is fraught with role conflict and ambiguity. They recommend that the causes of job satisfaction among chairs be investigated and addressed.

Seagren, A. T., J. W. Creswell, and D.W. Wheeler. 1993. *The department chair: New roles, responsibilities and challenges.* ASHE-ERIC Higher Education Report no. 1. Washington: The George Washington University, School of Education and Human Development.

This publication includes a summary of research conducted on the role of the department chair. The authors work from the research base to discuss the chair's role as a leader and evaluator of faculty performance. The report includes chapters on how politics, the institutional types, and the discipline influence the chair position. The authors conclude with a chapter describing the future challenges that department chairs face.

PART
TWO

• • • • • • • • • • • •

The Department and
Its People

CHAPTER

The Chair and Department Members

To lead a department effectively, a chair must take into account the characteristics and interests of the department's three primary internal constituencies: faculty, support staff, and students. Each group exhibits its own complexities, which pose management challenges for any chair. A chair's success in linking these constituencies in effective collaboration will determine the quality, productivity, and reputation of the department.

FACULTY

The Composition of the Faculty

In a representative department there will be variations in age, career stage, seniority of title, and disciplinary subspecialty of the faculty. There will be different races and genders. With increasing frequency, there will be differences in employment status as institutions make ever-increasing use of part-timers. The nature of the institution, be it a community college, private undergraduate college, state comprehensive, or research university will also affect the attitudes of faculty as they work together on the department's business. All these variations will color the attitudes of individual faculty, influence departmental culture, and affect collective decision making.

Challenge of Race and Gender

Department chairs committed to supporting faculty diversity soon realize that the challenge of productively integrating the department begins, rather than ends, with the hire of gender or race minorities. Faculty who by race or gender are in the minority are likely to hold opinions based upon their unique experience that differ from those held by other department members. Minority hires may require the chair's support to become fully participating members of the department. How the chair communicates with minority hires establishes the protocol for how other department members will communicate with them. If, for example, the chair dismisses the comments of a new female faculty member during department meetings, that chair licenses other department members to do the same. The chair can cultivate mutual respect among faculty regardless of gender or race through his or her own behavior.

The campus culture can facilitate or hinder the retention of racial and gender minorities. The governance structure and the leadership style of the administration contribute to the institution's culture. These elements help to establish the faculty's role in campus decision making. Chairs can help minority faculty have a voice on campus by nominating them to serve on important policy-making committees. At the same time, chairs may need to help shelter minority faculty from excessive committee service. When those who form campus-wide committees strive for diversity within the committee membership, it can result in heavier service assignments for faculty who are underrepresented by gender or race. Chairs can help new minority hires succeed in meeting standards for faculty performance by helping them know which assignments count toward promotion and tenure and making certain that they do not spend a disproportionate amount of time on committee service.

It can be difficult to retain racial and gender minorities even when the chair is sensitive to these issues. The community culture is also an important factor. Some minorities may elect to leave an institution because they fail to find social conditions to support family life in the area. Because the community environment, as well as the department and campus cultures, can influence a faculty member's persistence, a chair should seek to learn about community attitudes and resources that may impact the comfort of diverse faculty members. The knowledge gained should be shared with affected faculty; an honest picture in the long run is preferable to a Chamber of Commerce sales approach, which is likely to engender later disappointment.

Part-Time Faculty

Part-time faculty form a unique subculture within a department and they tend to perceive themselves as holding different status within a given department. They rarely hold tenure or tenure track appointments. They do not accrue the same benefits and have no guarantee of long-term employment even on a part-time basis. Traditionally, part-time faculty members have been used to meet unexpected needs for additional instructional staff when full-time instructors become ill, are given sabbaticals, or receive unexpected leaves of absence. They have been the typical source for teaching courses at night, on the weekend, in the summer, and off-campus through extension and continuing education programs. Part-time faculty most often teach one or more courses with no other assigned responsibilities. They are usually paid a lower salary than that of full-time faculty members because they have not been required to advise students, participate in the governance system, and so on. What is different today is that departments are using part-timers not only as "fill-in" faculty, but also to staff segments of the curriculum on a regular basis. When used in this manner, part-time faculty influence department quality and effectiveness. The degree of influence will vary with the percentage of part-time faculty, the centrality of the purpose they serve in the department's mission, and the proportion of part-time to full-time faculty in the department. Some departments, particularly in large urban settings, may employ many more part-time faculty than full-time faculty. Other departments rarely have more than the occasional part-time faculty member to cover the absence of a full-time faculty member. The presence of part-time faculty affects the composition and culture of the total department climate.

Faculty Performance, Attitudes, and Career Stages

The traditions of the academy provide faculty with significant independence and autonomy in carrying out their job responsibilities. Aside from meeting scheduled classes, department faculty structure their own workdays and agendas. This independence is an aspect of work life that faculty value. However, its practice has resulted in ambiguity about the focus of faculty loyalty. It has also led in many institutions to the fraying of collegiality and departmental cohesiveness. Depending upon the campus and department criteria for tenure and promotion, faculty may pursue activities that do not directly support department operations. For example, faculty at a research institution must invest a significant amount of time in pursuit of research and publication. That research focus may make faculty less accessible to students or unavailable for committee service.

The personal mission pursued by individual faculty will vary according to the stage of career development. An untenured faculty member at a research institution, for example, may be more focused on those short-term activities and achievements that will help to establish him or her as a researcher in the discipline. Tenured full professors at the same institution have greater freedom to select research projects that may not culminate in a final product or publication for several years. Thus, as chair, you may experience significant differences in the perspectives of tenured full professors and untenured assistant professors. These differences derive from perceptions of job security and standing in the department.

Academic training and professional experience, combined with career stage, can also contribute to different views. Faculty expectations for how a department should operate stem both from previous experience and cultural assumptions. Whatever the experience, the responses of untenured faculty are likely to be more flexible than those of veteran tenured faculty. However, for both groups, chairs can expect that specific actions or decisions that violate central values will engender conflict. For example, the need to standardize the content taught in multiple sections of the same course may be perceived as an infringement upon academic freedom, particularly by veteran faculty. The department chair seeking such a policy change would be more successful if s/he linked the proposal for a common syllabus to central values held by faculty. Faculty, for example, may be more accepting of the need to standardize the content taught in multiple sections of the same course if they perceive the proposal as a strategy to preserve instructional quality.

The institutional mission serves as a cornerstone for building faculty performance expectations. For example, an institution with a mission to offer quality programs to undergraduate students will demand teaching effectiveness but is less likely to expect faculty to engage in the type of scholarship that leads to publication. Carnegie I research institutions, however, will place greater emphasis on the use of publication and grant activity as two indicators of faculty success and accomplishment. The location of the institution also contributes to its culture. A large urban institution may employ faculty who commute a greater distance than those of a rural campus. Faculty who commute long distances or rely on public transportation may be less flexible in setting office hours or in being available for committee meetings. Finally, the presence of a faculty union can influence the institutional culture, which, in turn, affects faculty performance. Negotiated contracts that stipulate criteria for faculty promotion and detail performance responsibilities delimit the opportunity for department influence over the faculty role and participation in department business.

The culture of institutions of higher education as social organizations also influences faculty performance. As a social organization, an institution of higher education has elements of both collegiality and bureaucracy. This is a delicate balance for chairs to maintain, particularly in light of the increased demand for accountability imposed by external audiences. Pressures to implement measures of accountability tend to place constraints on faculty autonomy and limit faculty participation in organizational decisions. For example, departments at numerous institutions have needed to respond to externally imposed mandates to assess student learning outcomes. Such initiatives represent top-down decision making and, therefore, narrow the participation of faculty in shaping the policies of the institution. Department chairs often find themselves in the difficult position of needing to secure faculty cooperation on externally imposed initiatives. Faculty reaction to such initiatives is likely to vary according to the career stage of the individual. Untenured faculty, for example, are less likely to resist the implementation of new initiatives.

Discipline Orientation

Faculty often identify with the discipline or the professional area more than with a specific department or institution. Even within the same discipline, teaching and research specializations can contribute to a wide range of perspectives among faculty. Particularly with access to e-mail and other forms of electronic communication, faculty are linked to colleagues around the globe who share their disciplines and subspecialties. The culture of the discipline is an important source of faculty identity, and faculty frequently care more about their reputation within discipline associations than within the academic department. Further, the specific discipline influences the assumptions and norms accepted by faculty for performance within the discipline. These assumptions and norms help to determine department criteria for products of teaching and research quality. For example, some disciplines are more accepting of multi-authored work or a slower pace of publication. In some disciplines, scholarship leading to the publication of books is less frequent and, therefore, not the norm for academic promotion. As department chairs work to develop departmental procedures and criteria for promotion and tenure, they must find the balance between adhering to university standards and discipline expectations.

Engaging the Faculty

Department chairs must understand the composition of the faculty within their own departments if they are to cultivate effective communication among faculty. It is chairs' responsibility to encourage faculty to take an active role in department matters, and the extent to which chairs solicit the participation of all faculty will influence the total culture and climate of the department. Department chairs cannot afford to overlook any subgroup of department faculty whose performance helps the department satisfy some portion of the department's mission. Assuming that all faculty carry out assigned duties that are important to the department mission, every faculty member has a unique perspective to contribute to department discussions. The department chair must structure ways for faculty to interact in a productive manner and compare perspectives on department objectives. Productive dialog among faculty also requires department chairs to maintain a climate in which faculty are free to express their views without fear of retaliation. Only when chairs establish a positive climate that is conducive to a free exchange of ideas, and a department structure that ensures that all faculty have a forum from which to participate in discussions, can faculty engage productively in carrying out the business of the academic department.

Even in a healthy department, individual faculty will not be motivated in the same way or for the same purpose. Full-time tenure track faculty typically perceive themselves as pursuing careers. They are motivated to engage in activities that build their resumes or advance their professional reputations as teachers and scholars within the discipline. They are likely to be interested in service work on committees that promote their visibility within the college or on the campus. At the same time, full-time faculty may resist duties that seem to slow progress toward tenure and promotion. They may even see some service activities as the job of the department chair. Faculty who see their roles as teaching and research, for example, may question the appropriateness of assignments to help with student recruitment or retention activities. Some full-time faculty vocalize a desire to have the department chair make decisions and handle all paperwork. These faculty believe they should be spared any and all "administrative" chores. Yet, if the department is to be more than a collection of individuals with separate agendas, the department chair must engage all faculty in pursuit of the department mission. This does not license chairs to delegate the handling of routine paperwork. It does highlight the importance of having all faculty understand and subscribe to the department purpose and objectives.

It is very difficult to supervise part-time faculty members in the same ways as full-time faculty members. Part-time faculty often serve very specific short-term department needs. They generally cost less to hire and consume fewer department resources. Seldom does the institution or the department invest in the professional development of part-time faculty. They do not compete for limited travel funds or campus awards to support teaching and research activities. These cost savings are offset by the problems inherent in coordinating part-time faculty participation. For example, there can be a lack of program continuity between coursework delivered by part-time faculty and that staffed by full-time faculty. Sometimes part-time faculty are not available to meet with students or to serve on department committees. They often do not participate in department governance, and they may not be incorporated into the social structure that is likely to exist among full-time faculty. As for the part-timers, they perceive themselves as holding a second-class status within the department. With the growing reliance on part-time faculty to deliver significant portions of the department's academic program, there is a heightened need to incorporate them into the fabric of the department. Recognizing this, representatives from 10 academic associations who attended the Conference on the Growing Use of Part-Time and Adjunct Faculty, held in Washington, D.C., September 1997, developed a comprehensive statement that included specific policy recommendations for how to hire and employ part-time faculty in a manner that enhances academic quality.

This culture of ambiguity demands considerable skill from chairs. Full-time and part-time faculty seldom function as a cohesive group without the effective intervention of the department chair. There is a more natural tendency for part-time and full-time faculty to perceive themselves as different from each other, rather than to perceive themselves as all working to serve the same department mission. This is particularly true if part-time faculty are excluded from department meetings. A lack of social networking between full-time and part-time faculty can contribute to distrust between the two groups. As long as part-time faculty perform needed duties that, for whatever reason, are not performed by full-time faculty, they help the department meet its objectives. As chair, your conduct and attitude will impact the perceptions of both groups. Full-time faculty, for example, may suspect that part-time faculty do not invest sufficient time in course preparation. They may assume that part-time translates to half-hearted commitment to teaching. Part-time faculty may perceive full-time faculty as preventing their involvement in department governance. They may conclude that their views are not wanted or respected by full-time faculty. As chair, the onus falls on you to help shape these differing perspectives to a point where faculty respect and value the contributions of one another regardless of the employment status of each. In the same way that full-time faculty teaching in different discipline specializations may have different, but equally valid, views of the curriculum, part-time faculty teaching night and weekend courses may hold different, but valuable, views on the department curriculum. Effective department management makes full use of all faculty resources and expertise.

THE SUPPORT STAFF

Departments are complicated organizations and depend heavily on many different people to accomplish their work. Although chairs often think of faculty as the most important people in the department, others may play equally important but less visible roles. A large department may have a number of key staff people who do important jobs. In fact, the staff are often the ones who represent the department to students and the public. In some departments, staff with considerable seniority may effectively run things and constitute the department's *de facto* management. Chairs come and go, faculty come and go, but staff assistants stay on for decades.

It is important that department chairs assess the composition of their staff. Support staff may be administrative/professional or clerical, union or non-union, and full-time or part-time. Frequently, new department chairs inherit support staff who were hired by their predecessor(s). Even when chairs hire their own support staff, they must comply with campus policy for identifying and screening qualified applicants. If a staff position, for example, has a civil service or government job classification, the chair must fill the vacancy from a list of applicants generated by the campus personnel office. Tests and assessments made outside the department determine applicant qualifications and eligibility. Usually these job classifications have prescribed conditions and time limits for probationary employment and performance review. Although staff members work in and are supervised by the department, they are usually recruited, classified, hired, paid, evaluated, transferred, and promoted by a personnel unit. They may be members of a collective bargaining unit, or they may be covered by state laws and rules. If they have complaints or grievances, these are processed by specialists in the personnel department who ordinarily have little reason to be involved in the department's business.

A department chair may have very little to say about many aspects of staff employment because staff members are covered so completely by separate rules and regulations. Authority over staff may reside in a remote bureaucracy, and it is sometimes difficult to figure out who is really in charge. A department chair, for example, may discover that s/he has little to say regarding the approval of a request for an extended leave. Particularly if the staff support job classification is protected by a union, the department chair has no authority to alter work hours or working conditions beyond what is stipulated in the negotiated employment contract. The department chair must work with campus personnel administrators in managing special circumstances that may arise in the supervision of support staff.

Chairs usually have more control in hiring support staff for positions that are non-union or administrative. The quality of the applicant pool (and new hire) is determined by what the labor market has to offer and the position funding available to the department. Department chairs may discover that they either do not have sufficient funds to hire support staff with the skill proficiencies desired or that the local pool of qualified applicants is small. In these instances, department chairs may discover the need to train new support staff to handle their assigned responsibilities within the department.

The range of staff in a given department depends on its size and general importance to the university. Some smaller departments are lucky if they do not have to share a clerk/typist of the lowest job classification with two or three other departments. Others may be able to hire (in effect) a professional manager. This person may have a business degree and substantial experience, and can, with a minimum of guidance and supervision, effectively manage the entire scope of the department's routine business. Other staff may include professional-level people who advise students and assist in the academic administration of the department. In some disciplines, support staff replace faculty in doing some of the work of the department. A theater department, for example, may hire a technical director to oversee set construction for stage productions on a 12-month staff contract instead of a nine-month faculty contract. In some instances, administrative support staff may also teach specific courses in their areas of expertise. Administrative professionals who also teach can hold continuing appointments but are not eligible for tenure review and professorial rank.

Working with Support Staff

Although department chairs may expect to manage the staff, ironically, staff often "manage" department chairs. Staff with long experience are often the most knowledgeable in the university. They have control of files and information. They know who really makes decisions. They can anticipate the cycle of events. They know the quirks and idiosyncrasies of the system. They have seen it all before, and they know that every new administrator is bound to make avoidable mistakes. Savvy department chairs will take full advantage of their staff's knowledge and experience.

But staff can legitimately function only within the formal boundaries of their jobs. Department policies are essentially the province of the faculty, and staff need to be directed in the implementation of those policies. The chair is the link between faculty and staff, and between policy and implementation. Unless they get a clear explanation and clear direction, staff will not be in a position to either understand or implement department policies. The chair is usually the only person with the necessary authority to provide direction and guidance to staff. S/he must assume responsibility for seeing that the staff receives appropriate training and feedback. When new policies or rules are adopted, staff need to be counseled and advised about how to implement them. When new technology is adopted, staff will need opportunities to attend training sessions, and they will need to adapt their familiar work patterns to the new equipment. When job responsibilities are ambiguous or in conflict with others' responsibilities, staff need the opportunity to seek an authoritative resolution. The chair may feel it is inappropriate to act decisively and authoritatively, having absorbed the consultative norms of the faculty culture, but staff usually expect and need the chair to exercise direction and control. It is the only way they get clear signals about what they are supposed to be doing.

Managing Tensions between Support Staff and Others

Support staff have a unique relationship to the other department constituencies. Although support staff may not be directly involved in instruction, they may frequently be the department members that are most accessible to students. Students who wish to schedule an appointment with the chair or seek other types of assistance will leave a message for a faculty member or deal with the support staff in the department office first. Consequently, it is important that support staff know and understand the mission of the department and behave in a way that is consistent with its goals. In terms of the mission, faculty and support staff are on the same team and it is important for each internal constituency to recognize this fact.

In addition to being visible (and sometimes vocal) representatives of the department, support staff serve as the linchpins for department activity. Support staff sort and distribute mail, field incoming phone messages, duplicate instructional materials and other work requested by faculty, and assist the department chair in managing the day-to-day routine of the department. In fulfilling these duties, support staff can be congenial and facilitate a productive and positive work climate, or they can be obstacles to an efficient department.

It is important that department chairs facilitate an effective working relationship between the support staff and faculty. This is not always easy because faculty and support staff bring very different perspectives to the department. Faculty hold expectations for support staff performance that supports their work. Faculty seek prompt turnaround in the duplication of instructional materials and may fail to remember that support staff receive work from numerous individuals. On the other hand, support staff who watch faculty come and go as they wish may feel that short notice on projects are symptomatic of inefficiency and lack of planning. The chair will inevitably hear complaints from either side or both sides, and will sometimes have to intervene in a direct clash of wills between a faculty member and a staff person. The perceptive chair will anticipate this kind of conflict, and will develop a sense of when and over which issues it is likely to occur.

Conflict between faculty and staff can substantially weaken the chair's authority and effectiveness if it gets out of control. Staff, if they perceive that they lack the chair's backing and support, can bring the work of the department to a halt. They can also tie up the chair's time by going into a "passive-aggressive" mode: they simply stop taking responsibility and initiative, requiring the chair to direct and coordinate their every task. Faculty, on the other hand, will see management of the staff as one measurement of the chair's effectiveness. If they sense the staff has become unresponsive or unproductive, they will be quick to blame the chair, and they will also consume more of the chair's time with complaints. When they cannot see results, they will naturally question the chair's ability to do the job.

The chair's best strategy is usually to develop a good teamwork climate for the staff, to engage in regular planning and feedback sessions with them, and to signal that they have his or her support and commitment as long as they continue to perform in good faith. If they sense that the chair is approachable and they can discuss problems and solutions openly, they will respond. They can almost always appreciate the need to accommodate faculty and to adapt and change when unusual conditions arise. But they cannot (and should not be expected to) sacrifice their pride and their interests in a one-sided relationship in which the chair simply fails to consider or support them.

COMPOSITION OF THE STUDENT CONSTITUENCY

Students are the department's lifeblood. Ironically, they are both customers and "products." The department has fiduciary responsibilities to educate them, but it also has to satisfy them, or they will—practically speaking—take their business elsewhere. If the department fails to educate, it will be held accountable; if it fails to satisfy, it will lose student credit hours. While this poses a dilemma for the department in dealing with students, it also helps to define the unique characteristic of the student constituency. Institutions compete to recruit bright students and work hard to retain their student "customers." Simultaneously, institutions are involved in grading and assessing student learning as one important indicator of instructional quality and institutional effectiveness. Academic departments must also appeal to students as consumers while they remain diligent evaluators of student achievement. This dual task embodies inherent tension, which is further exacerbated by the diversity of the student constituency.

Most institutions work to recruit students of all races, differing ages, and, unless they are single-sex institutions, students of both genders. Each possible gender or race combination carries with it the potential for variation in academic interest and need. The educational background of students of the same gender or race can vary greatly depending upon the high school attended, the student's economic status, and even work or life experiences. The student constituency is more complex when one realizes that not all students pursue the same educational goals or can be satisfied in the same way. To consider how best to educate and satisfy students, one must understand the composition of the student constituency. Academic departments typically classify students as graduate or undergraduate. Each of these subgroups, however, contains a diverse grouping of students with further defining characteristics.

Graduate Students

Graduate students can be full-time or part-time and their age and experience can vary greatly within the same department. While some students enter graduate school immediately following the completion of their baccalaureates, others return to school to complete graduate degrees after obtaining work experience. Still others attend graduate school to alter or change their career paths. The journey that leads an individual to graduate school will shape that person's expectations and educational objectives.

Graduate students may be employed outside the department or by the department as teaching, research, or sometimes administrative assistants. Graduate teaching assistants may function as instructors with full responsibility for syllabus design and course delivery or they may assist faculty through the supervision of class labs, the grading of student work, or participation in instructional research. Graduate students employed as research assistants typically work for one or a few faculty. Usually the stipends they receive are funded through external grants and last only for the duration of the research project or grant support. Graduate students employed as administrative assistants typically report to the department chair and may work on a variety of administrative projects such as producing the department newsletter, helping with recruitment or development activities, or serving as additional staff support for administrative duties performed by the chair.

Undergraduate Students

Undergraduate students are typically classified as traditional or nontraditional. The "traditional" label is used to describe single students who pursue college education immediately following high school. These students are between 18 and 20 years old at the time they enter a college or university. Traditional students, however, can be divided into subgroups according to their academic interests and goals. Many enter college to earn baccalaureates. Others have plans to go to graduate school following completion of their baccalaureates. Still others pursue postsecondary education seeking particular expertises. Students in this latter grouping may, for example, want to take courses in real estate or computer graphics. That goal may include earning associate's degrees, or it may be limited to gaining professional expertise without the blessing of any degree.

Whatever the goal, there is a growing expectation among students and their families that a college education should lead to productive employment. Whereas students in previous decades may have sought college degrees for the purpose of becoming educated, the majority of undergraduate students today seek college education for the purpose of securing gainful employment. With employment as the primary goal, traditional students have a wide range of academic objectives. They may seek associate's or bachelor's degrees for employment or bachelor's degrees as preparation for graduate or professional programs. Many traditional students plan to complete their college education in phases, earning two-year associate's degrees to get better-paying jobs with the intent of going back to college to finish baccalaureates at a later date, and possibly on a part-time basis.

Traditional students vary greatly in terms of their financial need. The availability of financial aid can often dictate where a student seeks admission. The growing popularity of community colleges in some states can be attributed to the lower tuition and greater scheduling flexibility that allows students to work part-time while pursuing college coursework. Students who seek jobs on campus need to be able to enroll in classes that leave time for a work block. Students who pursue college education while holding jobs often need classes that are offered in the evenings and on weekends.

The "nontraditional" category encompasses returning students, single parents, married persons, adult learners, part-time students, and transfer students. Each of these descriptors identifies a subgroup of nontraditional students that possesses a unique perspective. For example, part-time students need courses that do not interrupt employment or other personal commitments. These students enroll in night and weekend classes. Transfer students typically seek a college or university that will accept previous coursework. These students hope to move from associate's degrees to baccalaureates without any loss of credit earned. While many institutions accept the two-year associate's degree as equivalent to the institution's core curriculum, the department often needs to review transfer students' transcripts to determine the equivalency for courses taken at the 300- or 400-level. Transfer students tend to be very goal-oriented and often exhibit remarkable maturity in making academic decisions and selections.

Returning students can have a variety of educational needs depending upon the reason for their earlier departure. Students find it increasingly necessary to interrupt their college education to work. These students are very thrifty consumers who seek to complete their degrees in the shortest, most efficient ways possible. Other returning students seek coursework that will enable them to change career paths and generally improve their employment status. Single parents and some returning students may seek to continue their education for the purpose of retraining for the job market. These categories of nontraditional students can overlap, in that it is possible for a single parent to be returning to college or entering college for the first time as an adult student. Similarly, returning students may be part-time or full-time. Regardless of the individual's circumstances, the growing number of nontraditional students places an increasing demand upon department and institutional resources. Nontraditional students require support services that traditional students seldom seek, including day care, night and weekend library hours, and accessible parking on campus.

Nontraditional students are also concerned with the cost of education. They view a college education as an investment in their future. More practically, they want to know that the money spent on a college education will translate into better earnings. And they look for bargains. Students living within driving distance of several institutions may enroll simultaneously at more than one institution. They build their curricula around work or family schedules with the goal of finishing as quickly and inexpensively as possible. A student may, for example, enroll in an English composition course taught on Saturday at college X, a history course on Tuesday evening at college Y, and a science class offered on Monday evening at college Z. All credit earned is then transferred to a single institution for degree completion.

Another category of students that can be either traditional or nontraditional is the "at-risk" group. These students enter a university on a provisional basis with recognized academic deficiencies. These deficiencies may be indicated through low scores on college admission exams, low GPAs in high school or other institutions, or a lack of seat time in certain subject matters. For example, the high school student who has not taken certain math courses may be admitted to a college or university with an identified deficiency in math. When a student lacks the required seat time in math (or other core subjects), the institution may require him or her to enroll in a remedial course before taking college math courses.

As state legislatures work to make college education more accessible to larger numbers of people, the at-risk students comprise a significant subgroup of the student constituency. These students may need remedial coursework, tutors, study sessions, and other support services. Depending on the services offered at a particular institution, academic departments may need to design and manage some discipline-specific services. For example, disciplines that require some technical proficiency may consider adopting a medical school model in which students are allowed to retake content until they demonstrate mastery without jeopardizing degree completion.

Working with Students

Most students do not need to see the chair on an individual basis. Much of the chair's contact with individual students will be to conduct routine business. Granting required approvals, signing forms, handling drop-add and late registration, providing routine academic advisement, and dealing with exceptions and waivers to rules are likely to be the usual reasons students see the chair. But much of this business can be, and often is, delegated to a support staff member.

Students, however, are quick to find the department chair when they have a complaint. A chair typically hears, and may need to intervene, when students and faculty have misunderstandings or disagreements and fail to reach satisfactory solutions. A chair may hear complaints about teaching styles, office hours, grading practices, course management, faculty behavior in or outside of class, and other related matters. Sometimes students seek to meet with the department chair for guidance and advice. Emotional support, career guidance, surrogate parenting, personal friendship, and intellectual exchange may all be reasons why students visit the chair. The chair has to decide how much time s/he wishes to spend visiting with students. A warm, engaging personality and an open door may attract students to the point where the chair is distracted from a normal work routine.

Sometimes a chair must deal with problem students. Incidents of cheating or plagiarism, for example, require the chair's involvement. It is important that the chair be familiar with the campus policy on student misconduct. Typically the campus policy prescribes a course of action that the chair must follow in managing instances of student misconduct. Similarly, the campus policy on sexual harassment, grading, and faculty conduct are ones that should guide the chair's action in responding to specific student complaints. The policy for each issue is likely to identify a campus office that can assist the chair in managing the application of a particular policy. For example, the office of personnel or legal counsel may have an individual who is available to advise a chair on how to manage a formal complaint of sexual harassment.

Department chairs also interact with students when department operating procedures provide roles for students in department governance. As student representatives on department committees, undergraduate and graduate students witness faculty interacting with one another and with support staff. Student presence on department committees will be embraced by some faculty but resented by others. When students do their homework and prepare for meetings they can offer an important perspective to department committees. Students are likely to ask the questions that faculty may not think to ask. Their presence forces faculty and staff to discuss issues with more clarity and reason. Short-tempered committee members are likely to exercise greater restraint during committee meetings when students are present. Those faculty and staff who believe students should not participate in department governance typically assert that students do not have a long-term vested interest in the welfare of the department. Some feel stifled by the presence of students and, therefore, believe that student participation in department governance produces an outcome reached by compromise rather than rigorous debate. It becomes the chair's responsibility to balance the various interests and perspectives held by students, faculty, and staff.

CONCLUSION

By assessing the particular composition of the faculty, support staff, and students in any particular department, the chair is in a better position to understand the full scope of perspectives. Departments succeed only when all the internal constituencies perform in a way that best advances the department's mission. When the internal constituencies work at cross-purposes, they jeopardize the department mission. The department chair needs to help each internal constituency understand its role in the department's operation and its value to the department's future. It also becomes the chair's responsibility to help each internal constituency understand and recognize the contribution of the other constituencies. Faculty need to understand the importance of support staff and support staff need to understand the essential mission of the teaching faculty. Similarly, faculty and support staff need to understand that students represent both the purpose and the success standard of any academic institution. The relationships among these internal constituencies are important yet fragile. When the relationships are productive, the department runs like a well-oiled machine.

REFERENCES

Austin, A. E. 1990. Faculty cultures, faculty values. *New directions for institutional research* no. 68: 61–74.
    Austin describes four primary cultures that influence faculty values and behaviors. The essay includes suggestions for institutional leaders on how to build on these various cultural values to improve institutional performance. Although Austin writes about institutional management, the primary cultures identified also affect department management.

Banachowski, G. 1996. Perspectives and perceptions: A review of the literature on the use of part-time faculty in community colleges. ERIC Document Reproduction Service no. ED 398 943.
    The author reports the results of an examination of the literature on the use of part-time faculty in two-year colleges available since the late 1980s in the ERIC collection. This position paper cites 50 sources.

Biles, G. E., and H. P. Tuckman. 1990. Managing part-time faculty. In *Enhancing departmental leadership: The roles of the chairperson*, edited by J. B. Bennett and D. J. G. Figuli, 83–90. New York: American Council on Education/Macmillan.
    The authors present a model for auditing part-time faculty human resource management and an action plan for improving part-time faculty human resource management policies and practices. The prescription includes suggestions for developing a part-time faculty human resource management policy and procedures manual.

Brodie, J. M. 1995. Whatever happened to the job boom? *Academe* 81, no. 1 (January-February): 12–15.
    The author examines changes in college faculty employment patterns since the 1970s and discusses the current lack of available full-time positions and the increase in use of part-time faculty.

Gappa, Judith M., and David W. Leslie. 1993. *The invisible faculty: Improving the status of part-timers in higher education*. San Francisco: Jossey-Bass.
    The authors describe the current environment for part-time faculty and identify the external forces and campus conditions that contribute to an institutional

reliance on part-time faculty. In part II of this text, the authors prescribe strategies for enhancing evaluation through the use of part-time faculty.

Green, M. F. 1989. *Minorities on campus: A handbook for enhancing diversity.* Washington: American Council on Education.

This handbook was written as a practical guide for trustees, presidents, and other higher education administrators. The handbook offers specific strategies for enhancing diversity on campus in seven areas: an institutional audit; undergraduate students; graduate/professional students; faculty; administrators; the campus climate; and teaching, learning, and the curriculum.

Higgerson, M. L. 1996. *Communication skills for department chairs.* Bolton, Mass.: Anker.

This text offers specific communication strategies for working effectively with faculty, staff, and students. The author prescribes *how* a chair might execute the supervisory tasks that chairs must manage.

Kuh, G. D. 1990. Assessing student culture. *New Directions for Institutional Research* no. 68: 47–60.

The author summarizes literature on student cultures and reviews approaches to assessing student culture that are believed to have a significant impact on many aspects of college life, including student learning.

Leslie, D., and J. Gappa. 1994. Education's new academic workforce. *Planning for Higher Education* 22 (4): 1–6.

The authors report the results of a study of part-time faculty and offer suggestions for how institutions of higher education might adapt their policies to the growing trend to employ part-time faculty.

Pearson, C. S., D. L. Shavlik, and J. G. Touchton. 1989. *Educating the majority: Women challenge tradition in higher education.* New York: American Council on Education/Macmillan.

This text begins with the premise that educating women involves more than admitting them to institutions originally designed for men. The 29 chapters contributed by leaders in higher education are organized into four sections: (1) understanding women's diversity and commonalities; (2) learning environments shaped by women; (3) reconceptualizing the ways we think and teach; and (4) transforming the institution.

Proceedings from the Conference on the Growing Use of Part-time and Adjunct Faculty. *Academe* 84 (1): 54–60.

Rhoades, G. 1996. Reorganizing the faculty workforce for flexibility. *Journal of Higher Education* 67 (6): 626–59.

The author reports the results of research involving the examination of contracts of 183 institutions and systems that address the use of part-time faculty. The study focused on two research questions: (1) To what extent do collectively bargained faculty contracts provide for managerial discretion or professional constraint regarding the use of part-time faculty? and (2) To what extent are part-time faculty's conditions of employment different from those of full-time faculty? The researcher concluded that there is extensive managerial discretion built into the contracts and that the conditions of employment for part-time faculty are relatively undefined.

Roueche, J. E., S. D. Roueche, and M. D. Milliron. 1996. Identifying the strangers: Exploring part-time faculty integration in American community colleges. *Community College Review* 23, no. 4 (spring): 33–48.

Working from organizational identification theory, the authors present a "Part-time Faculty Integration Model." They report the findings of a two-stage quantitative and qualitative descriptive analysis of a survey administered to a broad-based stratified random sample of colleges in the American Association of Community Colleges. Specific implementations and recommendations are drawn from the study.

CHAPTER 4

Recruiting the Department's Constituents

Nothing you do in your department is more important than the selection of faculty, staff, and students. Given the institutional tenure of most faculty, their selection represents a million-dollar decision. As for staff, they give the first, and last, impression of your department culture, receptivity, and productivity. Students are the ultimate product of your department, and it is through them that your department will be judged within your institution as well as outside it by external professionals and employers. Nothing is more critical to your department than its ability to recruit, hire, retain, and develop top-quality faculty, staff, and students. As chair, it is your responsibility to lead those efforts. But how do you go about doing that?

STRATEGIC DEPARTMENT RECRUITMENT

Recruitment of faculty, staff, and students should not be an *ad hoc* series of activities carried out in isolation, but an integral part of the department's strategic plan (chapter 10). The planning process provides the department with a sense of its strengths, weaknesses, opportunities, and threats. A personnel or human resource inventory serves as a tool to take action in the recruitment of its constituents. Today's rapid advances in technology, for example, challenge the traditional roles of secretaries hired to type manuscripts for faculty, of faculty performing a solo teaching function, and of traditional-aged students' dependence upon faculty for dissemination of knowledge. As it becomes commonplace for faculty to be equipped with computers, making them able to prepare their own teaching materials and manuscripts, the roles of department secretaries are changing. Over the past 10 years many secretaries have moved from being primarily typists to being program assis-tants and coordinators. Secretaries are now part of the department chair's office team. As faculty become involved in distance learning and technology-dependent instruction, their roles change as well. Teaching is becoming less a solo activity and more a team effort, particularly as technology becomes an integral part of the pedagogical process. When it comes to students, they are not demographically the same as those served by institutions a generation ago. Today students are older, more culturally and ethnically diverse, and have a variety of needs unlike those of students who walked the halls of academe in earlier decades. Without a vision of the future, departments will not be able to move into the twenty-first century with the human resources they need to survive and meet the needs of their respective communities.

As resources begin to shrink, replacement of faculty and staff will become more difficult. And as colleges and universities become more competitive for students, it is especially important that recruitment efforts be consistent with department goals and that the recruitment process be well organized and articulated. Furthermore, each department's recruitment plan should be in concert with the mission and goals of the specific college or university. Given the changing clientele, the department may have to make adjustments. More students now are nontraditional (older, more mature, more diverse, and employed), which necessitates adjustments in both teaching schedules to accommodate work schedules and teaching methods to reflect characteristics of the adult learner.

With the opportunity of attracting more diverse students also comes the challenge for advisors and recruiters to be sensitive to their special needs. Many departments have hired minority recruiters to pay attention to some of these issues. At both the undergraduate and graduate levels, students who are admitted do not necessarily choose to enroll. In today's competitive higher education market, it may take the extra effort of follow-up telephone calls, personal visitations, and recruitment trips not only to attract but also contract with students to enroll in your department. However, recruiting is only one part of the equation as retention becomes an equally challenging concern. Support programs such as mentorships and special scholarships are also needed to increase the chance of not only recruiting diverse students but also graduat-ing those recruits. This may require more coordination and involvement with university and college student service programs such as admissions and out-reach.

IN SEARCH OF UNDERREPRESENTED TALENT

Not only do department chairs have a moral and legal obligation to disallow any form of discrimination against women and minorities, they should feel compelled to recruit and select from the most diverse pool of candidates possible. Where it has been determined that underrepresentation exists, chairs need to engage in special recruiting efforts to help correct the problem. At the faculty level, the simple continuation of traditional hiring practices within the university or college tends to perpetuate the underrepresentation of women and minorities in academe. Failure to recruit, educate, and graduate a diverse student body undermines the future diversity of the professoriate.

The relatively low participation of minorities in American higher education has been a concern of the National Education Association (NEA), the American Association of University Professors (AAUP), and the American Council on Education (ACE) for many years. In particular, ACE sponsors several programs to encourage and recruit minorities into faculty and administrative positions. Even with these and other efforts, minorities are significantly underrepresented in colleges and universities (NEA 1993, 1).

All American-born minorities are underrepresented on the faculty of colleges and universities (Carter and Wilson 1996, 5). For example, one-third of the professoriate in America will retire by 2010. If that demographic turnover is to expand the numbers of minority faculty, minority students must be recruited now into doctoral degree programs. Today, only 5 percent, 7 percent, and 4 percent of the graduate students are African American, Latino/Latina, and Native American, respectively, while they represent 13 percent, 7 percent, and 1 percent of the U.S. population.

While insufficient women and minority participation of students and faculty represents a broader societal issue, departments must take responsibility for attracting more women as well as more minority students to study and major in their disciplines. Some educators recognize that they must look further back into elementary and secondary schools to identify potential academic talent. The groundwork may be laid by engaging in early recruitment and cooperation with public and private school systems. This expansion of opportunity requires the department's willingness to learn and adapt. It may even require a complete change in attitude. A report entitled "Achieving Faculty Diversity" identified five negative attitudes or assumptions about minority candidates: they aren't the best qualified; there aren't any of them out there; they'll want astronomical salaries; they won't want to live here; and we're already doing all we can (NEA 1993, 9). The logical inference from such statements is that effort spent looking for minority candidates is a waste of time and resources. If these attitudes exist in your department, the first challenge will be to change that culture.

There are external resources that you and your department can draw upon in seeking to build diversity. Some institutions collaborate in the establishment of national "vita banks" to assist in pooling names of minority students and faculty. Professional associations may also have networks dedicated to finding and promoting women and minorities for faculty positions. Some of the most successful universities "grow their own" by graduating women and minorities with the Ph.D. degree—and serve as fertile recruiting grounds for other institutions seeking candidates. When recruiting women or minority faculty, a department may be tempted to recruit established professionals from other colleges and universities. While viewed as an easier path by some, this solution is unproductive in the long run as it merely shifts the problem from institution to institution with no net gain in the number of minority faculty.

The culture of your institution will also have an effect on your efforts. Several studies on recruitment point to five key elements at the institutional level that affect the success of efforts to recruit minorities. As department chair you may want to promote and challenge these ideas within your own institution.

1. Leadership from the top—commitment from the president and board of trustees—is important to the success of minority recruiting at the department level. Even if your department is receptive to the goal of recruiting underrepresented minorities, it will be difficult to succeed if the president and trustees are not similarly inclined. Faculty will eventually undergo tenure review and if administrators up the ladder are not supportive, the department may find candidates are being blocked.

2. A sound plan addressing every aspect of faculty hiring—from central administration to each department—is helpful. The most reliable indication of institutional goals is a written plan that has been publicly circulated. Your department's recruiting efforts will fare better if departmental and institutional goals are in harmony.

3. An institution-wide approach to minority recruiting is valuable. The American Council on Education recommends this as the foundation for all departments and academic units for the strategic planning process and as a criterion by which individuals and units are evaluated. This institution-wide approach will provide each candidate with the assurance that s/he will not be a mere token, but rather an integral part not only of the department but also of the institution as a whole.

4. Expanding the pool by identifying potential and existing candidates is vital. Chairs and faculty do not always keep in mind that they are part of the solution. It is foolish to expect to find well-trained minority

candidates if efforts are not made at the department level to teach minority students.

5. Financial support for minorities early in the pipeline is necessary, from undergraduate through graduate school and postdoctoral work. The University of Wisconsin calls this need the "unbroken financial aid ladder" (NEA 1993, 11–12). Departments do have the power to affect the supply of minority candidates through the allocation of graduate fellowships. It is important to work with your department to exercise that power responsibly and effectively.

In conclusion, as we see adjustments in the legal definitions applicable to affirmative action, it is important to understand that the achievement of greater diversity, while a legitimate institutional and departmental goal, must not be pursued through the application of unlawful hiring quotas or preferences based on race, ethnicity, or gender. Rather, selection should be based on qualifications carefully defined to reflect the specific instructional and other programmatic needs of the department that the successful candidate will be expected to fulfill. The department should always hire the best qualified candidate, based on stated criteria relevant to its needs. Those might be defined to reflect a candidate's ability to work in a culturally and ethnically diverse environment, for example, without making minority status a determinative factor in the selection decision. Affirmative action efforts—to ensure that employees and applicants are treated without discrimination—should include outreach and other efforts to broaden the pool of qualified candidates where appropriate to any identified underrepresentation.

RECRUITING STAFF, STUDENTS, AND FACULTY

Hiring Staff

No department constituency is complete without the academic staff. Your productivity as department chair is critically affected by the quality of your staff. In addition, staff are the first line of visibility and service to your students and faculty. Staff need to understand your department's mission, and they need to support its values. Without that coordination, your department will project a conflicted image to all who come in contact with it. Just as with hiring of faculty, the process of staff recruitment is often regulated and regimented by university requirements. In some institutions, your ability to shape the initial pool of staff applicants may be more constrained than it is for faculty recruitment. But it is no less important to the productivity and image of your department to recruit staff with patience and care.

Selecting a staff member who best meets the work requirements and complements the character of the department from a list of similarly credentialed and experienced applicants may be difficult. However, the basic tools used when hiring quality faculty members are useful in staff selection: effective recruitment, interviews, and reference checks. Yet since the employment market for staff members usually resides within the university itself, most campuses have standardized procedures and applicant lists generated and distributed from personnel offices or human resources centers.

The first step prior to posting the vacancy is to review and/or create a job description by conducting a systematic job analysis; a process of determining the skills, knowledge, and abilities required for job performance. From such an analysis you should determine the essential job functions, minimum qualifications, preferred characteristics, and any special requirements. Now you are ready to prepare and distribute the advertisement and post the notice of vacancy on your campus and do some serious recruiting. Once you receive the applications it is essential to take the time necessary to conduct a thorough review of the applications, make the necessary background calls and checks, interview your top candidates, and select a member for your office team. While selecting faculty represents a million-dollar decision, hiring competent and collaborative staff members is an investment in your department's productivity and collective success. Creating an effective, efficient, and compatible staff team should be the goal in any departmental staff hiring. Using the department's strategic plan to drive the staff recruitment process will enable you to anticipate the course of events prior to the occurrence of vacancies and to avoid hasty, ill-conceived decisions at the time of hiring.

Recruiting Students

Department faculty and chairs do not necessarily see the recruiting of students as one of their primary responsibilities. Insofar as our institutions have developed elaborate specialization of functions, it has been easy for each structure to limit its concerns to its assigned task. What is increasingly apparent is the interconnection of all functions in the institution. While specialization of function is useful and necessary, particularly as the size of institutions increases, it is important to perceive where and how one unit can enhance the performance of another. Thus, with the recruiting of students, there are contributions that chairs and faculty can make. At the graduate level this function is easier to see, since admission to a program is controlled by that program. However, even at the undergraduate level, departments can contribute to the recruitment process. They can do so by furnishing assistance when and as requested by those formally vested with the task of student recruitment, namely, the staff in the admissions office. Chairs and faculty can also ease the burdens of recruitment by the kinds of external contacts they initiate and the ways in which they develop those contacts. Perhaps the most potent support chairs and faculty can give the admissions office is in their effort to retain students. The investment of time and money in the recruitment of students in private institutions represents a major piece of the institutional budget. However, even in publicly funded institutions, each student represents a significant investment. For every student who drops out before completing a program, the institution has effectively wasted a piece of its budget. Most admissions offices can give you cost figures for recruiting each student. Granted, dropouts do not occur for a single reason. Nonetheless, if you can help your department acknowledge that it can affect the retention of students, you will be more likely to come up with specific stratagems to improve student retention and graduation rates. The effects will be positive for both the department and the institution.

Faculty Recruitment

Setting the Stage

The current system in higher education stratifies faculty appointments based on preconditions of employment status. A tripartite classification stratifies faculty in the department into categories of: (1) tenure track faculty; (2) term appointment faculty; and (3) temporary and adjunct faculty. The tenure track faculty are further categorized into those with or without tenure as well as those with or without graduate faculty status. Faculty on term appointments serve in many capacities necessary to strengthen the department, from traditional faculty roles to the role of program administrator. Temporary and adjunct faculty provide resources in areas of current weakness whether due to position vacancies or unmet assignments.

The recruitment process for all three classifications of faculty may be quite different. In general, you may find that instructional and research positions of a continuing nature that are half-time or more need to be advertised following affirmative action guidelines. Make sure you know your institutional procedures. However, some positions, particularly those filling term or temporary positions, need not meet all the recruitment requirements. The following are classic examples of position vacancies that may not have to follow the strictest guidelines for recruitment:

1. selection of a chair or assistant chair from within the department (However, external recruitment of an outside chair does need to be advertised.)
2. a principal investigator or recipient of a contract or grant
3. an existing position with funding sources that have changed but with duties that remain the same (For example, a shift from a grant or contract to a regularly funded general budget. If the duties are redefined, the position needs to be advertised.)
4. visiting scholars or exchange professors

5. positions less than half-time during a term
6. "adjunct" or other temporary faculty who are appointed for less than one year

Given the exceptionality of each of the cases listed above and institutional idiosyncrasies in terms of hiring, it is futile to lay out principles for these kinds of hirings. Instead, the remainder of this chapter will focus on the chair's role in guiding the recruitment of the permanent, tenure track faculty member. Your major tasks as chair will be to: (1) establish the size and composition of the search committee; (2) create the timeline and secure approval of the position announcement; (3) ensure a market saturation of the vacancy announcement; (4) provide assistance in managing accurate search committee records and screening of applicants; and (5) coordinate the selection of the finalist with the dean and faculty.

Establishing the Search Committee

Before appointing a search committee, you should have in hand written authorization from your dean for filling a particular vacancy. You also need to work with the dean to ensure that you have support in that quarter for the committee you intend to appoint. While the size varies, committees of five to seven members work well for faculty searches. Fewer than five participants does not provide the range of views needed for an effective search, and more than seven will create serious coordination problems for the committee members.

There are several factors to consider in terms of the search committee. The first is its composition, which, of course, needs to take into account the symbolic representation of the department's constituency. However, it may also be important to have input from the population the department serves. If your department works on a continuing basis with another department, sharing students, projects, and overlapping curricula, you may want to appoint a person from that department. Often a search committee includes a student from the discipline. There may even be circumstances in which you will want to include professionals or stakeholders from outside the university or college. The major pitfall to avoid is to seek the path of maximum comfort by appointing individuals who always work well together and who represent the same ideology. The committee should reflect a balance of differences in attitude, philosophy, gender, ethnicity, and talent. What they do need to share is the mission to select the person best suited for the position given the needs of the department.

The appointment of a chair for the committee should also be thought out. You have two options: to designate the chair yourself or leave it to the committee to select its leader. The path you choose will vary according to departmental custom, institutional practice, and the particular circumstances of the search. Regardless of the manner of appointment, it is important for you to establish the expectation of regular reporting from the committee chair to you regarding the progress of the search. This will enable you to ensure efficient progress and a successful outcome.

During the appointment process, you will also need to establish a written charge. That charge should include: (1) the development of the position description; (2) a defined process for finding qualified candidates; (3) an agreed system for screening applications; (4) a procedure for contacting references; and (5) an organized protocol for interviewing final candidates. While the committee is responsible for the details of the search process, you should work out with the dean how the committee will report its recommendations to you as chair and to the dean. Although the charge to the committee should be in writing, you can set the tone and pace of the search by meeting with the committee to discuss the charge. You may also be able to offer the committee some tools that can enhance the efficiency of their work. A conversation at the initiation of the search will also give you the opportunity to emphasize that, ultimately, the function of the search committee is advisory to you and the dean.

Creating the Position Announcement and Time Line

One of the first tasks you should ask the search committee to perform is to create the job description, announce the vacancy, and establish a time line. Two kinds of announcements need to be prepared. The first is a short statement to advertise the position, and the second is a longer detailed description to be sent to all potential candidates and those responding to the advertisement. The short advertising statement should include the following basic information:

1. the name of the department and institution
2. particular mission or market niche the department serves, including types of degrees granted
3. the academic rank(s) of the vacancy(ies)
4. minimum qualifications and experience required
5. specialization or unique characteristics desired
6. appointment status—tenured or term
7. employment status—annual or academic year
8. salary range or competitiveness with peer institutions
9. starting date of employment
10. application papers required and to whom they should be sent
11. special statement encouraging women and minorities
12. closing date for application

The longer version of the job description repeats the same basic information but goes on to elaborate on the unique qualities of the institution as well as any other relevant information that may attract candidates to apply for the position. This is the place where you make sure the department markets itself and the vacancy. The degrees the department offers should be listed along with specializations. If the location of the institution is not well known, a cultural and geographic description should be included.

Instructions on applying and submitting credentials should be clear and precise. An application usually consists of a cover letter, three letters of reference (or names, addresses, e-mail addresses, and phone/fax numbers of references), and a current vita. Placement files are seldom requested but may be appropriate for staff or temporary appointments. Search committees may also wish the candidate to submit a sample of his or her research, teaching evaluations, or other evidence of performance effectiveness.

Candidates should not be asked to submit information regarding their race, national origin, gender, age, disabilities, family plans, or other items precluded under affirmative action guidelines. However, for monitoring purposes such information is typically requested under a separate cover from the college's or university's affirmative action office.

Marketing the Vacancy Announcement

Most institutions routinely advertise their openings in *The Chronicle of Higher Education*. While this might be the most convenient, comprehensive, and necessary vehicle to meet affirmative action guidelines, it is not sufficient. To attract a robust pool of applicants including minorities and women the department chair must encourage the search committee to act in a proactive manner and go beyond placing an ad in the *Chronicle*. Job registries are published by various agencies. These registries may have a wide circulation and are targeted to special populations. Also, many disciplines and professional organizations have state, regional, and national associations that publish position openings in their newsletters and journals. Advertising in metropolitan newspapers known to serve significant populations of women and minority scholars is another way to broaden the scope of the search.

Marketing the search to include underrepresented minorities should not end with the passive placement of advertisements but should include the active use of existing or new networks of minority scholars, department chairs, and professional associations. The committee can also solicit minority graduates, campus visitors, and friends to recruit actively from underrepresented groups. Some institutions have established contacts with predominantly African-American or Native-American colleges and universities, and have built a minority presence on their own campuses through faculty exchanges or minority student teaching fellowships. The minority fellows may be able to help in recruitment efforts and may even become potential candidates themselves. Finally, make sure your affirmative action statement on the advertisement is not limited to stating the perfunctory "We are an equal opportunity affirmative action employer." It should highlight something unusual or unique in your approach and commitment to recruiting underrepresented groups.

Managing Accurate Records: The Screening of Applicants

The importance of keeping complete and accurate records cannot be overemphasized. Litigation centering on sloppy search procedures is not uncommon. Careful record-keeping will do much to avoid potential legal difficulties with applicants. Designate someone in the department office as the records-keeper, with all materials kept in a specific location known to the committee and to you. All mailing announcements should be recorded, and when each application is received it should be dated and placed in individual folders. The applicant folders typically contain checklists to determine the completeness of each folder. As the closing date approaches, a candidate comparison spreadsheet should be developed, which should include such basic information as names, current positions, degrees and locations, experience, publications, and other vital information important for review by the selection committee and affirmative action office.

Once the files are in order and the closing date has passed, the committee is ready to review the material and rate the candidates based on the degree to which each person meets or does not meet the job requirements. As committee members review each folder they should read with the following questions in mind:

1. Does the cover letter clearly address the requirements established in the position description?
2. Does the vita contain clear information regarding the qualifications and responsibilities needed to screen the applicant? Are there unexplainable employment gaps? Does the vita raise suspicions or doubts about the authenticity of the candidate's achievements?
3. Do the reference letters specifically address the candidate's skills and knowledge? Are the sources of the reference letters credible?
4. Did the candidate supply the committee with unnecessary and unorganized paperwork? Are some supplemental materials included that are inappropriate, such as personal photographs (Gmelch and Miskin 1995, 31–32)?

The screening of potential applicants to the select few invited to campus for an interview and visit usually follows a three-step process. First, the committee separates the eligible from the ineligible based on the papers submitted. Eligibility of candidates is determined by how closely their credentials and experience match those listed in the position description. The second stage narrows the applicants down to a "long list" for follow-up reference calls. Finally, after comparing information obtained on each of the applicants from the long list, the committee selects the finalists to be recommended to the chair and dean for interviews. As department chair you may want to brief the committee on the screening process, as explained in more detail below.

Paper Screening Applications. The first laborious task of the search committee begins with the initial review of the applicant pool. At this initial stage the committee has to decide if any applications are ineligible due to incomplete information in the file or lack of prerequisite job requirements, such as an earned doctorate. It is vital that all members of the committee use the same explicit criteria and that they apply them consistently across all the files. A formal checklist is a useful tool during this stage. You will need to rely on ongoing contact with the search committee chair to see that these procedures, for which you are ultimately responsible, are fairly and consistently applied.

Reasons for finding candidates not eligible may be the lack of terminal degrees or the inability to meet state or institutional regulations. For example, some institutions have a strict policy of not hiring their own graduates because they fear the consequences of academic inbreeding. There is also the hazard that senior professors will continue to direct their former students' activities rather than accept them as equals. Conversely, some institutions deliberately employ alumni, particularly those who have distinguished themselves elsewhere, for the added benefit that they understand the tradition of their alma mater better than outsiders. Many times, special circumstances present themselves whereby graduates are hired on a temporary basis to fill a sudden vacancy, or on a permanent basis if the top minority or woman in the field happens to be from the same institution.

The end of the first screening process typically culminates in the candidates being placed in one of three categories: (1) "ineligible" in terms of qualifications or institutional or departmental policies; (2) "marginal" in that their files may not be complete or they do not quite meet all of the criteria for eligibility; and (3) "eligible" by meeting the basic qualifications and requirements. Files of ineligible applicants should be set aside with a note containing the reasons for the ineligibility.

From Long List to Reference Checks. Now the committee members prepare for the second cut. The goal of this stage is to reduce the field of candidates to a reasonable number (usually from 10 to 15 applicants) for the first set of reference calls. They may decide to consider "marginal" candidates, those who do not quite meet all the criteria but nevertheless appear to have better-than-average qualifications. In reviewing application materials, the committee members should keep in mind the affirmative action policies of the institution, retaining as many women and minority candidates as possible for consideration in the finalists' screening. The files of applicants who do not survive the second screening, for whatever reasons, should be pulled from further consideration. The remaining applicants meeting the minimum set of requirements become the official pool of "nominees" from which the best qualified will be selected.

Selection of the Finalists: Using Phone Interviews. Your goal in this stage is to generate sufficient data to narrow your field to the final three or four persons you wish to invite for interviews. The ideal way to conduct such a check would be by personal visit, but this is seldom possible unless you are attending a national meeting or discipline conference. Practicalities dictate that this process will be carried out by telephone. At this point it is both a courtesy and sound practice to call the applicants to let them know they are on your "long list" of candidates and inform them you will be making reference calls. It is also useful to conduct telephone interviews of the candidates. Committee members should team up and call at least three or four references for each candidate and, if possible, go beyond the list of references provided by the candidate.

The search committee should agree on a basic phone protocol to ensure that each interviewer covers the same core questions with each interviewee. Furthermore, callers should have the written protocol in front of them when they call. Since the objective is to learn as much about the candidate as possible, interviewers should follow up on interesting issues *ad hoc* as the conversation develops. The search committee will probably want to interview both the candidates and their references, so the protocol needs to be adjusted accordingly. The structure of the suggested protocol is derived from Elliot and Fortunato (1997, 17). Whether speaking with the candidate or a referee, your first task is to establish rapport with the person you are calling. It is important immediately to identify yourself, your position, and the university, and to state why you are calling. Then ask whether this is a good time to converse. Throughout the conversation, let the person talk freely, without interruption. Be alert for pauses or subtle clues that invite questions, then follow up and probe.

In interviewing the candidate, be sure to state that s/he is in the "first-cut pool." Then verify that the candidate is still interested in being an applicant. Review the position and its qualifications, and then pursue an open-ended conversation about the position and explore the reasons for the candidate's interest. Ask the candidate what questions s/he might have about the position, and inform the candidate of the next steps in the search procedure. Before you end the interview, review your checklist of questions to be sure everything was covered.

When speaking with references, it is important at the outset to assure the references that all comments will be kept confidential. Before asking questions about the candidate, review the position and its qualifications. Then ask how well the candidate would meet these qualification. From there, progress to more specific questions. A good concluding question is, "Would you reemploy the applicant?" Again, review your protocol to ensure that you have asked all the questions and then thank the interviewee for his or her time and assistance.

What should one look for in these phone interviews? Reference letters rarely uncover critical information people might give either in person or by telephone. Thus, your goal should be to press beyond the statements made in letters of reference. Interviewers should probe for the candidates' levels of competence in specific areas; their weaknesses, as well as their strengths; and their ability, or lack thereof, to work with colleagues and students. Questions about the candidates that may have come up during discussion of their files may be resolved in the telephone interviews. Personal contact with candidates and references establishes credibility and reliability of information provided in applications and adds another dimension to candidates' profiles.

Once the reference calls are completed, the search committee should meet to prepare its recommendations for you as chair. You, in turn, will carry these to the dean. It is worth knowing whether the dean wants candidates ordered by rank or simply listed alphabetically. You should also know the maximum number of candidates the dean will fund for campus visits.

The Campus Visit. The campus visit is the crucial penultimate step. Careful thought should be given to the orchestration of this process. Remember that the candidate is taking the measure of your department, institution, and community just as you are taking the measure of the candidate. Before the first candidate reaches the campus, you should have worked with the search committee to set up the visit protocol. Each visit should be made as identical to the others as possible. Chairs should discuss with the search committee what the basic components of the campus visit will be. That conversation can be held at any time before candidates are invited to campus. The plan must be agreed to before invitations are proffered, because as part of the invitation the candidate should be informed of the procedure and given the opportunity to prepare in any way that may be necessary. There are several basic questions that need to be sorted out. One is the duration of the visit. How long will candidates spend on the campus? With whom will they meet, and will those meetings be in groups or on an individual basis? What kinds of contact will there be with students? Do you wish the candidate to teach a class or give any sort of formal presentation? At what point should a meeting with the dean or vice president of academic affairs (VPAA) be arranged? Who will answer terms of employment and institutional benefits? What parts of the campus and community is it important for candidates to visit?

Mechanical details are also important. If well arranged, they can help make candidates feel comfortable and positive about the institution and department. If left to *ad hoc* arrangements, everyone can become frustrated and irritated. Those details include arranging to meet the candidate upon arrival, as well as return him or her to the airport at the end of the visit. If you have not already done so, the candidate will appreciate receiving on arrival a printed interview schedule with names of all the people s/he will be meeting. If the candidate has not been provided with basic institutional documents, such as the course catalog, these should also be in the candidate's arrival packet. Be sure all visit details have been coordinated, inlcuding housing for the candidate and guides to take the person from one interview to the next. During the visit, be prompt, follow the schedule, and provide an attractive location for the interviews.

Ideally, the visit protocol should provide time for an individual interview with you as chair, a group visit with the search committee, individual and group visits with faculty members with whom the candidate will be working, and time with student representatives. Assuming the interview process takes more than a day, there will be the opportunity for informal canvassing of the committee members. If the search committee agrees that a particular candidate is one they may wish to recommend for final hiring, the dean, and perhaps a member of the central administration should have an opportunity to meet the candidate. Although the protocol design should provide for such a visit, it is a step that does not need to be included in the visitor's initial agenda. There will be some interviewees that the search committee will quickly agree they will not want to recommend. The dean can then be spared an unnecessary interview. Obviously, this arrangement should be coordinated with the dean.

Generally, not long into the campus visit, the search committee will identify a candidate about whom they are truly enthusiastic. When that happens, it is worth giving thought to special courtesies and interventions that may make a crucial difference in the candidate's decision making. For example, if time permits, s/he should be taken on a tour of the city and shown appropriate residential areas and other interesting and attractive features of the community. With more and more faculty hirings involving spouses, some institutions are making an organized effort to accommodate their needs. If this is going to be an important factor in a candidate's decision, s/he will probably have made that clear during the telephone interview. If so, you and the search committee should be prepared to guide the candidate in exploring employment options for his or her spouse. Schools for children may also be an important consideration. If the department has faculty with children of comparable age, they can be helpful in discussing schooling options in the city. If no profile in your department matches that of the candidate's family, look for help from faculty in other departments.

The heart of the campus visit is a series of interviews. Interviewing is both art and science. While some have the artistic instinct for drawing out others, there is no question that much of the technique can be learned through practice. Insofar as interviewing is not generally a core skill for professors who are trained to be subject experts, the following suggestions may be useful for discussion by the search committee and as a guide to individuals to review before meeting with a candidate or conducting a telephone interview. If you have a colleague in your department or on the campus who is professionally skilled in interviewing, you may wish to solicit suggestions from that "expert." Absent that resource, there are some common sense measures you can use to help the search committee. One basic rule is to see that meetings, whether group or individual, are scheduled in a space that can be protected from extraneous interruptions. For example, for interviews held in an individual office, be sure that there will be no telephone interruptions or casual drop-in visitors.

There are also some principles for the process itself that can enhance the quality of the interview. Typically academics are not trained in, nor skilled at, interviewing candidates. Many interview sessions are filled with rhetorical questions or statements attempting to impress the candidate with one's own stature. Your goal, after all, is to learn as much as you can about the candidate. Thus, listening is more important than speaking. The kinds of questions asked will make a crucial difference in the quality of information you obtain from the candidate. Open-ended questions will invite comment from the candidate while closed-ended questions will elicit "yes" or "no" answers that provide no substantive insight into the candidate's views or skills. For example, closed-ended questions can begin like this: "Do you feel qualified for this position?" or lead-in phrases, such as "Did you . . .?" "Were you . . .?" or "Have you . . .?" Open-ended questions seek to elicit substantive responses. Such a question is: "How would you assess your qualifications for this position?" Open-ended questions invite description. For example, ask: "In what ways . . .?" "Why did you . . .?" or "Describe how . . .?"

Questions to be avoided include any that violate fair employment practices, such as health status, religious preference, spouses' employment, family status, clubs and organizations, or other non–job-related questions. This does not mean you need to cut off a candidate's responses if s/he brings up such matters. There are also some behaviors to avoid. You do not want to turn the interview into an interrogation. You also need to avoid hasty judgments about candidates who do not fit your expected mold of behavior or appearance. Ultimately, it is the chair's responsibility to see that the search committee understands these "rules" and remains consistent, fair, and legal as it interviews candidates.

A good interview has a structure like any productive meeting—an introduction, substantive discussion, and conclusion. During the introduction the goal should be to put the candidate at ease by welcoming him or her, introducing members of the selection committee, and establishing the purpose and format of the interview. As the interview progresses, clarify any expectations the department has in mind for the successful candidate. Be sure to allow the candidate time to ask questions. What the candidate asks might, in fact, reveal a good deal about his or her concerns and values. Thus, it is worthwhile for at least one interviewer in a group interview to keep track of the candidate's questions.

The closing of the campus visit is an important moment. The protocol should have made clear who will see the candidate last. In the case of someone the committee senses it may wish to recommend for hiring, the closing contact is critically important. The candidate should leave with a clear idea of the next steps that will be taken and when s/he might expect to hear from an institutional representative. The search committee will also want to know something about the candidate's decision process. If the candidate has made other visits that could result in an offer, it is worth knowing when these might come to fruition. Even candidates that the committee feels it will not be recommending for an offer deserve the courtesy of knowing when a hiring decision might be forthcoming.

At the end of or during the interview process for each candidate, the committee chair should distribute a simple evaluation form to all those who participated in the candidate's interview and visit. The form could simply provide space for comments on the candidate and an overall three-part appraisal of "do not recommend," "recommend," or "highly recommend." That tally should be included in the report you make to the dean indicating the committee's recommendations for hiring.

The Dean's Choice and Job Offer

After deliberation with the department chair, the dean may either reject the list of finalists or approve an offer to the leading candidate. A hiring offer works best when deft coordination exists between dean and chair. In most cases the chair will not have legal authority to make an offer on behalf of the institution. The authority to commit institutional dollars to pay faculty salaries generally resides with the dean. Hence, it is the dean who needs to make the offer. However, the candidate will likely have little contact with the dean in his or her future worklife at the institution. The person who matters to the candidate in that regard is the department chair. It is also the chair who during the interview process will have learned most specifically about the needs and desires of the candidate. The chair needs to communicate those facts to the dean so that the dean can present an offer that is realistic in terms of the institution's resources and standards and that matches as closely as possible the employment goals of the candidate. Conditions of employment beyond salary and rank are critical, such as teaching load, support for scholarship, travel funds, and computing or laboratory start-up funds. Some of these employment components are under the control of the chair. Most importantly, if the candidate accepts the position offered, that person will be working on a daily basis with a particular department. Thus, once the dean has made the formal offer on behalf of the institution, it is important for you as chair to follow through by calling the candidate and welcoming him or her as a colleague. The candidate may want to explore certain details about the work situation that cannot be readily explored with the dean. At this point, you should be prepared to offer assistance with housing, schooling for family members, and possible employment for his or her spouse.

Retaining Your First Choice

Remember, even after the offer is accepted and your new colleague comes to campus, this is only the beginning. Assuming faculty have little mobility in their professional careers, you have just participated in a million-dollar decision of possibly indefinite duration. Now you need to develop your investment with every support possible to ensure your new colleague's success as a faculty member and community member. New faculty, just like new staff and students, want to feel part of your department. They need to be included in social and professional events. Your future tasks, as discussed in chapters 3 and 6, are to develop the talents, support the interests, and advocate the advancement of your department's new colleague.

CONCLUSION

Recruiting department members is an important responsibility for chairs. Except in the rare instances of the start-up of a new institution, you will be refining the mix in your department. However, each addition will make a difference to the culture, productivity, and success of your department. Top quality staff who work as members of the department team greatly enhance the success of the department. Top quality students attract their peers. In that regard, however, it is wise to remember that the goal of education is to enhance and build on the talents of students. If they "knew it all" they would have no need of your department's ministrations. An important measure of your department's effectiveness is its ability to build the capacities of its students, something it is unlikely to do if it assumes its students to be dunces. As for the faculty, they are the long-term resource of the department. The recruitment and care of quality faculty must be one of your most important endeavors as chair.

REFERENCES

American Association for Employment in Education (AAEE). 1997. *The higher education job search: A guide for prospective faculty members.* Evanston, Ill.: American Association for Employment in Education.

The American Association for Employment in Education is the only national organization that works actively to facilitate the process of securing teaching positions in colleges and universities. This manual covers everything from preparing for the academic job search, writing curriculum vitae, preparing for the interview, and negotiating the job offer. It also includes advice for the first-time faculty member. The booklet is available for $8.00 from AAEE National Office, 820 Davis Street, Suite 222, Evanston, Ill. 60201-4445.

Carter, D. J., and R. Wilson. 1996. *Minorities in higher education.* Washington: American Council on Education.

Now in its fifteenth edition, the Annual Status Report on Minorities in Higher Education provides the most recent information on minorities in higher education. The report includes data on current trends including high school completion, college participation rates, college enrollments by race/ethnicity, educational attainment, degrees conferred, and employment trends.

Elliott, J. M., and R.R. Fortunato. 1997. Conducting a telephone preempolyment reference check. *Interviewing and selecting employees,* edited by K. Zucco-Gatlin and D. Schmidt. Pullman, Wash.: Human Resource Services Employee Development.

Gmelch, W.H., and V.D. Miskin. 1995. *Chairing an academic department.* Thousand Oaks, Calif.: Sage.

Based on national research of department chairs, this book explores the four key roles of departmental leadership: faculty development, scholarship, management, and leadership. The book describes the basic tools necessary to being an effective academic chair.

National Center for Education Statistics (NCES). 1997. *Minorities in higher education.* Washington: U.S. Department of Education, Office of Educational Research and Improvement.

The National Center for Education Statistics is the primary federal entity for collecting, analyzing, and reporting data related to education. This volume addresses minority issues in higher education, including preparation and course-taking patterns, college enrollment rates, college access, participation, persistence, and completion rates.

National Education Association (NEA). 1993. *Mentoring minorities in higher education: Passing the torch.* Washington: National Education Association.

This publication is the result of a joint meeting of NEA and the American Association of University Professors on the topic of mentoring minorities in higher education. It first provides an overview of the status of minorities in higher education. It then cites recruitment programs that work and suggests how to assist minority students and faculty.

CHAPTER 5

Faculty Work and Workload

BASIC ISSUES

Faculty work and workload is one the most challenging areas of change in higher education. For department chairs acculturated in a simpler, easier time when workload questions were straightforward administrative issues, the subject can be particularly fraught with ambiguity. Impetus for change is coming from the external world, from within the institutions and their departments, and from the impersonal force of technological change. An indication of the intensity of concern about the subject of faculty work was the launching by the American Association of Higher Education (AAHE) of its Forum on Faculty Roles and Rewards in January 1993.

Managing the Course Schedule

Despite the new challenges, there are still important administrative considerations that need to have a part in how you, the chair, help the department manage its teaching load. Managing the course schedule is a primary task of the department chair. Because it is the interface between the collective work of the department and the individual responsibilities of faculty, it can raise contentious issues both for the department and for faculty as individuals.. As chair, you have an important role in both arenas, the collective and the individual. Theoretically, you could approach first either the collective or the individual issues. However, there are benefits in beginning with the collective considerations. A point we have made throughout this volume is that the chair's most potent power is in guiding the process of discussion within the department. The ambiance and content of any departmental discussion is the foundation for the department's culture. If you have inherited an effective department you will want to preserve that culture. If you are struggling to repair damage in a dysfunctional department or are trying to enhance the energy of a tired department, how you guide departmental decision making will be critical. The advantage of beginning with collective issues is that it helps focus the discussion on factual matters and away from personalized quarrels, which are the foundations of dysfunctional departmental cultures.

Unless your department is a newly formed unit, you will inherit an existing operating pattern. That does not mean that you can afford to proceed on autopilot to replicate the schedule of years past—or the past year. There are some initial organizational questions that are useful for you to review. You may even find it beneficial to take the entire department (or a committee, if you have a large department) through the review. The questions parallel those that emerge in a discussion of the curriculum (see chapter 8). As you look at scheduling you will need to consider the courses you will carry in the department curriculum, the frequency with which each course needs to be taught, and the question of the need for multiple sections. Although your concern may be with the formulation of the coming year's schedule, it is wise to look at the preceding year and your projections for the following year as well. The department may have arranged for a curriculum that carries different course units each year. Some may fall into a regular, predictable rotation. Should that be true for your department, it is crucial that you understand that pattern and see that it is, indeed, implemented; otherwise students may have their studies needlessly prolonged. Once you have a good command of the "facts," you will want to engage the department in the discussion. How and where you begin that dialog will make a difference in the outcome of your review. If you begin with faculty preferences of what they want to teach and when they like best to teach, it will be impossible to avoid the personalization of questions of scheduling. And you can be assured that no one will be satisfied, be it the department faculty, the students, or the institution's administration. Today, you might need to add the state legislature to the list of malcontents!

Having established an inventory of courses, the next question to answer is when—in terms of time of day and annual sequence—those courses should ideally be taught. The answer to these questions lies beyond the confines of the department. Questions of time of day need to address the characteristics of your department's student body. If the department is serving adult students, their time availability will be different from that of residential undergraduates. It is important to keep in mind that reasonable time availability of classes can affect the rate at which students complete a given curriculum.

Thus, decisions on scheduling can impact retention and graduation rates. Regardless of the level of enrollment (undergraduate or graduate), your best scheduling options will be affected by whether students are predominantly full-time, part-time, or some mix of the two. In some cases, a class may need to be offered more than once, but in different time slots. Other external audiences are those departments that make use of your courses to supplement or support their majors. A discussion with the appropriate chair colleague is vital to avoid scheduling conflicts for students. The final external element you may need to consider is the availability of space. If your department needs laboratory or studio space, the timing of courses will need to be coordinated with others (not all of whom will be departmental colleagues) if you are to avoid conflicts. If your department has courses that need general institutional space such as an auditorium, large lecture hall, or special seminar rooms, the coordination will need to take place with the administrative office that assigns class space. Once you have a grasp of the collective geography, you can turn to the matter of linking individual work assignments to the department's proposed schedule.

Assigning Workload

When assigning workload, you should first review the basic facts about your department. If your department operates under a collective bargaining agreement, your role in assigning workload may be quite explicitly defined. Lacking such explicit standards, you can be sure that through years of practice, your department has evolved policies to cover a number of individual contingencies. In that case, you can exercise your prerogative as chair to make certain assignments, or you can use the occasion to focus the department's attention on questions you find to be important to the management of the department. The former may be tempting for its efficiency. The latter is the one that will enable you to establish a department-wide climate of decision making. Among the policy issues to review with the department are standards for work assignments for new faculty. For example, does the department support the notion that it is appropriate to design a schedule that will relieve a new faculty member from preparing new courses for every teaching slot? Does the department have an explicit policy on granting course relief for senior faculty who may be undertaking a particularly heavy community task, such as writing the institutional self-study report for accreditation? There are advantages to having the department discuss and set these kinds of standards. While you may have the authority as chair to make such decisions, if they are made on the basis of your individual judgment, they could be subject to criticism for being based on personal preference, favoritism, or whim. As for the department, it will be a far stronger unit if you have led a discussion affirming the collective responsibilities of the department to provide the curriculum that best serves the interests of the institution and its students.

In assigning particular individuals to scheduling slots, institutional policies may also come into play. These standards may be in the collective bargaining agreement, they may be stated in a faculty handbook, or they may exist through years of institutional habit. Because of the nature of faculty work, these can be quite complex. Laboratories and beginning foreign language classes are usually given a different workload measure than that for a lecture course. Your institution (or department), may have particular workload definitions for undergraduate independent study arrangements, for the supervision of undergraduate theses, for graduate seminars, and for the supervision of graduate dissertations. Studio courses and individual instruction in music will have their particular workload definitions. These issues will come into play at the point where you link particular faculty to the department's scheduling map. The issues that will shape your decision making will be affected by the nature and historic practices of your department.

A chair must be concerned with not only each faculty member, but also with the department's total functioning and how its workload can be distributed equitably among all the faculty. The chair must not only keep in mind the needs of individual faculty members but also assess the affect each person's assignment may have on the other faculty members in the department. If, for example, a faculty member is assigned to teach a course for the first time and is given some released time from other teaching responsibilities for course development, who will assume the teaching responsibilities of that faculty member? The chair will have to assess each faculty member's skills and competencies to make sure the workload is spread equally among those who can best perform it. For the most part, department chairs carry out this equalization process in an informal manner.

However, it is important to keep in mind that the assigning of workload to individual faculty also has contractual implications. This is particularly evident when a new faculty member is hired. The appointment letter will usually specify the kinds of duties that are expected. These expectations, in turn, become part of the future reappointment, promotion, and tenure standards that will be applied to the individual. As the formal employment relationship between faculty members and the institution evolves, however, the salary letter often becomes merely a notification of salary award, whereas the contract document becomes the actual instrument of notification of employment and salary level. The contract document may contain a variety of other information, including a detailed statement of requirements in legal terminology. The assignment in the contract still may be given in functional terms (i.e., teaching, research, and service), but it may also list specific tasks (i.e., teaching one graduate course off-campus). In preparing a contract, the dean's office may solicit information from the chair about any special assign-ment terms to be entered in faculty contracts. At the same time, a chair should check with the dean's office to make sure that a faculty member is not assigned activities that are not likely to be required or performed—for ex-ample, a faculty member who has been assigned teaching as a full-time workload should not be assigned any research or service activities. That point can become important if a faculty member receives a federal grant that specifies that a specific percentage of time be devoted to the project. If the faculty member concurrently holds a full-time teaching contract, the federal granting agency can withdraw funds for failure to meet the contract with the agency.

Already the topic of faculty workload is remarkably complex. It is not a mere matter of assigning work obligations to individual faculty. It requires the development of a shared culture within the department concerning how work will be distributed and how individuals will support the mission and goals of the department. As chair, you need to be familiar not only with departmental custom and/or policies, but also with institutional standards. Both the chair and department members must be cognizant of the needs of students and faculty of related departments. Ultimately, the process of completing the teaching schedule may require a mathematical wizard to put all the pieces in place. But we are far from the end of the workload story. So far we have not progressed beyond the universe that has been in place for many decades. In fact, the reality in which these decisions need to be made is in the process of fundamental change.

A NEW LANDSCAPE

A Changing External Environment

Three components of the new landscape are now clear enough to identify. These are changes in the external environment and its expectations; internal institutional changes that include the emergence of a new cadre of part-time faculty members and changes in attitudes toward tenure; and changes in how as faculty we carry out our work. While we can begin to describe what is happening, the process is still dynamic, which means that there are no agreed-upon norms and certainly no prescriptive solutions. Furthermore, as a chair, the urgency with which you face any of these issues will vary by virtue of your institution, its history, and the immediate context within which it operates. You can be most helpful to your colleagues by understanding that the universe in which the department functions is evolving into new patterns both within the institution and within higher education as an enterprise. Intrainstitutional turf battles between departments can no longer be shrugged off as the "norm," because they can endanger the institution as a whole. And to remain oblivious to changes in our legislatures, communities, and society is to create the conditions of intellectual isolation, aggressive external intervention, and possibly even extinction.

The External Context

The alteration in external expectations has created the most visible pressure on higher education. Russell Edgerton described those "changing conditions" as comprising "new and sharper public expectations for quality; an ebb in nearly all the major sources of revenue for higher education; and a more elusive but quite real erosion of public trust in higher education" (Edgerton 1993, 12). If Edgerton's assessment is correct, the effects will penetrate all the way to departments. These demands have been generated by state legislatures and reflect concerns about quality, which higher education is no longer trusted on faith to provide; and use of resources, which the public is no longer willing to devote as liberally as it once did to education. The assumption that supports these demands for accountability is the view that the professoriate may be working hard, but it is working at the wrong things. These new demands for accountability are leading to the development of departmental assessment approaches as discussed in chapter 13.

This disjunction between expectations and perceived performance is more historical artifact than the product of explicit intention. As Edgerton has pointed out in his editorial, in the 1950s and 1960s:

> Americans wanted two things from our universities: dramatic expansion of opportunities for access—with few questions asked about the kind or quality of education universities offered—and dramatic expansion of scientific research and training capability—with few questions asked about how all this related to particular social needs. (Edgerton 1993, 5)

Today, Edgerton goes on to point out, "America is in a different place..... While access to college remains a crucial goal, the public now cares deeply about the kind and quality of education students are given access to" (Edgerton 1993, 5). The most pressing issue is the quality of the workforce, which means that we now face a greater sense of public urgency about applied social fields than we do about abstract scientific disciplines.

How does that change in conditions affect departments, chairs, and the assignment of faculty workloads? The preceding paradigm, which valued access and scholarship, created the academy's current reality. American higher education opened its doors to participation to an extent unrealized at any time in history and without parallel in any other country of the globe. In the United States we have seen the effects of massification in the net increase of students enrolled in postsecondary institutions as well as in the change in the composition of the student body (a matter discussed in chapter 3). In

arranging workloads, chairs need to be cognizant of class size. With burgeon-
ing student bodies, departments and chairs need to have concern for the total
number of students an instructor is responsible for, as well as the number of
classes (labs, etc.) s/he may be teaching. Furthermore, chairs must ask
whether workloads are equitably distributed among the members of the
department. Are faculty asked to teach beyond their area of expertise? How
frequently are they asked to prepare new courses? If the department needs to
furnish bridging courses for underprepared or transfer students, the chair
should have concern for whether those burdens are appropriately shared
within the department. All these issues flow from the decision to provide
maximum access. While massification is an issue that other nations are just
now addressing, the United States is already facing the next question: How do
we demonstrate the quality of our results?

The public, largely through the work of state legislatures, has become
fixated on quality and accountability. In effect, they are delivering the
message that instructors may be working hard, but they are working on the
"wrong things." Those "wrong things" are the scholarly research that has
become the definition the academy has used to set its standards of quality. As
noted from Edgerton's observation earlier, that pursuit of scientific research
was a response to public demand during World War II and the Cold War. In
the last 40 years, that emphasis on scientific research has impacted every
institution in the country. The scholarship of discovery, which was pioneered
by the nation's research universities, has become the norm in state
comprehensives and even liberal arts colleges. It has touched every field, not
just the sciences. Despite the work of Ernest Boyer (1990) in *Scholarship
Reconsidered*, many institutions are still caught in that fever Small liberal arts
institutions, which pride themselves on the excellent quality of their teaching,
are now demanding that their faculty also publish. And that product is
weighed and measured in terms of the quality of the journals in which work
appears, as well as the quantity of output. Ironically, this is going on at the very
moment that research institutions are trying to give greater emphasis to
teaching quality.

Chairs need to be prepared to deal with both current and emerging realities.
The current reality still emphasizes the importance of scholarly output. Thus,
colleagues' efforts to sustain their research is important and needs to be
encouraged. New faculty need guidance in allocating their time so that they
retain the opportunity to keep alive the original work they pursued in earning
their graduate degrees. Concurrently, as chair, you will need to respond to the
emphasis on the importance of teaching. That topic needs to be part of the
collective dialog of the department, as is mentioned in the curriculum discussion in chapter 8. Because these issues cannot be sorted out exclusively at the
department level, you will need to keep track of the institutional dialog as well.

A shift in the balance between research/scholarship and teaching cannot be pursued without dealing with the whole topic of institutional rewards. Standards for promotion and tenure need to be reviewed and will need to be changed at the institutional level if this new emphasis is to become effective. No single department can afford to take off on its own to make these new definitions; for if it does, its faculty will be punished within the operant institutional principles of tenure and promotion. Chairs have a major responsibility in helping colleagues succeed under current institutional rules at the same time that they may participate in an institutional dialog that may change those rules.

Intrainstitutional Change

The intrainstitutional change in faculty workload involves the emergence of a new cadre of part-time and non-tenurable faculty and a change in attitudes toward tenured employment. Part-time faculty have long been part of the educational labor force. They have been called on in emergencies or to cover sabbatical vacancies. What is different today is the increase in their numbers and their contribution to maintaining departmental curricula. Judith Gappa and David Leslie pointed out, in a study for the American Association of Higher Education, that by the early 1990s more than one-third of faculty in the United States worked as part-timers.[1] But the changes are more extensive and startling than that. In a 1996 AAHE report, Gappa stated that:

> Fully 26 percent of all full-time faculty are not eligible for tenure, either because their institutions do not grant it or because their appointments specifically state that tenure is not available. (Gappa 1996, 2)

This new reality, of course, affects departments, since that is where all part-time teaching takes place. In informal surveys of participants at the American Council on Education's workshops for department chairs, an interesting pattern is visible. Virtually all departments have some part-time members. For a plurality, the numbers are modest *vis-a-vis* the size of the department. However, a substantial number of chairs indicate that they have about half as many part-timers as full-timers and 10–15 percent indicate that they have *more* part-time faculty than full-timers. The groups attending these workshops are relatively small—no more than 300 in a year—and about 60 percent of the participants come from one band of institutions—the state comprehensives. Nonetheless, these data conform with the more exhaustive reports from Gappa and Leslie.

The impact on any department chair is significant. It is no longer feasible to think of departmental leadership as focusing on building an effective body of faculty colleagues who work together on a daily basis. The part-timers may now constitute a significant part of the department's teaching resources. How can or should a chair seek to integrate part-timers into the department? The answers are, unfortunately, not simple. As you consider this problem for your particular department, it can be helpful to keep in mind that there is more than one variety of part-time faculty member. Gappa and Leslie (1993, 49, ff) suggest the following four categories of faculty: career enders; aspiring academics; freelancers; and specialists. Their characteristics and interests are markedly different. Career enders are those who are retired from a prior full-time career, often at the same institution. These faculty have no interest in working full-time. If your department has such part-timers, they can be an invaluable resource because they know your department, have been active in it, and continue to have an interest in its welfare. At the chair's discretion, they can be included in departmental meetings. They should certainly be included in its social functions. The opportunity to continue employing career enders can even be an asset when the discussion turns to retirement. While some faculty look forward to being relieved of all professional duties, many are eager to continue their relationship with an institution and colleagues who have been part of their lives through long professional careers. Department chairs are in a far better position to get wind of these interests than is a distant dean or provost's office. It is the chair who may have the opportunity to link together individual interests with those of the department and the institution.

The aspiring academic is a very different person. This is someone who has completed a doctoral degree, who wishes to pursue an academic career, and who is unable to find a tenure track or continuing appointment. Despite the hope that there would be a multitude of openings in the 1990s as older faculty chose retirement, the academic labor market has still not opened up. For example, *The Chronicle of Higher Education* (1997b) carried a discouraging report on science Ph.D.s who were "spending an increased amount of time in temporary, low-paying postdoctoral positions." More alarming yet was the finding that in 1993 "only 13 percent of people who were holding their first postdoctoral appointments had achieved tenure-track academic posts two years later." In addition, "18 percent of people with doctoral degrees were still working in temporary, postdoctoral positions five to six years after they received their Ph.D.s" (*Chronicle* 1997b). Eight professional associations, the American Association of University Professors, and the Community College Humanities Association held a special meeting in September 1997 to address the matter of part-time faculty[2] (*Chronicle* 1997c). It is the sorry condition of this segment of the faculty that draws this kind of bitter protest letter to the editor in *The Chronicle of Higher Education* in 1996:

> ...what is needed is a wholesale restructuring of colleges and universities so part-timers and full-time working poor are paid on a moral basis. That is, don't pay them merely as little as you can get away with paying them, but rather pay them what they need to live a safe and healthy

life. To begin with, pay part-time faculty in direct proportion to the work they do in comparison to full-timers. (*Chronicle* 1996)

For a chair, the aspiring academic is a significant problem. The personal and the institutional interests are entangled and are often at cross-purposes. The aspiring academic may also raise uncomfortable issues of your own personal values. With the part-timer, you may be dealing with frustration and bitterness. This will escalate if the person is also place-bound. If you are dealing with the frustrated spouse of a university faculty member or, worse yet, of a department colleague, the personal dimensions of the dilemma will be very difficult to handle. Your personal values will color your reactions, but it is vitally important to separate those from institutional policy. There are several layers of standards that come into play in the hiring of part-time faculty. It is important that as chair, you talk to your dean and to the human resources professionals of the institution. These people will know both institutional policy and state law. Unfortunately, part-time employment brings up complex questions regarding benefits, workers' compensation, and unemployment payments[3] (*Chronicle* 1997c). All of these represent dollars in the institution's budget. Once you know the "facts" for your institution, you can then look at how to integrate the part-timer into the department. There is a fine line between humane professionalism and building false hopes or assumptions into the relationship. While you may wish to work for changes in institutional employment policies *vis-a-vis* part-time faculty, you must not give false hopes to part-timers by suggesting employment arrangements that will not be upheld by the institution.

Gappa and Leslie describe the third part-time model as the freelancer. This person is probably place-bound. However, they are not likely to have the frustration of the aspiring academic. Freelancers have other interests and aspirations. However much they are interested in their teaching, it is not their only occupation. In fact, freelancers can easily blend into the fourth category of the specialists, whom departments like to tap. As the title implies, the specialist has an active—perhaps even full-time occupation. Teaching for them may be a source of intellectual stimulation and excitement. It provides a link to professionals with whom the part-timer can explore her or his craft. For example, business departments often use professional accountants to teach accounting courses. The rationale is that this is a professional field and that it is appropriate to utilize a practitioner to teach the skills in question. Artists are often pleased to work part-time. Teaching is stimulating, and it may provide at least a minimal level of remuneration that they can count on. Freelancers and specialists can be a source of tremendous stimulation to both faculty and students of a department. In fact, these categories of part-timers may develop a long-term, continuing relationship with a department. In that case, you may want to consider how to make that linkage most effective for the specialist and the department. Martin Wachs (1993, 10), an urban planner has suggested that "Professionals with practical experience should be integrated into the academic department in regular-ladder faculty ranks, not relegated to part-time adjunct status."

The point at which the conversation on part-timers founders is that of compensation. Part-time faculty have never been paid on the same basis as full-time faculty. The argument has been that they do not carry the same burdens of institutional governance, departmental administration, and student advising that their full-time colleagues carry. This has justified a different (lower) pay scale. It has also led to the practice of keeping part-timers at arm's length from department business. In the interest of socialization, it did not seem defensible to ask them to carry any of the department's general work obligations. But reality is changing. Departments are using more part-timers than in the past. Part-timers are even carrying some of the core requirements for department majors. Some are becoming quasi-permanent. While general policies may need to be set at the institutional level, it is department chairs who are living the new reality. Only chairs will know whether their part-timers are "career enders," "aspiring academics," or "freelance specialists." It is chairs who will have the sense of what kind of relationship will work best with part-time faculty. It is only chairs who will have any idea of whether continuing part-timers need to be encouraged to keep up in their disciplines by attending professional meetings. As new work patterns emerge for the professoriate, department chairs have an opportunity (and obligation) to participate in creating suitable policies.

New Questions

The Taboo Subject of Tenure and New Employment Models
The standard career for faculty members has been the six-year probationary period at the end of which one undergoes a rigorous tenure review. If successful, the faculty member is tenured during the seventh year and, barring program closure, financial exigency or unprofessional conduct, expects to remain at the institution for the remainder of his or her career. In that scenario, the task of the chair has been to mentor, guide, and shape the novice in preparation for acceptance as a permanent member of the faculty. In devising workload assignments, chairs can (and should) make sure that promising new faculty teach a representative array of courses, from introductory to specialized, and should see that they have a full spectrum of experience with large and small classes, research seminars, and tutorials. The similarities to the process of entering a monastic order are not surprising, given the origins of the modern university from the Church-dominated culture of the Middle

Ages. However, current reality is evolving into what may well be fundamentally new patterns. These changes are being propelled from within and without U.S. higher education institutions. The internal impetus to change is what may best be called adaptive behavior. The external pressures, on the other hand, combine explicit legislative demands as well as changed public assumptions.

The expansion in the number of part-time faculty is creating a different internal reality. However, that is only part of the story. As Gappa's findings reveal, non-tenure track appointments, which have long been the norm for part-time positions, are now being used for full-time appointments as well. This is a clear sign that employment patterns for faculty are evolving to create an array of options. In an attempt to start mapping this phenomenon, Judith Gappa in 1996 set about the task of describing "Six Models for Full-Time, Nontenurable Appointments." The changes in practice that Gappa described do not affect all institutions to the same degree. In medical schools the use of non–tenure track appointments, both full- and part-time, have become part of their employment norm. This "adaptive behavior" has been precipitated by the rapid reorganization of the nation's health care system and the proliferation of health maintenance organizations (HMOs). But college/university institutions are also making more liberal use of non-tenure track full-time appointments, with private institutions making greater use of non-tenure track appointments than public institutions (Gappa 1996). The adaptation, as in the case of medical schools, is fiscally propelled. However, the practical goals are different. While medical schools are adapting to realigned demands, private institutions are seeking to maintain a greater degree of fiscal and programmatic flexibility. While they may need the full-time faculty members, these institutions do not want to be locked into indefinite fiscal obligations. They also perceive a need for being able to adjust their program offerings in response to "customer" demand. Private institutions feel the effects of changes in students' interests immediately as enrollments fall or rise, with instant impact on operating budgets.

Although in the estimation of these authors, tenure is not likely to disappear in the foreseeable future, we do believe that we will see increasing variation in employment practices. But that does not need to be a negative development. In discussing Gappa's six models, one can see a positive rationale for each variant. For example, model 1, or teaching appointments, covers full-time appointments that are limited in time and often nonrenewable (Gappa 1996, 2). These appointments can provide flexibility to departments and provide full-time teaching positions that afford experience for new faculty. If your department is responsible for doctoral students who are seeking academic careers, it may be beneficial to establish connections with other institutions that can offer opportunities for limited full-time appointments as a means of gaining teaching experience. Or your department may be in a position to offer such appointments to new graduates from other institutions.

Three other models that Gappa has identified would not be covered by tenure as currently defined. Model 2 describes what Gappa calls "professors of practice." These appointments are often used for clinical appointments. They are appropriate in any discipline that is professional in nature, from business to the arts to mass media. We have noted that part-time faculty are used extensively to cover various applied fields. The difference with Gappa's model 2 is that "professors of practice" are employed full-time but without tenure. Model 3, "research professors," covers another variant of full-time professionals who do not hold tenure. These are appointments one finds in professional fields such as medicine, natural sciences, and engineering. Model 4 covers the "distinguished senior lecturers." These appointments appear more frequently in universities, but they can also be found in small colleges. As the title suggests, these individuals have usually had distinguished careers, for example, in public life. They often lack the standard academic credentials, but they bring with them extraordinary hands-on experience that can appropriately be shared in the academic context.

For the chair, the question is whether any of these models can enhance the work of your department. There has certainly been a tilt toward professional programs, a shift that has impacted undergraduate curricula. If that is the reality for your department, then it may be fruitful for your department to discuss employment variations that go beyond tenure. The institutional climate will affect the freedom you have to devise new employment relationships. However, do not start by assuming that change is impossible. Circumstances are so fluid today that the premium is on insightful creativity more than it is on maintaining the *status quo*. As for the research professors, these appointments will be tightly governed by the nature of your institution. Only large research universities can use such faculty, who may have no or very limited teaching responsibilities. The "distinguished professor," on the other hand, is a possibility for any number of departments. History and political science departments can always use a distinguished public figure to extend their curricula. Literature departments, both English and foreign languages, can benefit from a writer in residence. Music departments can be enhanced by having resident musicians singly or in small chamber groups. Whether a campus has this kind of participation from distinguished practitioners will depend greatly on the interest of departments and your energy as chair in pursuing such possibilities. Money will undoubtedly become a consideration and fiscal assistance will need to come through the institution, probably marshaled in collaboration with the development office. (See chapter 14.)

Gappa's last two models are institution-specific. One is model 5, the "limited tenure situation," where an institution defines an employment system that specifies that certain positions will not be tenure eligible. Model 5 can be seen as a variation of model 1, with greater specificity built into it. It is a model that by definition needs to be shaped at the institutional level. Chairs need to be privy to discussions if such a system is being contemplated, and if it exists institutionally chairs may wish to apply it to their departments. The last model, model 6, which Gappa describes as "integrated tenurable and nontenurable tracks," are specific to medical schools. While this model is currently idiosyncratic to medical schools, it will be interesting to see if such a mixed model becomes generalized within higher education.

Post-Tenure Review

Another new development has been the imposition of post-tenure reviews. While some institutions already have such provisions in their handbooks, the major energy behind this practice has come from state legislatures demanding greater accountability. Exasperated by reports of senior professors reluctant to teach basic undergraduate courses, some states have required workload reports from all faculty. And they have pressed for post-tenure reviews. The probabilities are that this practice will become the norm in the United States. In 1995 Cathy Trower produced a paper on post-tenure review for the American Association of Higher Education. In a survey of 87 institutions, Trower found that 23 percent of the institutions were carrying out post-tenure reviews. For most, the review cycle was every five years (Trower 1996).

Changing Realities for Chairs

Depending on the type of institution and the specific local circumstances, changes in employment patterns may affect your work as chair. For example, you may face a more complex group of faculty than you first anticipated. Two important points should be kept in mind. The first is that you are chair for *all* the faculty, whatever their employment status. Regardless of whether a faculty member is full-time or part-time, tenure eligible or permanently nontenured, a junior or senior member of the department, all are professionals who are hired to deliver a sound education. How you as chair treat these faculty will set the tone within the department as a whole and will affect both individual and collective success. As Gappa (1996, 25) has observed, "The role and beliefs of department chairs are ...critical to the success of nontenurable faculty." It may be easier to work with a homogeneous group. However, social patterns are currently evolving in diverse (sometimes divergent) directions and as chair you will need to establish a standard that honors and respects the contributions of faculty, whatever their contractual relationship may be to the institution.

Second, it will be useful for you as chair to acknowledge the possibility of more than one employment model. Leaving aside the external pressures, the fact is that the needs and concerns of department colleagues will vary.

Academic couples may be interested in job sharing. Women faculty who have delayed childbearing to complete graduate work may wish to stop the tenure clock to have a child. As for part-timers, their needs and interests we already know are varied. There is no doubt that those who accept part-time employment while they wait to find full-time continuing academic employment may be exploited. There are other part-timers, however, for whom intermittent teaching contracts suit their lives and career styles. As chair you will be the first to face requests for adjusting employment practices, and your attitudes will affect your colleagues' reactions to such requests. You can create the circumstances and climate in which new employment models can be discussed in non-polemical terms. Whatever direction these conversations take in departments, within institutions, and even nationally, the people with the practical knowledge that will be needed for creating new models are and will be the department chairs.

Changes in How We Work

The third area of change that affects faculty work and the distribution of workload is what can be broadly referred to as the teaching/learning revolution. Two streams of development are merging. One is the change in focus from a teaching-oriented perspective to a learning-oriented perspective. We have been accustomed to focusing on the teacher as an individual, a practice that has led to a fixation on degrees earned, the statistics of courses taught, and papers published. The tables are now turning and the focus of higher education is settling on the student, what each learns, and what each can do as a result of being "taught." This development is meshing with the technological revolution that is changing the process of becoming educated.

Since the founding of universities in Europe in the eleventh century, learning has been transmitted through the lecture. Though later supplemented by the printed book (Gutenburg set off that revolution in the fifteenth century), education has remained a process of transmission from older, sager persons to a younger naive generation. Technology has for the first time introduced the possibility of building an education in a fundamentally different manner. Technology opens the horizon to a learning process that is bound neither by place nor time. It enables us to access immense amounts of data that are beyond the scope of mastery of any individual. That fact undermines, or at least alters, the position of the teacher as an authority. It is not only that the quantity of available information is now overwhelming, but also that information is continually changing as it is both augmented and/or outdated. Professors no longer hold a monopoly on knowledge and students are no longer postulants awaiting admission to an anointed society. The process of education is becoming much more an act of collaboration where the lines between teacher and learner begin to blur. What the teacher now brings is experience that includes practice in analysis and judgment. The teacher is a crucial guide to resources and to the process of establishing meaning for what is learned (Oblinger and Rush 1997).

If technology is changing the relationship between teacher and student, it is also changing the work world of instruction. For millennia teaching has been a solitary activity. We have lived with the concept that a teacher's classroom is his or her castle. Much of what we cherish as academic freedom is entangled with that concept. The change that technology is pressing on us is the reality that courses are neither conceived or delivered by a single individual. Just as Japanese ukioye prints are not the sole work of the individual artists whose names we revere, so, too, the course delivered through distance learning or with the aid of a Web site is not the sole creation of the individual professor whose name may appear in a college catalog. Ukioye prints may have been conceived by Hiroshige, Hokusai, or Utamaro. The prints we cherish today were created through collaboration with wood-block carvers who transposed concept into concrete form and the deft work of printers skilled in the application of color in the multiple pressings that produced the marvelous colors we enjoy today. Similarly, courses that use Web sites may be the creation of more than one instructor and have certainly been actualized with the assistance and support of one or more technical experts. Teaching is ceasing to be a uniquely solitary practice and is instead emerging as a collaborative activity.

What do these realities mean for a department chair? Again, the impact will be modulated both by your institution and your department. Institutions are moving with varying pace into technology. A few have actually mandated that all courses make use of a Web site.[4] Some institutions are developing technology policies and are seeking to embrace this revolution. Others are still hanging back. Whatever the state of mind within your institution, it is more than possible that your department will have its own particular views. In the past 20 years we have examples of disciplines that have taken up the use of computers with enthusiasm. These "early adopters" have been enthusiasts from the first moment that computers became available to them. Not surprisingly, many "early adopters" have come from science and mathematics. If you are leading a department that has taken to technology with enthusiasm, your leadership issues will fall in the area of how to make the best use of the resources to enhance student learning. You will not have to face the issue of getting your faculty to work with the medium. Numerically, there are more chairs who are still dealing with departments that make minimal—or even no—use of technology. Chair leadership in those instances will require patience, persistence, and an ability to help colleagues grasp the nature of the learning revolution that is taking place. This could be the most difficult task you may face as a chair.

The "work" of teaching is also changing as the line between theoretical instruction and application erodes. In this instance, we may be returning to an older landscape, namely, the apprenticeship model which was the training/ educational system for most young people through much of human history. We are seeing a return of the phenomenon in the proliferation of internship programs. The link between study and work has become an urgent question in the minds of students, parents, and the public. These issues face departments regardless of the discipline involved. For chairs, a primary leadership function is to assist departments in talking through these issues. And the results of the dialog will affect faculty workload. For example, as work linkages become a greater concern, the array of faculty "teaching" tasks will need to include the oversight of off-campus experiences. In some departments this may mean devising and implementing appropriate off-site experiences for students. It may mean leading an overseas study trip. It may mean helping to identify off-campus opportunities ranging from working at archaeological sites, to volunteering in social agencies, to interning in local businesses. It may mean arranging collaborative projects outside the university. Whether or not faculty actually carry out the off-site work involved, they will be collectively responsible for maintaining the quality and credibility of those experiences. Faculty, as advisors to their students, will remain responsible for helping students create meaningful and effective learning experiences.

CONCLUSION

As the nature and format of faculty work change, the issue of assigning workload is no longer limited to arranging a suitable time pattern. Effectively, what we are moving toward is a redefinition of faculty work itself. While change has been incremental and/or gradual so far, the pace is accelerating and the implications of the changes are becoming increasingly visible. Tenure may remain as the basic employment model, but it is clear that a range of other models are becoming part of the academic menu. Furthermore, these new employment models are manifestations of rational, adaptive behavior. The process of teaching is also going through the most profound alteration that we may have experienced since the emergence of universities in the Middle Ages. The relationship between teacher and student is being altered and the boundaries between concept and application are fading. For chairs the relatively simple days of devising fair workload assignments are being turned topsy turvy. Perhaps the most valuable contribution any chair can make is in guiding the processes by which change takes place. Changes in employment practices are bound to raise passionate feelings. It is important that these changes be respectfully discussed without resort to invective that blurs reason. In a context in which change is rapid and unsettling, chairs can make important contributions by their willingness to support experimentation—with its inevitable stumbles and dead ends. Chairs will also make an immense difference in the culture of their departments if they succeed in developing an atmosphere that welcomes and integrates part-time and non-tenured faculty into the core of the department's life.

NOTES

1. According to Gappa and Leslie (1993, 20), by 1992 270,000 faculty in the United States were working part-time. They comprised 34.6 percent of the faculty in the country.
2. Some newer figures from Gappa (1996, 2, ff) are available in a report (*Chronicle* 1996) cited in the references. The tenor of the statistics is synchronous.
3. Text of the statement endorsed by this body is available on the *Chronicle* Web site (*Chronicle* 1997c). Following a description of the current situation, the group agreed on a set of standards that they recommend be applied by institutions in employing part-time, non-tenure track faculty.
4. *The Chronicle of Higher Education*(1997a) reported that the University of California, Los Angeles, was requiring that every course in the fall of 1997 have a Web page. According to the *Chronicle*, this mandate has required the "hiring of 69 to 80 technology consultants, most of them students, to construct Web pages and teach professors how to use them."

REFERENCES

Boyer, Ernest. 1990. *Scholarship reconsidered: Priorities of the professoriate*. Ewing, N.J.: The Carnegie Foundation for the Advancement of Teaching.
   This has become a classic statement on the matter of the varieties of scholarship.

The Chronicle of Higher Education. 1996. Letters to the editor. (20 September): B 6.

The Chronicle of Higher Education. 1997a. (1 August): A21.

The Chronicle of Higher Education. 1997b. Postdocs and career prospects: A status report. From a study by the Commission on Professionals in Science and Technology, (12 September 1997).

The Chronicle of Higher Education. 1997c. Statement from the Conference on the Growing Use of Part-Time and Adjunct Faculty, 26–28 September 1997. <http://chronicle.com/che-data/focus.dir/xtra4415.dir/part-time.htm>, 1 December.
   Web site posted by the heads of eight disciplinary organizations, the American Association of University Professors, and the Community College Humanities Association. This will doubtless emerge as a critical statement on the matter of policies *vis-a-vis* part-time faculty.

Edgerton, Russell. 1993. The re-examination of faculty priorities. *Change* (July-August).
   Edgerton's excellent introduction prepares the context for a series of articles on faculty work.

Gappa, Judith M. 1996. Off the tenure track: Six models for full-time nontenurable appointments. *New pathways: Faculty careers and employment for the 21st century: Inquiry #10.* Washington: American Association for Higher Education.

This monograph is a contribution to AAHE's ongoing examination of the issue of faculty roles and rewards.

Gappa, Judith M., and David W. Leslie. 1993. *The invisible faculty.* San Francisco: Jossey-Bass.

This is a rare study of an important new reality in U.S. higher education, the appearance of the part-time faculty member. This work provides a profile of that new segment of the professoriate.

Oblinger, Diana G., and Sean C. Rush. 1997. *The learning revolution: The challenge of information technology in the academy.* Bolton, Mass.: Anker.

These essays arranged in three parts lay out a map for current developments in technology and its impact on teaching and learning, describe several innovative responses to that new reality, and conclude with projections on what the future will hold for higher education. Oblinger's and Rush's article "The Learning Revolution" and Michael Hooker's "The Transformation of Higher Education" paint a particularly clear picture of current developments.

Trower, Cathy A. 1996. Tenure snapshot. *New pathways: Faculty careers and employment for the 21st century: Inquiry # 2.* Washington: American Association for Higher Education.

This is a contribution to the AAHE's ongoing study of faculty roles and rewards.

Wachs, Martin. 1993. The case for practitioner-faculty. *Bulletin* (November): 8–10. American Association of Higher Education.

This brings the voice of a practitioner faculty member into the dialog about faculty work.

CHAPTER 6

Developing and Evaluating Department Members

THE CHAIR AND PROFESSIONAL DEVELOPMENT

One important task of the department chair is to foster the growth and development of faculty and staff members within the department. In this context, performance development refers to structured activities and experiences that improve or advance the performance capabilities of individual faculty and staff. Put more simply, professional development enables faculty and staff to do their jobs more effectively. Professional development activities might include learning new skills and technologies or engaging in self-renewal activities that rekindle an individual's motivation to do quality work. Virtually any activity or experience that improves or advances performance capability can legitimately be considered professional development.

Importance of Professional Development

We have long assumed that the continuing professional development of individual faculty and staff is important. However, we have been slow in recognizing an inherent tension in the goals of development. Is it the interests of the individual we have in mind or those of the department? The fact is that both are important. What is often lacking is an explicit connection between the two. The challenge for you as chair is in ensuring that the link between individual development and departmental goals is made effective. A key datum is the department's policy in regard to individual development. Does it have such a policy? If not, this is an appropriate matter for you to bring up as chair. If such a policy already exists, it merits review to see if that policy does foster a link between individual and departmental development goals. If your department has an ongoing program of professional development, it will afford you an ideal vehicle through which to monitor and offer counsel on individual job performance. Absent a departmental program or policy for professional development, individual faculty and staff are left to invest their time and energy in development activities that accrue personal benefit, without regard to departmental interests.

In times of scarce resources, how the department spends its discretionary monies is of great importance. Ideally, professional development should foster individual professional growth at the same time that it enables department members to help the department pursue its mission and objectives. Whether that involves training all department members on a new software installation or helping individual faculty members improve the delivery of courses, professional development activities that improve individual performance help advance the mission of the academic department. Where funds are invested should also reflect the collective values of the department. The relationship between individual professional development and the department mission is most apparent when the department chair suggests or encourages specific professional development activities. For example, if as chair it is your call to allocate department travel funds, your sponsoring attendance at a conference on teaching methodologies reinforces the notion that quality instruction matters to the department. On the other hand, tensions may arise if the connection between individual development activities and departmental objectives is not made articulate. In that case, the opportunity to attend conferences and workshops may be seen as a perk if not a reward.

In looking at a departmental development policy/program, it is appropriate to keep in mind that the department is served by staff as well as faculty and that faculty are not a homogeneous body. Depending on the size of your institution, training opportunities may be available for staff, in which case your contribution may be no more than ensuring that staff members have time to take advantage of such opportunities. In smaller institutions you may need to inquire of staff what training assistance they may need, and then see how that might be proffered. As for faculty, their development needs will be affected by their employment status and career stage. Part-timers will have different needs from those of full-time members. Pre-tenure faculty will have different needs from those of mid-career faculty, and senior faculty will have yet other needs. Professional development opportunities guided by departmental policy, and wherever possible, supported by department funds serve to demonstrate that individual faculty and staff are important to the overall achievement of the academic department.

Who Should Engage in Professional Development

Every department member has tasks to perform that are essential to the department. Effective utilization of human resources requires that individuals continue to learn and grow as professionals. Hence, professional development should not be limited to untenured assistant professors and new staff hires. Nor should professional development be limited to department members whose appointment is probationary or whose performance is seen as problematic. All department members need continued professional development, including full-time and part-time faculty and staff, faculty at all professorial ranks, staff at all points on the seniority continuum, graduate assistants, and the department chair.

Not all institutions have comprehensive professional development programs that encompass all department members. Depending on the campus culture for ongoing professional development, chairs may find varying degrees of receptivity to a program of ongoing professional development for all department members. These tensions and strategies for combating resistance will be discussed later in this chapter. Chairs who mentor and encourage department members to pursue professional development opportunities may neglect developing an ongoing professional development program for themselves. Unfortunately, chairs may have to seek their own development opportunities, but strengthening their skills as chairs is a facet of department development they should not ignore.

Resources for Professional Development

With finite (and often shrinking) department resources, department chairs need to make full use of all available internal and external fiscal and other resources. These resources include, but are not necessarily limited to, external funding support for professional development, campus training programs, release time to engage in specific professional development activities, and opportunities to practice and improve specific professional skills.

Typically colleges and universities have some centralized professional development opportunities. These may include competitively awarded stipends to support concentrated efforts to improve teaching or support research. The provost, for example, may offer summer salary support for faculty to develop new instructional methods to improve the delivery of a core course such as English composition or math. The college dean may offer financial support for faculty to design an interdisciplinary course. The graduate dean or campus office for research may offer funding support to faculty who conduct research that is likely to improve that faculty member's ability to secure external funding for future research. Department chairs help to promote department excellence across the campus when they encourage faculty to apply for such campus programs. Applications from department members in these campus-wide competitions bring positive visibility to the academic department. Further, when department members receive financial awards from outside the department, the chair succeeds in increasing the department budget. While such awards are earmarked for specific purposes, these stipends free department funds to be used for other purposes. In addition to formal campus programs for professional development, chairs need to learn if the various administrators have biases for supporting certain types of activities. For example, the president may have a special interest in supporting activities and programs that yield positive press for the institution within the region. The president's interest could translate into financial support for the staff member who seeks training that would lend support to the advancement of a highly visible program. This might include, for example, travel for a theater faculty member to learn how another institution developed and now manages a touring theater company. These potential sources of funding become professional development opportunities for individual faculty; they are the means of stretching department resources; and when properly chosen, they can forward the development goals of the department.

Chairs also need to be aware of the professional development activities held on campus. Typically these events address skill needs that are specific to a particular campus or that contribute to more general career development that improves the institution's ability to achieve basic goals such as the delivery of quality instruction, securing external funds for research, or achieving more effective use of the campus information system. This might include orientation programs for new faculty, training seminars on how to write grant proposals or guidance on use of specific software packages, or teacher training workshops for new graduate teaching assistants. These resources save time and money for the department. New faculty, for example, can become proficient in accessing and using the campus computer capabilities and library search procedures by enrolling in available workshops. Similarly, department responsibility for training new graduate teaching assistants can be lessened if the department's graduate students participate in the orientation program offered by the graduate school. Chairs can often influence the campus agenda for providing training and other professional development opportunities for faculty and staff. Chairs, for instance, may request campus training on topics related to the implementation of new administrative mandates or policies. Depending on which campus initiatives are most salient, chairs might request college or campus training on such issues as student recruitment and retention, learning outcomes assessment, or fund raising. Virtually any new initiative imposed by central administration becomes a reasonable subject for training to implement and manage the new program initiatives more successfully.

Department chairs need not be limited by campus policy and practice in planning professional development opportunities. By taking full advantage of campus opportunities for professional development, the department chair reserves more flexibility in using the department budget to support remaining professional development needs. And not all development opportunities will cost money. With electronic mail, faculty can engage in professional discussions with colleagues at other universities regarding teaching methods or research findings without ever leaving campus. Sometimes there are good professional development opportunities within a single department. The resident computer expert, for example, might conduct informal training sessions for other department members. More time-consuming professional development activities might be incorporated within the department calendar and made part of the faculty or staff member's assignment. For example, course assignments might be scheduled to allow individual faculty a one-course load reduction every fifth or sixth semester in order to award time to work on some agreed-upon professional development activity. Reductions in individual course loads can be managed over an extended time period without altering the university's expectation for average course assignment. In such instances, time in the form of a course or workload reduction becomes a professional development opportunity for individual faculty and staff.

Support for professional development activities can also come from sources external to the department or campus. *The Chronicle of Higher Education* carries announcements of competition for postdoctoral study, fellowships, and grant opportunities. Unless individual faculty and staff read *The Chronicle of Higher Education* on a regular basis, the department chair will need to alert individuals to these opportunities. The campus office on research typically offers information and assistance to departments and individual faculty who wish to learn more about grant opportunities. Community, state, and regional agencies are another potential source of professional development support. The state agency on aging, for example, may be willing to fund a special professional development activity for a faculty member who conducts research that is relevant to the population served by this agency.

It is the department chair's responsibility to assess professional development needs and priorities relative to the department mission. The chair then needs to coach individual department members to apply for external funds to support specific professional development activities, establish internal mechanisms to ensure that department members engage in important ongoing professional development activities, and manage the department's budget to support professional development experiences that advance the unit's mission. In short, department chairs must assume responsibility for professional development if the department is to have an ongoing program of professional development for individual department members that benefits the department.

Resistance to Professional Development

Department chairs may find it difficult to implement a program of professional development depending upon the initial department and campus climate for such activities. It is possible that some individual department members will see professional development activities as personal business. Some may perceive the spending of department funds on individual professional development opportunities as a misuse of department resources. Others may perceive encouragement to pursue professional development opportunities as more work on top of an already heavy workload. Department chairs need to consider the degree of change needed to implement an effective program of professional development. If faculty and staff are accustomed to receiving funds for professional travel or other professional development activities then there may be little, if any, resistance to the establishment of a department program of professional development. However, if there is no history of spending for professional development, department members may perceive professional development activities as an unnecessary expense that results in unwanted extra work. Similarly, if campus policy for performance evaluation does not include tenured full professors or senior staff, then some are likely to perceive professional development as irrelevant and unnecessary. If the campus culture recognizes (and rewards) faculty for engaging in special professional development activities including fellowships and training seminars, then faculty at all professorial ranks will be more receptive to the chair's encouragement to pursue specific professional development opportunities.

The implementation of a department professional development program will inherently involve some change. Resistance is likely to correlate directly with the degree of change needed. Department chairs should assess their own department's receptivity for change while keeping the following caveats in mind.

Aim for Cooperation

For professional development to become an ongoing process, it must be a cooperative effort involving the department members, department chairs, and other administrators. Lack of support at any of the three levels could result in wasted effort. Chairs who expect resistance to an ongoing program of professional development will want to begin by helping faculty understand the need and benefit of such a program. In departments where faculty and staff perceive professional development opportunities as a perk, the chair will want to make certain that all understand the basis upon which individuals secure these advantages.

Think Big, but Start Small

A well-planned activity for a small group of interested faculty members is more likely to be successful than a large-scale, general effort, which may suit no one. A low-profile, low-key approach keeps expectations at realistic levels and provides a better basis to begin working with faculty members. A hard-sell approach tends to alienate or intimidate many faculty members and thereby creates difficulties in working with them later. A small group of satisfied and motivated volunteers will soon set an example for their colleagues. The results, however, should be significant. The initial activity should carry a direct benefit for all participants. This will help faculty and staff recognize the intrinsic value of ongong professional development.

Involve Department Members in Planning Development Activities

This approach will help ensure content validity for the participants and enhance their commitment to follow through. The cliché "begin where people are" is as pertinent when working with the faculty as with any other group of adult learners. The goals to be achieved should be set by the faculty members themselves, not by other persons in the academic hierarchy. Given adequate performance counseling, faculty members should assume the ultimate responsibility for determining the direction and nature of change. Also, when faculty and staff set the agenda, the potentially sensitive issues become more manageable. It is one thing, for example, for faculty to plan a workshop session on improving computer-assisted instruction and another for a department chair to ask faculty to attend a session on the same topic before the faculty express a desire for the information.

Be Eclectic in Approach

When planning a professional development program, the department may be tempted to concentrate on a single new technique. No single technique is suitable for everyone, however, and a variety of possible techniques would enable department members to choose some that suit their own style and needs. The department is comprised of individuals who are at different stages in their careers and, therefore, in need of different professional development activities. Even a group of untenured assistant professors can have different professional development needs. Some may need help in mastering effective teaching strategies whereas others may need help on how to write grant applications.

Start Where the Chances of Success Are High

First impressions are crucial, and a few small but highly successful efforts will soon pave the way for more ambitious projects and activities. This will help build momentum and enthusiasm for continuous professional development. Follow-up is important. If the professional development activity does not translate into a meaningful experience that improves work performance, then it will be difficult to persuade department members to participate in future activities with sincere commitment.

Institutionalize Professional Development Efforts

A meaningful program of professional development must address itself to the question of long-term efforts and how these can be formalized to ensure longevity, adaptability, and relevance. Ideally, professional development should become a way of life for all faculty and staff. When this happens, every member of the department invests energy in continuous improvement. They tend to be more motivated and innovative. In departments characterized by continuous professional development, faculty and staff are generally more optimistic about the department's future and less resistant to change.

Implementation of Professional Development

As chair you do not need a mandate from central administration to implement a department policy on professional development. Chairs who wish to accrue the departmental benefits of professional development can do so by cultivating within the department a practice of ongoing professional development. By encouraging faculty and staff to engage in professional development activities, department chairs help individual faculty improve professionally while satisfying department objectives. Chairs also demonstrate their genuine interest in the continued professional development of all department members, an action that is likely to earn respect and appreciation for the chair. Lastly, well-constructed professional development programs help build a healthy collaborative culture within the department, which in turn will provide the foundation for collective success.

PERFORMANCE COUNSELING: THE CORNERSTONE OF PROFESSIONAL DEVELOPMENT

Performance counseling offers the department chair a valuable communications tool that, properly used, can significantly enhance relations with faculty members and improve the department's chances for obtaining its goals. Performance counseling is here defined as a regular although not necessarily formal contact between the department chair and individual faculty members for the purpose of discussing successes and failures in completing assignments and duties. We use the term performance *counseling* with full recognition that campus policy may prescribe performance *evaluation*. Often these terms are used interchangeably. The terms, however, imply different actions. A chair, for example, may evaluate a faculty member without offering any counsel or advice. Also, a chair may offer counsel that is not derived from a formal evaluation.

Working with Campus Policy

Many institutions have policies requiring formal performance evaluation for faculty and staff. Often campus policy prescribes who is evaluated, by whom, when, and on what criteria. For example, campus policy may require the annual evaluation of untenured faculty but have no such stipulation for tenured full professors. The procedures for evaluating staff are typically more inclusive. Campus policy is likely to require the department chair to conduct performance evaluations of all staff on a regular basis. The institution's policy may also stipulate how performance evaluation is to be documented. For example, the evaluation of staff performance may require the completion and submission of a standard form that is used across the campus. Often department chairs need to file their evaluations of staff members with a central office of personnel services. Evaluations of untenured faculty may need to be forwarded to the academic dean. At some institutions, department chairs are required to use specific forms for the purpose of evaluating faculty. At other colleges and universities, policy may require the chair and faculty member to cosign a letter that summarizes the content of the performance evaluation. Still other institutions may have no formal requirement for documenting the performance evaluation session.

Department chairs need to recognize that the campus policy for conducting performance evaluations for faculty and staff serves as the minimum requirement. As the administrator responsible for the success and development of the academic department, the chair has the authority to implement strategies to safeguard and cultivate department success. A program of ongoing performance counseling should be one of those strategies. The department chair can structure a program of ongoing performance counseling even when the campus policy does not require regular performance review or performance review for all department members. The chair can also implement procedures for documenting performance counseling even when campus policy does not require it.

Making Performance Counseling Productive

Many department chairs admit that the task of evaluating faculty and staff performance is uncomfortable. As Higgerson (1996, 106–7) points out, that discomfort is understandable for two reasons. First, department chairs perceive themselves as "criticizing" one time faculty and staff colleagues. Second, for many department chairs there is a natural fear of confrontation. Higgerson suggests that department chairs conceptualize the task as one of "coaching" rather than "criticizing" department members. The term "performance counseling" is more appropriate to the task than the term "performance evaluation" because it implies that the ultimate purpose is to help individuals succeed. When individuals satisfy performance expectations, the department is more likely to achieve its mission. Department chairs are responsible for reviewing needed improvements as well as achievements. By working from the initial premise that the chair wants individual department members to advance professionally, the task of suggesting areas of needed improvement is more palatable for both chair and department member. Criticism or suggestions for improvement are easier to hear and accept when it is clear that the department chair believes the individual department member can satisfy performance expectations and succeed professionally. Consequently, trading the role of critic or judge for that of coach not only makes the task of reviewing individual performance more comfortable, it makes the outcome more positive for both the chair and department member.

Performance counseling is a person-specific activity in that individuals are not seeking to achieve the same goals, nor are they motivated by the same rewards. Further, not all department members have the same job responsibilities and, therefore, individual achievement cannot be measured by the same criteria. It is also unlikely that all individuals will be at the same stage of their careers. Tenured full professors must be approached differently from untenured faculty in tenure track appointments. Similarly, department chairs are likely to review full-time faculty using different criteria than they employ to evaluate and coach part-time faculty. In short, department chairs need to approach each faculty and staff member differently. The starting point for each department member should be that individual's job description. It is impossible to review job performance without full knowledge of that individual's assigned duties and responsibilities. Job responsibilities become the standard against which performance should be assessed. The other important element is the university standard for promotion. For example, a new assistant professor may be hired with responsibilities for teaching, conducting research, and service. It is the specific criteria for obtaining tenure and promotion to the rank of associate professor that guides the untenured assistant professor in knowing what activities and achievements are expected. Using information about job responsibilities and promotion criteria, the department chair can coach individual department members to determine specific and manageable performance goals. Since part-time faculty have little, if any, opportunity for promotion, department chairs may substitute criteria for professional advancement for promotion criteria. For example, the part-time faculty member may need to complete a doctorate to be qualified for a full-time continuing position.

In the case of staff, new staff are usually hired with a probationary period of some specified length. During this period, the department chair may have a good opportunity to work closely with an employee who is motivated and receptive to suggestions. Although it sometimes takes a considerable investment of time and energy to orient and train a new employee, that investment may pay important dividends. Expectations are made clear, lines of authority and communication are established, performance standards are set, and the new employee learns enough to be able to perform his or her functions independently. The personal contact one invests in a new employee can also result in a healthy bonding of that person to the department. Competence and loyalty are two of the products of such a healthy induction process.

Performance counseling is a time-consuming activity in that department chairs must work individually with all department members. Effective performance counseling requires more than the usual annual meeting with an individual department member. When faculty perform well, continuous performance counseling serves to acknowledge good performance and encourage more of the same. In instances of unsatisfactory performance, continuous performance counseling serves to remedy problematic performance and motivate the individual to invest the effort needed to improve. Although time consuming, ongoing performance counseling is more effective than a program of annual review because the evaluative comments are more timely and, therefore, more beneficial. Both positive and negative evaluative statements carry more meaning when they are delivered in relation to a specific event and not tucked in a file for discussion at some future review.

Addressing Unsatisfactory Performance

Unsatisfactory performance is handled most effectively if it is identified early. Early detection of an unhealthy situation allows time for diagnosis and remediation. Even when the campus policy requires, for example, only an annual meeting with untenured faculty, the department chair must meet on a more regular basis with a faculty member who is not making acceptable progress toward tenure. Particularly in instances when faculty are not making satisfactory progress toward tenure and promotion, the chair will want to document the ongoing performance counseling efforts. This documentation should include specific information regarding the need to alter or improve performance and the suggestions made by the department chair for doing so. Higgerson (1996, 133–34) notes that it is especially important for documentation of performance counseling to be written with "third-person clarity." In other words, anyone should be able to tell from the written record what issues were discussed, the weight given to each issue, and the specific recommendations made for improving performance. This document serves as a guideline for the individual who needs to improve and becomes a benchmark for assessing that individual's future achievements.

Dealing with unsatisfactory performance need not be uncomfortable for either the department chair or the department member. Higgerson (1996, 108, ff) offers some specific communication strategies for managing face-to-face performance counseling sessions. Several of these strategies are particularly useful when engaged in performance counseling with a department member who has unsatisfactory performance.

Make Performance Counseling a Year-Round (Not Yearly) Activity

This reduces the anxiety that might be associated with an annual performance evaluation session. Higgerson points out that by "increasing the frequency of evaluation, it is easier for a department chair to keep performance counseling in a 'coaching' mode. It is much harder to shed the role of 'judge' or 'critic' if once each year the department chair summons the faculty to a formal evaluation session and it is the only time in which they hear evaluative comments about their job performance" (Higgerson 1996, 108, ff).

Offer Both Formal and Informal Evaluations of Job Performance

Higgerson notes that "delayed praise is rarely effective. In the same manner, constructive suggestions for improved performance have less impact if the chair withholds them until the annual performance evaluation session" (Higgerson 1996, 109). Some department chairs begin each department meeting with announcements of achievements. These positive evaluations might include statements such as, "A special thanks to Professor McCauliff who conducted an invaluable training session for beginning teaching assistants." Praise delivered publicly gives special recognition to the individual receiving it. Public praise also sends a clear signal concerning what is valued in the department. On the other hand, suggestions for improvement should never be made in front of colleagues. Not only is the individual in question embarrassed, but also colleagues are left uncomfortable wondering when they might be similarly humiliated in public. Public criticism of individuals is a good way to destroy trust within a department. Also keep in mind that evaluative comments, whether positive or negative, will be more genuine and have greater meaning if they are offered in the context of the activity being observed.

Make Job Performance Expectations Clear

When department members do not understand the expectations of their job performance, it is difficult, if not impossible, to satisfy expectations. Sometimes unsatisfactory performance can be remedied by helping the individual understand the expectations for job performance. New faculty, for example, need help understanding the institution's guidelines for promotion and tenure. The campus policy is usually written in general language so as to apply to all disciplines. The department chair needs to help faculty translate such general phrases as "demonstrated record of teaching effectiveness" into specific behaviors and achievements that will satisfy the standard.

Make Performance Goals Specific and Manageable

This is especially important in dealing with unsatisfactory performance. Improvement is more likely if the steps to improvement are specific and manageable. For example, the faculty member who is not performing satisfactorily in the classroom may first need to learn how to write a syllabus. The performance goal of writing a syllabus that the faculty member may review with the department chair is a specific and manageable performance goal. This prescription is more likely to result in improved job performance than the charge of becoming a "better teacher."

Focus Evaluative Comments on the Person's Performance, Not Personality

Most people are better able to accept constructive suggestions and review their own performance objectively when they are not defensive. By focusing comments on performance rather than personality, department chairs make it clear that the behavior needing remedy is not an inherent character defect in the individual. It is easier for those with unsatisfactory performance to hear what they should do in very specific terms than to listen to how they are "ineffective" or "deficient."

Link Evaluative Comments to Specific Examples

This strategy will also help reduce defensiveness. It also helps the individual faculty or staff member understand what behavior needs to be remedied. Most important, it gives the individual something to change. It is one thing to tell a faculty member that students perceive him or her as inaccessible, and quite another to tell a faculty member that students are more likely to perceive him or her as inaccessible if office hours are not posted on the door and kept. The former is a label that is likely to make one defensive and the latter is a specific action that one can take.

Link Self-Evaluation and Goal Setting

Faculty and staff need to leave performance counseling sessions with a commitment to follow through on constructive suggestions. This is less likely to happen if department chairs merely present individuals with a list of goals. The more that faculty and staff are involved in generating their goals for the next performance counseling session, the more likely they will take ownership of them and have a commitment to carrying them out. Some chairs find it useful to have faculty come to a performance counseling session with a list of goals. Others deduce goals from the discussion with faculty. The best list of goals will be one that the faculty member believes is manageable and that the chair knows will result in acceptable progress toward tenure and promotion.

Offer Specific Suggestions for Improvement

Department chairs need to realize that unsatisfactory performance often causes the individual to be frustrated and anxious. General suggestions are useless and may only aggravate the situation. Department chairs need to be very specific in offering suggestions for improvement. When counseling an individual with unsatisfactory performance, it is imperative that the individual know precisely what to do and how to begin. Together, the department chair and individual can review possible actions and decide what is feasible and helpful. This too serves to build the individual's commitment for improving performance.

Establish a Time Frame for Achieving Goals

Department chairs need to structure an ongoing review process particularly in the case of unsatisfactory performance. By setting a date for reviewing progress, department chairs make it clear that performance counseling will be ongoing and that the individual is expected to try the suggested improvements. It is important that the time frame is appropriate to the remedy being tried. If the suggestion is to work on a course syllabus, the chair needs to show samples and give the faculty member sufficient time to draft a syllabus. The effort will be maximally effective if the chair and faculty member can review the syllabus before the next semester begins. In general, suggestions for improved performance carry more meaning if they are timed with the activity to which they relate.

Recognize and Reward Positive Achievement

It is particularly important to notice progress in individuals who have unsatisfactory performance. Even when the action doesn't completely remedy the situation, acknowledgment of the effort made, recognition of even limited improvement and additional suggestions for continued improvement can help motivate faculty and staff to continue working to meet expectations. This also has the effect of making individual improvement (and eventual success) a team effort. It places the chair alongside the faculty or staff member as they strive to remedy unsatisfactory performance.

Benefit of Performance Counseling

Effective performance counseling is a key ingredient in building an effective department. When department members perform at optimal levels in behavior that supports the department mission and objectives, they contribute to the department's success. Further, performance counseling serves as a vehicle for chairs to make sure that every individual department member understands how her or his job contributes to the welfare and success of the entire department. Through performance counseling, department chairs can clarify the department mission and individual job responsibilities. This helps individual department members perceive themselves as members of a team with responsibility to the total department and not merely independent agents who happen to be housed in particular units. As chair you will also reap important benefits from your consistent pursuit of ongoing performance evaluation. The common understanding of the department mission and sense of teamwork translates into less department conflict, greater acceptance of change, and a more productive department culture. In addition, department chairs who engage in effective performance counseling bolster their credibility with department members. Performance counseling provides an opportunity for department chairs to demonstrate their genuine interest in the welfare and professional development of every department member. In this regard, even individuals with unsatisfactory performance are likely to appreciate the efforts of a department chair to help them improve and succeed in meeting department and university criteria for promotion. Furthermore, by working reflectively with an individual who is not meeting expected standards, you may have the opportunity of helping that person rethink his or her goals. It is then possible for departure to take place as a positive initiative on the part of the individual rather than as a negative rejection by the institution.

Individual department members benefit from effective performance counseling in many ways. They do not need to guess at performance expectations or wonder if they are making satisfactory progress toward promotion and professional advancement. This in turn reduces the potential for grievances filed by department members who do not understand why they were denied promotion or tenure or why they received a low merit rating. Department members benefit from learning the department chair's assessment of their contributions. This information helps department members prioritize their activities. They know how to invest their time effectively and efficiently in assignments and activities that are consistent with performance expectations and that will lead to tangible rewards. When department members fail to satisfy performance expectations, they benefit immeasurably from hearing their chair's suggestions for improvement. This consistent coaching can be a lifeline for those who initially have difficulty meeting performance expectations.

LINKING PERFORMANCE COUNSELING AND PROFESSIONAL DEVELOPMENT TO DEPARTMENT DEVELOPMENT

Earlier in the chapter we spoke of the desirability of working with your department to create a development program, particularly for faculty. One of the hazards of individual professional development is that in some instances individuals have pursued their goals on the basis of personal benefit and interest without regard to the mission and goals of the department. Linking the two is a delicate balancing act between supporting and encouraging individual achievement and ensuring that the needs of department and institution are met. That is where an explicit articulated department development program for individuals can be helpful.

For example, if excellence in teaching is to be a key standard in the department, that is a goal that should be publicly understood and acknowledged. The implementation of that goal can be pursued both collectively and individually. Collectively the department can sponsor team efforts to improve teaching by monitoring individual success as particular techniques are applied.

Pedagogy can become an important department agenda item. Focusing on individual faculty, the improvement of teaching can include attendance at workshops, individual coaching, and classroom visitations.

If research excellence is an important standard in the department, this, too, can be pursued both at a departmental and individual level. Research can be a costly affair. Departments can achieve more if there is discussion of the kinds of research that will be pursued and the equipment that may be needed and that may potentially be shared among projects. Encouraging an individual to pursue a line of research that cannot be effectively supported by the institution and/or department can lead only to quarreling and dissatisfaction within the department. In smaller institutions where research may involve community linkages, it is especially important to discuss where the focus will be so that there can by reinforcement between the curriculum presented to students and the research interests of faculty. It is wasteful to have faculty energy expended in a way that is disconnected from the department curriculum.

CONCLUSION

Developing and evaluating faculty is a key chair responsibility. The faculty, individually and collectively, is the department's major resource, as well as its major investment. It is the faculty who are the foundation of the department's quality. A faculty who works synergistically together produces more than the sum of its individual efforts. It is, therefore, important for chairs to give careful consideration to the matter of developing and evaluating the department faculty. In fact, performance counseling, when carried out with department goals in mind, links with strategic planning—a topic discussed in greater detail in chapter 10. Although there may be aspects of performance counseling that are uncomfortable and tempting to avoid, this is perhaps the key area that determines whether as chair you are a titular head for a short period of time or an effective leader.

REFERENCES

Baiocco, S.A., and J.N. DeWaters. 1995. Futuristic faculty development: A collegiate development network. *Academe* 81, no. 5 (September-October):38–39.
     Based on a survey of current practices at 5,436 colleges and universities, the authors propose that institutions adopt a new conceptual model for faculty development. Instead of leaving individual faculty to "shop" for conferences, workshops, or other professional development opportunities, the authors propose a Collegiate Development Network prototype for offerings that link faculty seeking assistance with mentors either on campus or nationwide.

Cashin, W. E. 1996. *Developing an effective faculty evaluation system.* IDEA Paper no. 33. ERIC Document Reproduction Service no. ED 395 536. Manhattan, Kans.: Kansas State University Center for Faculty Evaluation and Development in Higher Education.

The author offers 20 principles or steps in an effective faculty evaluation system that are repeatedly in the literature on faculty evaluation. The principles collectively call for an institutional commitment to faculty development.

Crawley, A. L. 1995. Senior faculty renewal at research universities: Implications for academic policy development. *Innovative Higher Education* 20, no. 2 (winter): 71–94.

The author describes a survey of coordinators and directors of faculty development programs and selected academic affairs administrators representing major research universities across the United States. The results demonstrate the need for policies and programs to support senior faculty, development, and renewal. The results also evidence the initiation of polices to increase the supply of new and more diverse faculty by increasing retention and recruitment efforts.

Higgerson, M. L. 1996. *Communication skills for department chairs.* Bolton, Mass.: Anker.

In chapter 4 of this text, the author addresses performance counseling and offers specific strategies for department chairs on how best to conduct and document face-to-face performance counseling sessions. The chapter includes four short case studies and the author walks the reader through them so as to demonstrate how to put the strategies into practice.

McHague, M. 1996. The teaching resource center: A catalyst and resource for chairs and dean in the quest for faculty/staff development and excellence. ERIC Document Reproduction Service No. ED 394 595. Proceedings of the 5th Annual International Conference of the National Community College Chair Academy, February, Phoenix.

The author explains the importance of a Teaching-Learning Center (TLC) to faculty and staff development. Teaching-Learning Centers should provide seven specific services: (1) orientation for new employees; (2) workshops and other professional development opportunities to improve the instructional skills of faculty; (3) materials to help internationalize the curriculum; (4) support for advancement activities; (5) resources related to the formative evaluation activities of faculty; (6) facilitation of partnerships with other educational institutions; and (7) advocating efforts to improve the teaching and learning environment.

McKellar, N.A. 1996. Comprehensive professional development plan for a college in education. *Innovative Higher Education* 20, no. 3 (spring): 201–16.

The author describes the professional development plan for a college of education and the process used to develop the plan. The author offers an assessment of why this comprehensive professional development plan was successful.

PART THREE

• • • • • • • • • • •

The Department and Its Operations

CHAPTER 7

The Department as a Collectivity

BUILDING A COLLECTIVE CULTURE

Impetus and Impediments

Scholars and administrators alike speak about a leadership crisis in higher education at multiple levels, including the academic department. With nearly 80 percent of all administrative decisions in universities taking place at the department level, there is a growing realization that the leadership crisis at the department level may be the most important. That, in turn, thrusts a level of responsibility on chairs that is unprecedented. Unfortunately, chairs are apt to assume their positions absent any leadership training, without a clear understanding of the ambiguity and complexity of their roles, and without an awareness of the long-term cost to their academic and personal lives. There is a fundamental redefinition of roles that needs to take place as you become a chair. The theme that unites the transformations is the metamorphosis from being responsible for yourself as an individual to being responsible for a group. These changes are manifest in your life as you cease being a solitary individual and start being a social person; from someone essentially autonomous to one held accountable publicly to others; from an authority who can proclaim to an entrepreneur who must persuade; from the scholar immersed in research manuscripts to a communications practitioner who must succeed in writing effective public memoranda (Gmelch and Miskin 1993, 16). The bottom line is that as a chair your challenge is to create a dynamic collective culture in your department. Under any circumstances this would be difficult to achieve. The process is complicated today by the fact that in trying to create a coherent departmental culture you may be faced with the challenge of bridging cultural differences of gender, race, and ethnicity.

The benefits accruing to such an effort are significant. The Pew *Policy Perspectives* (1996), quoting a report from the Stanford Institute for Higher Education, noted that departments that function most effectively have demonstrated an ability to work collegially, both in formal matters such as deciding promotion and tenure and informally through sharing research findings. Even though faculty reflected diversity in age, gender, ethnicity, and philosophy, these effective departments were defined by a community of interests. Faculty saw themselves as a collective whole: "a team, really, whose members talk openly about their different strengths and weaknesses as they go about the business of allocating energies and efforts of different players" (Pew 1996, 2).

Unfortunately, such departments are more the exception than the rule. Therefore, as chair, if you set yourself the goal of building teamwork within your department, you are more likely to be starting from the vicinity of ground zero. Hence, it is well to temper idealism with reality. The fact is that neither the university/college environment nor the practices of your department may encourage a culture conducive to teamwork. Ironically, while we talk about the importance of collegiality, the realities of academic organizations interfere with collaborative effort and/or teamwork. For example, while academic departments are discipline-driven, a commonality that might lead to a strong collective culture, the fact is that these same disciplines are the repository of multiple subspecialties that generate diverse/divergent faculty interests. Current departmental governance policies and practices provide strong inhibitors to effective teamwork. Subcultures built on traditions of autonomy, independence, and individual rewards render the building of a departmental collectivity difficult, if not impossible. At the university/college level, faculty may recognize the need to meet department challenges, but they are also aware that they receive recognition toward tenure and promotion for their *individual* research or teaching effort. Collective effort lacks a standard of value in the academy. External pressures add to the penchant for fragmentation. Turbulent and changing environments make short-term goals seem more realistic than long-term ones. At the institutional level goals may be multiple, contradictory, unclear, and imposed without consultation. Stakeholders and constituents contribute further to the process of fragmentation with pluralistic and unpredictable demands (Gmelch and Miskin 1993, 22).

Such conditions create departments portrayed by some as *clans of arrogant experts*, accountable first to their own agenda, second to their discipline, and third to their institutions. Others cast departments as professional guilds seeking to sustain individual privilege at the expense of departmental needs (Pew 1996, 2). There are even those faculty who treat their institutional appointments as convenient sites from which to operate active consulting lives. Given the tension between faculty autonomy and collective department interests, how can you as department chair move your department toward a collaborative/collective culture? Drawing on the recommendations of the Pew *Policy Perspectives* and applying the experience drawn from case study reports by Jon Wergin (1994), we suggest four factors as critical to building effective collaborative departments: purposeful facilitative leadership at the department level; a commitment to teamwork; a faculty that make teaching, research, and service the subject of collective dialog, inquiry, and practice; and assessment and reward for departments for their collective product. Our ensuing discussion will focus on what these findings may mean for you as a chair.

The Conditions for Leadership

Serve as Purposeful, Facilitative Leader

We have identified the need for a purposeful facilitative department leader as a necessary foundation for developing a collaborative collective department culture. But what in practice may that mean? A series of five case studies carried out by Jon Wergin in 1992-93 during the time he was Interim Director for the American Association of Higher Education's Forum on Faculty Roles and Rewards found that departments that had consciously pursued a collaborative agenda encountered four pressing issues. These were "balancing group, 'corporate,' interests with individual interests; developing academic communities as 'teams'; redefining evaluation of individual faculty members; and evaluating and rewarding group productivity" (Wergin 1994, 1).

All of these issues lie within the purview of chair leadership and can serve as a concrete framework for purposeful, facilitative leadership. How you conduct yourself as chair provides the link between policy and implementation. For example, the rationale for your decisions can help foster a collaborative/collective culture. If your colleagues understand that you weigh departmental and institutional needs when you are approached with individual requests, they will adapt their behaviors to those standards. If in department meetings you consistently raise the question of departmental interests when issues are debated and voted on, you will set a standard for collective decision making. A crucial factor in your leadership will be your stamina and persistence in articulating the importance of collective interests. Through persistence you can help create a collaborative culture. You also have potential influence in terms of setting the standards for departmental debate. It is important that you ensure that divergent views are heard; that boundaries are set for those who may have a propensity to dominate and overwhelm more reticent colleagues; and that in pursuing problems collaborative solutions are sought.

Foster Faculty Teamwork

Both the Pew policy paper and Wergin's case studies speak to the importance of fostering teamwork among department faculty. Some departments, like elite professional sports teams, behave like a *collection* of scholars, recruiting known stars in their disciplines or even developing/promoting their own stars. Like a high-priced sports team, a department may be ranked nationally, but that does not guarantee that it performs synergistically as a championship team. Rather than hiring a collection of scholars with "hollowed collegiality," departments are better served to think of themselves as a *community* of scholars, shifting their thinking and actions from *my* work to *our* work.[1] A concrete way in which to get this to happen in your department is to pick up on the Pew admonition that an effective collaborative department was the one that succeeded in making teaching, research, and service the subject of collective dialog, inquiry, and practice. As chair you have the position from which to see that such a dialog takes place in your department. If the department meeting agenda has become a prisoner of "administrivia" and individual turf wars, it will take conscious effort to change those habits. But if as chair you do not attempt to reshape the dialog, you cannot expect it to emerge spontaneously from your colleagues. What you can look for is a gradual shift in the content of the department dialog and the gradual emergence of support for your leadership in these matters. The result will be a more unified and effective department.

As part of the process of developing a collaborative department, you may also find it important to broaden the base of decision making. Broadening the decision-making base of departments to the point where teams emerge is, in some respects, similar to leading a jazz band to its full potential—that of making beautiful music. A jazz band leader works with an eclectic group of individuals, experts in their own right, determined to make their own marks. DePree (1992, 8–9), in an explanation of this leadership metaphor, suggests that the jazz band leader draws on the individual strengths and talents of band members, providing each with the space and time needed to add something special to the ensemble. In this way, the leader accommodates improvisation—the creative contributions of band members. Jazz improvisation may initially sound discordant, but over time it leads to synergistic creativity among band members. In essence, it is teamwork (Wolverton 1997, 2–3). Together the members of departments must put their collective expertise to work to meet today's challenges. This means moving away from directive control of academic isolates to collaborative, collective leadership of your community of scholars.

As you seek to move your department toward a more collaborative mode, there are some questions to ask of yourself. Do you value each faculty member's contribution to your department's mission? If so, how do you make that clear to each individual and how do you let the department know the importance of individual contributions? What do you do to ensure that each faculty member reaches his or her potential? How does the department as a whole support this value? How do you encourage the individual creativity of your faculty and what do you do to see that that creativity enhances the department's agenda and vice versa? Is the link between individual entrepreneurship and the department's agenda discussed collectively in the department? Do you encourage faculty to learn from and support each other in their professional activities? Do you and the department make the adjustments necessary to carry out collaborative work, be it in teaching or research? How do you react when faculty take risks but do not perform perfectly? Do you allow room for some failures to occur? Do you and your colleagues hold each other to high standards of professional performance? More to the point, have you sought to clarify what standards the department members hold in common? In cases of illness or crisis do colleagues lend support to each other in the interest of maintaining collective performance? Do you consciously decide which issues should be treated one-on-one and which need to be treated collectively?

Focus on Collective Dialog, Inquiry, and Practice

Our third criterion was highlighted in the Pew policy paper when it stated that to develop an effective collaborative department it is necessary to see that faculty make teaching, research, and service the subject of collective dialog, inquiry, and practice. Campus culture does not make this an easy proposition. Faculty see themselves torn between loyalty to their disciplines and loyalty to their institutions (Roberts et al. 1993, 69). The loyalty to discipline tends to win, in part because of institutional culture itself. With rewards handed out on the basis of individual achievement, faculty find the road to success in recognition within the discipline, which in turn is rewarded by the institution. Pew *Policy Perspectives* suggests a way to bridge that chasm by noting that the discipline is itself a double agent, acting as the intermediary between institutional missions and faculty interests (Pew 1996, 5). We note that it is also through the agency of the department that disciplines communicate with the public, which in this case is students. That "public communication" will be more effective if as chair you are able to move the department toward collective inquiry, collective dialogue, and collective practice. Much like a diversified investment portfolio with blue chip stocks, bonds, and real estate holdings, an effective departmental portfolio showcases a mixture of complementary faculty collectively producing excellence in teaching, service, and scholarship. Chair leadership functions as a catalyst that drives such a departmental portfolio of excellence. But what provides the collective glue that binds the work together? The last condition for departmental collectivity suggests that faculty should be assessed and then rewarded collectively, not exclusively individually.

Reward Department Faculty Collectively

When one asks what faculty behaviors get rewarded, the management axiom "what you pay attention to, you reward" seems appropriate. The partnered statement is that "what is rewarded gets done." Higher education has developed considerable expertise in rewarding individual performance. The same is needed for departmental accomplishment. Even if the institution does not recognize this reality, a chair can foster a culture of collective accomplishment. By using a portfolio of faculty responsibilities (integrated model of faculty responsibilities) and employing an annual department evaluation, many valued faculty members can work collectively toward common goals— and be recognized within the department for that contribution. The use of an annual unit evaluation helps you as department chair negotiate faculty work assignments and responsibilities in such a way as to maximize what is accomplished collectively by the faculty in your department. If reinforced at the institutional level, departments that are most valuable to the institution can be rewarded and publicly recognized (Krahenbuhl 1997, 10).

How can departments evaluate and reward collective productivity? One argument for moving to a system of collective responsibility is that higher education institutions already are evaluated that way by the public (Langenberg 1992, A64). Although true, this becomes problematic as the public and institutions debate the definition of quality measures. However, if each academic unit is able to define for itself how it will meet the institution's mission and articulates the measures it will use to assess quality and outcomes, then financial incentives can be used to stimulate teamwork and a sense of collective responsibility for outcomes within a department. Wergin's AAHE report logically argues that

> ...if academic units are to define themselves as collectives, and if they
> agree to be held accountable as collectives, then the unit as a whole
> must accept responsibility for what it does and for the impact it has.
> The only way for this to happen is for departments to function as teams
> in which there is both individual and mutual accountability. (Wergin
> 1994, 3)

WORK GROUPS AND TEAMS

Committees, councils, and task forces are common in the academy, but teams are more than traditional department committees or faculty meetings. When we speak of academic teams we usually have in mind research teams or teams preparing for accreditation. What is a team? How do they differ from effective groups and how and when can/should your department unit seek to operate as a team?

Definitions and Impediments

Too often the choice between working group and team is neither recognized nor consciously made. The basic distinction lies in how performance actually occurs. A working group relies primarily on the individual contributions of its members for group performance. For example, the sum of each faculty member's individual efforts resulting in national rankings become measures of departmental prestige. In contrast, a team strives for the synergistic achievement of its members working together in their individual roles. Current department culture is predominantly that of working groups. For example, research and teaching many times are seen as solitary activities with rewards assigned for individual achievement. Faculty are accustomed to operate in hierarchical academies where individual accountability counts the most. This is why departments are more likely to perform as work groups—not teams—in colleges and universities. This is not to say that faculty do not come together to share information, make decisions, help each other achieve goals, or reinforce each other's individual performances, but the focus is usually on individual performance, accountability, and rewards. Faculty do insist on defining a common purpose and on establishing a clear understanding of how performance will be evaluated and rewarded. But unlike teams, a working group focuses primarily on delineating individual roles, tasks, and responsibilities and does so in such a way that participants take no responsibility for results other than their own (Katzenbach and Smith 1993, 88–89).

Teams differ from working groups in requiring both individual and mutual accountability. Teams share well-understood goals and they carry out their work through open discussion and consensual decision making. They share information readily and fully and there is no room for running hidden agendas. When functioning well, there is a high level of trust among team members. Teams are not just an ideal model of human organization. Their value and appeal lies in the superior performance they deliver, which is probably why there is so much talk about fostering teamwork within the academy and particularly within departments. But as Katzenbach and Smith (1993, 89) point out, the team choice demands a leap of faith, and one that is particularly difficult in the academic setting. Rugged individualists—and there are many in academe—cannot contribute to real team performance without taking responsibility for their peers and letting their peers assume responsibility for them. Teams may promise greater performance than working groups, but they do exact a price that can be particularly stiff in the individualistic culture of higher education. Good teamwork can require faculty to take the risk of entrusting at least a part of one's individual reputation and rewards to the performance of colleagues. However, if our higher education institutions are to respond effectively to current public demands for accountability it will be necessary to develop teamwork as a normal aspect of departmental life.

Although the emphasis of this chapter is on developing effective teamwork, this should not imply that work groups should be denigrated. Much institutional life—which often revolves around committees—will continue to take place in groups. In fact, except for small departments with 10 or fewer members, you cannot expect the department to function continuously as a team. (See below, "Size of the Academic Team"). However, the skills perfected in performing as a team are transferable to a group setting and can markedly improve the performance of groups. As chair a question you will need to sort out periodically is whether to approach an issue from a team or a group perspective. However, the discussion that follows assumes your goal is to organize your department—or a subgroup within a larger department—to adopt a team approach to its work.

Building a Department Team

There is an extensive literature on teams, team building, team characteristics, etc., which has been developed both in the business world and in the volunteer sector. Among the basic elements of a team are specifications for size, purpose, and processes. The definition provided here has been adapted from Katzenbach and Smith (1993, 45) and applied to the academic setting. For purposes of clarity, an academic team can be defined as *a manageable number of faculty with multiple perspectives, complementary skills, and compatible group processes who are committed to a common purpose and hold themselves mutually accountable for its results.* A review of each of the elements in the definition follows.

Size of the Academic Team

Within institutions and across the country academic departments range in size from a few faculty in small discipline-specific departments to a few dozen in comprehensive departments, such as math and English. Overall, size of departments varies among disciplines and within institutions, with the average number of faculty per department ranging from 16 to 18.6.[2] In practice, the smaller departments tend to be run by consensus while larger departments (more than 24 members) have more layers of decision making (Ryan 1972, 475). But what is the right size for your academic team? There is no right answer as the optimum size fluctuates depending on common purpose, specific goals, complexity of tasks, synergy of skills, and mutual accountability. While an entire department of 30 can theoretically constitute your academic team, from a practical and operational standpoint larger departments would be better suited to break into sub-academic units/teams rather than trying to function daily as a single team. Why? Because large numbers of faculty may have difficulty constructively interacting as a group. Teams of eight to 10 faculty perform more effectively since they are better able to develop a common purpose, goals, operations, and mutual accountability.

Diversity of Perspectives and Skills
Rather than developing a team based on personal compatibility, teams should have complementary, diverse perspectives represented in terms of discipline, experience, tenure, age, ethnicity, and gender. They should also have the right mix of technical/discipline-specific, problem-solving, and interpersonal skills. In a small department of up to 12 faculty you will need to exert your effort to create a departmental team. In a medium to large department you will have the latitude to structure teams that match tasks with talents and that balance skills and expertise.

Agreement on Common Group Processes
Faculty need to agree on how they will work together to accomplish their common purpose. When faculty approach a task—especially in an academic setting—each already has preexisting professional assignments as well as personal strengths, weaknesses, experience, talents, personalities, and perspectives. A department functioning as a work group becomes a team when faculty develop and agree on the best way for the department to achieve its goals and common purpose. While faculty may not always agree, they must "agree to disagree" and develop a social contract or common set of beliefs (see chapter 10) as to how all faculty can work together.

Commitment to Common Purpose
While it is important for the department chair to set the direction and boundaries for the department or academic team, the team itself must have the flexibility to allow for modifications in forming a common purpose. Groups of faculty that fail to become teams seldom develop their common purpose. Many times faculty need a "rallying point" to bring them together under a common purpose or cause. The periodic task of preparing an accreditation report or engaging in a faculty search represents common purpose around which faculty teams may form.

If the department wants to rely on teamwork as the foundation of its general operations, it will need to take the last step—which is mutual accountability.

Mutual Accountability
The final element distinguishing an academic team from a collection of scholars is the necessity of holding itself accountable for its results. The subtle difference between "the chair holds faculty accountable" versus "we, as fac-

ulty, hold ourselves accountable" is the difference between an academic team and a group of faculty. The transition entails altering faculty members' understanding of the concept of responsibility. If there is to be mutual accountability, responsibility for success must become an acknowledged collective commitment. If your department is not committed to mutual accountability then it will not be able to sustain itself around a common purpose. You should not expect to create this commitment instantly. In fact, the best you may be able to do is ensure that as specific decisions are made that each conforms to the standards of mutual responsibility.

When and How to Use Teams

In summary, academic teams don't just happen. Your department is certainly a group, but groups are not necessarily teams. To what extent should you and can you develop teamwork within the department? The size of your department will certainly affect that decision. Much of the team literature suggests that from eight to 12 participants is about what is needed. If the number falls too low, it will be impossible to balance individual talents. If the group becomes too large, consensual decision making becomes impractical. Whatever the size of your department, there will be some decisions that must encompass all individuals. The organization of the curriculum is one such element. The details of implementation, however, may be better handled by organizing subgroups as teams. It is one of the challenges to you as chair to decide when and how to organize your colleagues into teams. If you decide on that path there are some basic questions to ask of yourself. Is your group the right size? Are faculty skills and perspectives complementary and diverse? Does the group have a common purpose and set of goals? Have the faculty members agreed upon how they will work together to reach their common goal? Have they determined how they will evaluate their progress toward their goal? Will they hold themselves individually and mutually accountable to achieve the desired results?

Stages of Development in Shaping Department Collectivity

One choice a chair needs to make is between presiding over a *collection of colleagues* or of leading a *department collectivity*. The latter is both more challenging and more rewarding. Infusing a team concept into your department will require you to take the risks and face the obstacles involved with team development. Again we can turn to the team-development literature to help understand the stages through which teams pass. Tuckman (1955, 384–99) has articulated a four-stage process that offers a useful conceptual model. The assumption is that these stages begin whenever a team is formed. In fact, every time a new person joins a "team" the process will be revisited. However, before reviewing Tuckman's stages, we should note that you will need to adjust the role you play as chair depending upon whether you are an active member of the "team"—as would be the case in a small department of 10 or fewer faculty—or whether you are a "team manager"—as would be the case when you delegate tasks to teams functioning as subunits in larger departments.

Forming

The first stage Tuckman described is *forming*. In this stage the "group" takes its internal measure. Participants identify the issues for which they will be responsible and get a sense of how they will work together. Academic departments, of course, already exist. Furthermore they have a shared history and ingrained habits of dialog. However, there are a number of stimuli that a chair can use to lead the transformation of group into team or the evolution from a collection *of colleagues* to a *department collectivity*. Taking over as a new chair is one such opportunity. The start of a new academic year or even semester is another convenient moment. Institutionally induced crises, such as downsizing and budget reductions or pending external academic reviews, can offer the window of opportunity that creates a need for purposeful leadership to pull together in a unified way—into a synergistic academic team. It is important at its inception that the team views the task, gathers information about the nature of the task, and explores acceptable interpersonal behaviors. Basically members of the team must make tentative decisions about goals, membership, roles, and procedures. At this stage the department chair assumes a more directive role by helping the group set the boundaries and standards of decision making. As faculty roles and team rules begin to be clarified, the forming stage merges into storming behaviors.

Storming

Tuckman describes the second stage in team formation as *storming*. At this stage you can expect evidence of conflict as people react with emotion to the tasks at hand. This is a delicate stage of development where teams can become stuck. Success in this stage will establish the basis of trust within the group that will make it possible for the team to be productive. A key role an effective chair or team leader plays in this stage is not to suppress conflict but to manage it productively, at times being a referee or mediator. Your reaction to conflict will make the critical difference. If you are fearful of conflict, you will limit departmental dialog to trivial matters. If, on the other hand, you permit conflict to run amok and be expressed in personalized terms, you will find your colleagues dropping out of the discussion or, worse yet, physically avoiding department/team meetings. Trust emerges when participants realize that they can debate issues freely and frankly without inducing flight in their colleagues.

Norming

Tuckman describes *norming* as the stage of team development in which participants establish conscious standards for their work and agree on who will be responsible for which tasks. They also look at how their work will be implemented. Dialog will be open and trust will be assumed. The fundamental change is that the group is shifting focus to the issue or problem at hand rather than on the dynamics among individuals. What you will probably see during the norming or cohesion stage is that conflict over goals, procedures, and roles are worked out and faculty start working together by sharing ideas and showing respect for individual contributions. The group develops norms for how problems will be solved, plans to implement solutions, and measures to assess their success. Faculty members will then resolve their differences after an open exchange of interpretations and opinions and begin to act as a cohesive group. Unfortunately groups of faculty often do not reach this stage; they instead revert back to protecting individual differences. Your role as chair during this stage of development is to act as an assertive coach bringing the team together. You may need to focus on keeping the group from reverting to personalized conflict, which if allowed to reassert itself will destroy trust within the department.

Performing

Tuckman describes *performing* as the phase in which the team concentrates on completing its defined tasks. What you can expect to see is that the faculty group, be it the department as a whole or subcommittees, now begins to act as an academic team. They will resolve issues and begin to assign roles that match the team's needs for leadership and expertise, as well as faculty's abilities. They will work together to achieve goals they identified. There will be cohesion in this performance stage. As faculty develop rapport and closeness they will interact more informally. The variable to watch for at this stage is that informality does not revert into an "old boys" or "old girls" network. When that happens a department is left with a governing group of insiders who interact informally and consensually while other members of the department are left hanging on the fringes. Assuming real teamwork has emerged, the sense of trust, informality, and cohesiveness may make it possible to move from exchanging ideas and proposing solutions face-to-face to interacting through technologically enhanced meetings via e-mail or teleconferencing. At this point your role as chair in a high-performance team becomes one of consultant and mentor.

Transforming

You might think that the *performing* stage was the final step in team formation. In fact, there is a fifth stage we call *transforming*. One of the differences between a team and a group is that a team focuses on particular tasks. When these are accomplished the team has no further reason to exist. Groups, on the other hand, have no specific beginning or ending point. In that sense departments are more akin to groups. Therefore, if your goal is to encourage a culture of teamwork in the department it is important to guide the transformation process. Tuckman has pointed out that teams, once their task is accomplished, need either to dissolve or to re-form around a new task. Applying this wisdom to an academic department suggests that as one task is brought to conclusion as a team effort, it will be important to explicitly identify the next task that will be treated in that manner. Translating this to your work as chair, the team development model suggests that team transformation will be an ongoing process in your department, since all teams come to a re-form or regeneration stage as they finish one work assignment and prepare to initiate another. To continue its existence, the team will need to define a new purpose and propose a new set of goals. Before it can do so, the team may also go through a stage of "mourning." You could liken this to the down feeling commonly experienced after someone has put in a particularly outstanding performance, given a premiere lecture, or received a coveted award. Teams may pass through such a phase, particularly if they have successfully completed an especially challenging task. It is not inappropriate to organize a celebration of such accomplishment. In fact that can be a means of rewarding and recognizing team success.

The team will also have to re-form itself with any change in its membership. In this fifth stage when the team transforms or reorients itself to other tasks and responsibilities, it will recycle through the stages of development, albeit often more rapidly the second time. It is useful for you to be aware of this cycle of transformation, because it will be an ongoing process in any department, driven by the cycle of the calendar and the comings and goings of faculty members.

The transforming stage does not need to sacrifice continued department performance. The hand-off of recommendations to others, arrival of new faculty members, departure of old ones, and changes in department leadership enable most departments to expand their performance even further.

Your department will pass through normal stages of growth as it realizes its collectivity. Departments can get stuck at various stages of development if they lack clear goals, when faculty members have incompatible goals, or when the department leadership is not facilitative. Each department must find its own path to its own unique performance. The challenge for chairs who attempt to build successful collaborative departments lies in the need to perform multiple roles as director, referee, coach, mentor, and consultant through the repetitive stages of academic team development. When you take the helm of a department, you may need to guide it through a transformation from a collection of scholars to a departmental collectivity. Your role changes in each of these stages from that of being a director (forming), to referee (storming), to coach (norming), to mentor (performing), and finally to change agent/facilitator (transforming).

BEYOND TEAMWORK

There are two other issues that connect with the process of departmental team-building, but that also stand as independent considerations. One is the general topic of decision making and the other is conflict management.

Decision Making

One of the transformational changes involved in becoming a department chair that we have not yet mentioned is decision making. Individual faculty members certainly talk to colleagues as they make decisions, but these "consultations" are *ad hoc*. In many cases, faculty make decisions entirely independently. Student grades are a good example. As a chair there are few decisions you will make in the professional context that do not have an effect on other people, individually or collectively. That means that chairs need to consult systematically. They also have to perfect their skill in listening to disparate voices attentively, even when they find them discordant with their own views. A factor in assessing the success of a department chair is to look at the quality of decisions made. Are they made in a timely manner and do they hold, or are they attacked and recycled?

With the emphasis given to building good teamwork in the department you might conclude that the more consultation the better. Effective team decision making does not mean a team (department) meeting must be held every time a decision has to be made. In fact your colleagues are likely to become quite exasperated with such an approach. One of the good deeds faculty want from their chairs is to be freed from as much bureaucratic paperwork and e-mail as possible. Other decisions will be yours by definition of position, and these you can expect to have specified in writing at the institutional level. Then there are areas of department life where you want your colleagues to acknowledge explicitly decisions that they delegate to you. It would not be unwise for you to revisit those decisions periodically to make sure that opinions have not changed. Context is never static, and it would be unwise to assume that a particular departmentally delegated responsibility has been handed to you as a "forever" proposition. There are some standard questions you can ask yourself when decisions are asked for that are not covered either by institutional delegation or by any explicit departmental consensus. These questions include:

1. Is the issue to be discussed and decided important to the achievement of personal faculty members' goals? If yes, then you should consult in a formal manner.

2. Do you have adequate information and, if not, do you know what is missing? The answer to whether you need consultation in this instance will not be clear until you have the missing information.
3. Are faculty on the team (in the department) likely to accept the decision and commit without participating? If the answer is "yes," you can proceed, but be careful in making assumptions about others' reactions.
4. Do you and the faculty members share common goals needed to solve the problem? Again, if the answer is affirmative, consultation may be in order.

Creative Conflict

Conflict management and decision making become entwined when you face making a decision you anticipate will precipitate contention in the department. If conflict is likely, that does not mean that you should avoid consultation. In fact, this may be an important time *to consult*. Your task as leader will not be eased by permitting conflict to fester unacknowledged. Departments and faculty often find themselves in disagreement over roles, procedures, resources, values, and goals. As chair you will be able to deal more effectively with conflict of all types if you know the interests of faculty and the strengths and weaknesses of different approaches to conflict resolution. If faculty are engaging in dysfunctional differences, you may need to bring faculty together to air their differences and reach agreement. If you step in as an intermediary or mediator, it is crucial that you *remain both neutral and impartial*. You will also need to know when to be appropriately assertive and knowledgeable enough to help generate options, alternatives, and possible solutions. Should you have the opportunity to receive some training in conflict management either in your institution or in an external workshop, take it.

In managing conflict between individuals, it may be necessary to establish ground rules or procedural guidelines that will protect the integrity of each individual. The key here is to separate people from the problem. If you can do that clearly for yourself, you can assist the parties in a conflict to learn the same skill. There is also much you can do by clarifying misunderstandings and miscommunications through active listening, questioning, paraphrasing, and reframing of the questions and options. Once you sense that the parties may be receptive to resolution you can ask for proposed remedies or points on which they agree. As you examine these with them you can help them isolate the issues that need resolution. In soliciting solutions from faculty it is important to involve all parties in generating proposals so that responsibility for resolution is shared and divergent needs are met. The more you can help people in conflict to develop their own solutions, the more likely they will feel committed to long-term resolution.

CONCLUSION

The essence of chair leadership lies in your ability to develop a functioning collectivity. Your skill in team building will make the difference between a department that functions as a work group of autonomous individuals accidentally thrown together under a discipline heading and an effective, productive collectivity that is able to meet the needs of the institution, its students, and society at large. Like any leadership task, team building is an ongoing process in which the collective focus evolves and must be repeatedly renewed. The end result should be the commitment of the department—you and your faculty—to building itself as a functioning collectivity.

NOTES

1. The term "hollowed collegiality" (Pew 1996, 4) was first used by William F. Massy et al. in Departmental Cultures and Teaching Quality: Overcoming "Hollowed Collegiality." *Change* (1994, July-August): 11.
2. McLaughlin, Malpass, and Montgomery (1975, 252) report an average of 16, while Carroll (1990, 95) records an average of 18.6.

REFERENCES

Bensimon, Estela Mara, and Anna Neumann. 1993. *Redesigning collegiate leadership: Teams and teamwork in higher education.* Baltimore: Johns Hopkins University Press.

Bensimon and Neumann offer a different perspective on academic teamwork, focusing on the complex ways that members of a leadership team interact, wield power, use language, and create meaning. They describe the team as a culture and argue that effective team leadership depends on expecting, understanding, and appreciating the differences among individuals.

Carroll, J. 1990. *Career paths of department chairs in doctorate-granting institutions.* Unpublished doctoral dissertation, Washington State University.

When the literature was silent on the roles and career paths of department chairs, James Carroll conducted an insightful study of academic leaders from research and doctoral granting institutions. His primary investigation was on career paths of chairs but his research also delved into differences in disciplines and department organizations.

DePree, Max. 1992. *Leadership Jazz.* New York: Dell, 8–9.

Gmelch, Walter H., and Val D. Miskin. 1993. *Leadership skills for department chairs.* Bolton, Mass.: Anker.

Gmelch and Miskin address three major challenges facing department chairs: (1) to develop an understanding and clarify the motives and roles of department chairs; (2) to understand the strategic planning process for creating a productive department; and (3) to develop key leadership skills required to be an effective department chair. The latter two parts of the book provide background and exercises for developing and maintaining the department team.

Katzenbach, J.R., and D.K. Smith. 1993. *The wisdom of teams.* Boston: Harper Business.

Katzenbach and Smith focus on actual team stories from the corporate world, many of which have applications for developing teams in the academic setting. They provide an excellent definition of a functioning team and tell how to change the performance within an organization through teamwork.

Krahenbuhl, G.W. 1997. The integration of faculty responsibilities and institutional needs. Working paper, Arizona State University.

Krahenbuhl's working paper has provided many university and department teams with a critical analysis of the work of faculty. He addresses the traditional view of faculty responsibilities in teaching, research, and service and explores the synergy of overlapping these responsibilities and devising new ways of rewarding the department collective.

Langenberg, D.N. 1992. Team scholarship could help strengthen scholarly traditions. *The Chronicle of Higher Education* (2 September): A64.

Lucas, Ann F. 1994. *Strengthening departmental leadership: A team-building guide for chairs in colleges and universities.* San Francisco: Jossey-Bass.

Ann Lucas provides a practical guide for department chairs in how to manage their departments. Chapter 8 in particular addresses the issues of "Team Building through Supportive Communication."

McLaughlin, G.W., L.R. Malpass, and J.R. Montgomery. 1975. Selected characteristics, roles, goals, and satisfactions of department chairmen in state and land-grant institutions. *Research in Higher Education* 3, 243–59.

Parker, Glenn M. 1996. *Team players and teamwork.* San Francisco: Jossey-Bass.

Parker addresses the fundamental question: What makes a good team player? He looks at the personalities of team players, illustrates four different types, and explains how they successfully work together. The book offers several resources for practitioners: team development survey, action planning guide, team player survey, and team player styles.

The Pew Higher Education Roundtable, The Pew Charitable Trusts. 1996. Double agent. *Policy Perspectives* 6, no. 3.

Roberts, A.O., J.F. Wergin, and B.E. Adam. 1993. Institutional approaches to the issues of reward and scholarship. In *Recognizing faculty work: Reward systems for the year 2000.* San Francisco: Jossey-Bass.

Ryan, D.W. 1972. Internal organization of academic departments. *Journal of Higher Education* 43: 464–82.

Tuckman, Bruce W. 1955. Development sequence in small groups. *Psychological Bulletin* 63, no. 6: 384–99.

Wergin, Jon F. 1994. *The collaborative department: How five campuses are inching toward cultures of collective responsibility.* Washington: The American Association for Higher Education.

Jon Wergin begins this AAHE monograph with an 18-page essay on how we can change the traditional view of academic departments as bands of individual entrepreneurs pursuing professional self-interest to academic units as self-directed collectives working cooperatively toward institutions' goals. The essay is followed by five cases highlighting how department collectives have worked in universities.

Wolverton, M., W.H. Gmelch, and L.D. Sorenson. 1998. The department as double agent: The call for department change and renewal. *Innovative Higher Education* 22, no. 3: 203–16.

CHAPTER

Curriculum, Pedagogy, and Student Advising

TEACHING AS A DEPARTMENTAL TASK

The central task of all U.S. postsecondary institutions is teaching, with the purpose of intellectually preparing new generations of profession als and citizens. This is true whether we refer to an undergraduate college or a research university, for unlike European universities (e.g., those in France) the United States has not segregated research in independent institutes. Today the public in the United States sees teaching as the primary mission of our institutions, an assumption that is a major factor behind the current external scrutiny and demands for accountability from institutions of higher learning. However, teaching is not a single activity. Teaching, as embodied in our institutions of higher education, encompasses curriculum, pedagogy, and advising. Curriculum is the structural organization through which we teach, pedagogy is the tool we use to convey that curriculum, and student advising is the mechanism by which we connect curriculum to individual needs of students. If institutions are to respond adequately to changes in public expectations, all three components of teaching need to be subjects of organized concern within departments.

At the same time that the change in public climate has escalated the urgency of these subjects, it has also altered the context in which that discussion is held. The shaping of that discussion within the department is one of the most important responsibilities of any chair. It is not unusual for chairs to lament their lack of power. The fact is that the power to design dialog is one of the most potent forms of power available to any leader. If the essence of leadership is the ability to focus collective energy to accomplish productive tasks, the means of exerting that power in the academy is through dialog—in both its content and its ambiance. Before you begin to lead the department dialog, whether at the beginning of a new academic year or even as you prepare for the next department meeting, it is helpful to reflect on the customary content and ambiance of those meetings. Personal reflection can furnish some of that picture, and a review of departmental meeting minutes can enlarge its perspective. Ask yourself what topics were handled. Several months' run is a more reliable indicator than the evidence from a single meeting. What proportion of the department's time has been devoted to discussions on curriculum? If curricular discussions were limited to reviewing individual courses, your department may be overdue for a more comprehensive discussion of the curriculum. When and how were issues of pedagogy debated? If they were seldom discussed, you may conclude that the department dialog needs some refocusing. How does the department advise its students? Has the process of advising been discussed at a department meeting and, if so, have colleagues concentrated exclusively on mechanical/procedural issues or has the department also considered issues of principle? If advising has been isolated as an individual task, it is time for the department to review its collective philosophy on that subject.

THE BASIC COMPONENTS: CURRICULUM, PEDAGOGY, AND ADVISING

The Curriculum

The curriculum is the structural tool that disciplines use to impart their knowledge to a new audience. In terms of historical heritage, Western education produced its first curricula in the Middle Ages in the form of the *trivium* and *quadrivium*. These furnished the medievalists' basic general education from which they could go on to specialize in theology or canon law. On this continent, where the institutional isolation of the frontier made education more a process of private study—Thomas Jefferson is one of the most remarkable examples of that process—individuals found their way from text to text, building their "education" from their personal interests and correspondence with like-minded souls. The tightly structured curricula prevalent in our institutions today grew up hand-in-hand with the evolution of our modern disciplines and of the institutions in which they were bred. In fact, without our formalized disciplines, it is difficult to imagine a curriculum. The development of recognized disciplines—which have proliferated in the twentieth century— has imposed a remarkable degree of standardization across all varieties of institutions in the United States. Each discipline has its recognized components and as you thumb through catalogs from different institutional types across disparate regions, you will find clear similarities for the undergraduate curriculum. More variety will appear at the graduate level, for departments will often develop particular strengths in subspecialties of a discipline.

Structured versus "Open" Curricula

Before initiating a discussion of the curriculum in your department it is sensible to ask yourself some initial questions. Is your discipline sequential or "open"? Some disciplines must be approached at the outset in a tightly sequenced manner. This is particularly true in the scientific and mathematical fields. It is also true of basic language study. For these disciplines there may be several courses students must take in sequence before they can begin to explore the subject in a more "at will" fashion. Then there are fields, such as economics and psychology, in which it is important for students to master a basic vocabulary before they can participate in the intellectual discussions of those disciplines. In such cases a basic introductory course may be sufficient to open the doors to a variety of topics in the discipline dialog. There are other fields, particularly in the humanities, where one could characterize the curriculum as "open." It may be sensible to enroll in a survey course of American history, but it is not absolutely necessary to do so before taking a course in the American Revolution. A survey course in art history may provide a valuable contextual background for a specialized course in art of the Flemish Renaissance, but that omission will not make the specialized course impossible to grasp.

The nature of your department's discipline will affect the dialog you structure with your colleagues. The more tightly sequential the discipline, the more important it becomes for the department as a whole to agree on the topics that must be covered in each required course. That agreement is crucial, because everyone in the department is dependent upon that introductory work as a foundation on which specialized courses will be based. It is a waste of both student and faculty time if detours need to be taken to fill in gaps in basic knowledge that appear as yawning potholes obstructing the progress of an advanced course. Furthermore, in a tightly sequenced discipline the introductory work really needs to be a department-wide concern *and* responsibility. That means that as chair you need to see that time is made in the department's agenda to discuss this part of the curriculum in detail. You may also find it necessary to open up discussion on the assumptions your colleagues make about that collective responsibility for core courses. If your senior faculty has been in the habit of shifting the teaching of entry-level courses either to the youngest members of the department or to a fluctuating cadre of part-timers, you may have a difficult—and necessary—debate ahead of you. You will want to think through the steps of that dialog with care and, if your plan is to change the existing dynamic, you will need to be prepared for resistance and be willing to persevere to its conclusion.

It is not our purpose to suggest that the only satisfactory solution is to have everyone in the department teaching introductory courses on a rotational basis. Nor do we mean to urge that these courses should be taught by senior faculty. Circumstances and opportunities will vary by department. What is critically important is that the entire department take responsibility for defining the specifics of its introductory curriculum. It also means that the department should reflect with care on the consequences of adopting a particular staffing pattern. Beyond the course content and staffing, the department as a whole needs to take interest in how that curriculum is taught—which means taking an interest in those who are teaching it and the problems and issues they are facing in the process. It should mean that the syllabi, assignments, and tests for those basic courses become "public" resources within the department and that whoever teaches those courses purposefully builds on the experience of those who have preceded in those duties. It means that the department should be informed of the progress students are making and that faculty not teaching in those introductory courses should be accessible for advice and troubleshooting to those who are. The fundamental change is one of attitude. Those courses that are the platform to specialization in a sequential curriculum need to become the intellectual property—and responsibility—of the department as a whole. It is especially necessary in teaching these courses to abandon the myth that teaching is a private, disconnected act. If your department already functions with these principles, your task will be that of maintaining the vitality of that collective dialog. If these principles constitute a new framework for your department, you will have to give thought as to how to guide the dialog.

If yours is a discipline that can be openly accessed, the dialog will need to be organized differently. It is periodically advisable to purposefully revisit the faculty's view of the discipline and how it should be taught. Even in a curriculum that can be accessed at will—English literature, for example—department members may have strong feelings about requiring an introduction to literature course as a prerequisite. You can be sure that if there is support for a common introductory course there will be plenty of variety in opinion about its specific content. Because there is no absolute answer to these questions, it is important to revisit the question periodically. The membership of the department may have shifted, a fact that would make it important to review the dialog so that newcomers become knowledgeable supporters of the department's position. Student clientele may change over time and that fact may affect faculty opinions concerning an introductory course. The climate of public debate may have evolved in a manner that invites rethinking curricular structure.

If your department supports an "open" curriculum, it is even more important to develop a consensus on the mega-messages of the discipline. Is the department seeking to develop student skills in analysis? Do they want to encourage critical thinking? Is the ability to write fluently and argue rationally an important student outcome? If your colleagues see their discipline as process oriented, then the department dialog needs to focus on how the desired intellectual skills will be enhanced *throughout* the curriculum. That in turn will make pedagogy, a topic covered ahead, a key focus for the department.

The Curricular Audience: A Rainbow of Students

Another dimension of the curriculum dialog is the nature of the audience. For most departments, the issue of audience is complicated. The most basic cut is between undergraduate and graduate students, with the former being more complex than the latter. At the undergraduate level most departments face five possible audiences: the potential major, the browsing generalist, the major, the student taking a prerequisite for another department, and the student fulfilling a general studies requirement. As chair you can assist this segment of the dialog by bringing to the department recent data on the characteristics of your enrollees.[1] Such data are important, because the aggregate facts may not comport with individual experience or assumptions.

In these days of tight resources, most departments want to strengthen their stream of majors. Enrollment is the key to departmental survival in the form of funding and replacement positions. If the need for enrollment strength comports with your department's reality, then an ongoing interest in the curriculum's entry points should be a vital concern to every faculty member. All should be concerned with the content taught. Basic topics should be agreed upon. Sequencing should be discussed. Pedagogy should be monitored to see what methods bring the best results. The choice of who is to teach which course should be addressed collectively. Finally, the department should agree on the process of making contact with individual students to assess and encourage their interest. This step will be further addressed ahead in a discussion of student advising.

A close cousin of the would-be major is the browsing generalist. The most highly sequenced disciplines will not see many of these, but the "open" curriculum departments will. The difference between the two is that while the would-be major begins with an asserted interest in the subject matter, the browser comes only with basic curiosity. However, the similarities are more potent than their differences. Neither is yet committed to the discipline. Both will need some personal attention and encouragement if they are to persist. In some ways the would-be major presents the greater challenge. If that student does not meet success, s/he will likely choose another major. While this may, indeed, be a student problem for which the department should not take responsibility, departments are ill advised to make that a blanket assumption. There have been too many changes in the demographics of our student bodies to make such a *laissez-faire* attitude acceptable. See ahead the discussion on student advising.

The major is the student that any department will readily identify as "their" student. Here we have someone who has declared an interest in the discipline and has become an intellectual disciple. This is the student for whom the department feels most responsible. But what kinds of majors are enrolling? Are these students seeking degrees that for them are an end goal? If you are chairing a department in a community college, are your majors intent on transferring to baccalaureate colleges? If you are in a college or university, is your department preparing a significant portion of your majors for graduate school? The answers to these questions deserve to have major influence on your department's curriculum, and they are answers the department will find only if it is effective in its advisement of students. The chances are that your department is handling a "mixed" audience of majors. The question is the proportion in the mix. If most of your potential graduates will be exiting to the work world with faint expectation of pursuing further study in your discipline, then the curriculum design needs to be framed in the context of "what do we need to do to prepare engaged, effective citizens?" This is a vitally important task in any democracy. If your students are intent on moving from two-year institutions to four-year degree programs, the chances are that many of them will do so locally. It then behooves the department to contact the destination institution with the objective of integrating curricula. This means that curriculum needs to be discussed across institutions, a more complicated but also exciting process. Planning, facilitating, and sustaining such a dialog will fall to the chairs at both institutions. Such linkages are being built between community colleges and nearby baccalaureate institutions. Those conversations are eased when both parties are state institutions, but dialogs across the public-private divide are neither unheard of nor impossible.

For the four-year institution that sees its students moving on to graduate school, the "transfer" task is trickier. There are some articulation programs—those referred to as three-two engineering programs are a good example—where transfer to a linked degree program is effectively guaranteed to students in good standing. However, in most instances graduate "transfer" involves preparing a student to survive the graduate admission process at another institution that your department does not control. For the students, it means that it is vital that they have mastered a carefully structured course of study taught to high standards. It means that they need to have experiences that will be the foundation of success in graduate school. For most disciplines this includes the ability to write effectively and some experience with library research. In the sciences students should have some hands-on laboratory experience. It is certainly helpful if the department faculty has kept current in the field, publishing, attending professional meetings, delivering papers, and maintaining contact with their own graduate departments.

A fourth possible audience is the student enrolled in your department for the purpose of fulfilling a prerequisite in his or her intended major. When this occurs, it is likely to affect specific courses. For example, a psychology major may be required to take a statistics course, but psychology majors may never be found in any other course in the math department. The necessary dialog you lead as chair may need to take place between departments as much as within the department. To play the service role effectively, it is important to seek out specifics from your "client department." We are so used to considering our disciplines sacrosanct that we find it difficult to think of ourselves as furnishing a service to someone else. Perhaps an effective way to pursue this conversation within your department is to think of this as a "consulting contract." You have a client who needs your knowledge. In this case the pay is the credit hours generated by your department. A consideration that is bound to arise is the feasibility of teaching a subject such as statistics to the needs of the psychology department while still enrolling math majors. This is a point upon which the conversation often generates more heat than light. The situation is certainly different if your department takes on its "consultancy" role exclusively with psychology "clients" or if it must teach its own majors concurrently. As chair you have the opportunity to introduce other solutions than the apparent either/or offered in the usual considerations of this dilemma, a possibility that will be addressed ahead under pedagogy.

The fifth and last group of students your department may meet are those fulfilling general education requirements. The manner in which you meet these students' needs will be dictated by the shape of your institution's general studies requirements. If you are in an institution that supports a basic core curriculum with specific courses—often interdisciplinary—with, at least temporarily, dedicated faculty, the department dialog will revolve around who are ready to take their turns in this institutional effort and how the department will re-adjust its internal teaching load. In part because of ease of delivery, institutions are content to specify a distributional system for fulfilling general education requirements. Some institutions screen those courses by requiring that students build certain skills such as writing. Courses approved for general studies will then be tagged with a special designator to signal students that the course will fulfill a university requirement. Under the distributional design your department will want to sort out which courses they want to open to general students. There is certainly a positive benefit in broadening the audience for the discipline. However, there is also risk in bringing in students unfamiliar with the vocabulary and methodology of courses where the novices will slow the process of teaching. As chair it is important for you to guide the discussion along the lines of institutional goals, student educational needs, and the department's obligations to the educational enterprise as a whole. No faculty member should remain permanently aloof from contributing to the general good. What you will want to encourage is a culture in which the department sees general education as one of the components of its ongoing curriculum.

If you work in an institution with graduate programs, the curriculum obligations of your department are further complicated. History and habit may have divided the department's faculty into senior veterans who spend all or most of their teaching time with graduate students, leaving the undergraduates to novice faculty and part-timers. As a chair, you certainly need to know your department's history, but your role as a leader may necessitate moving beyond that history.

Content of the Curriculum

There was a time when everyone "knew" what should be in the curriculum. One of the more disconcerting developments since the 1960s has been the barrage of demands both for expansion and realignment of the curriculum. The debate has unfortunately drifted toward the slough of "political correctness," creating a climate of strident battle that distracts from the process of rethinking the content of what we teach. It would be hard to deny that we are realigning our assumptions about our universe. Science and technology created mechanisms of destruction that have redefined the role of war. Science and technology have also permitted us to see our planet from a perspective— outer space—that our predecessors could not begin to imagine. Within the arts, humanities, and social sciences we have been beaten into acknowledging that there are people we have never "seen" before, including women and a range of ethnic groups. The globalization of the world economically and technologically is challenging us to look at all disciplines in a new light. Boundaries we assumed were immutable are dissolving. The impact on our intellectual endeavors is that our taxonomy of specialization is breaking down. We are as aware of the connections between fields and disciplines as we once were of their separateness. Chairs are frequently coping with attempts to teach in an interdisciplinary manner, with the creation of new designations and components for departments, and with the amalgamation of once separate disciplines into new combined units. All disciplines are potentially affected by each and every one of these changes. The task for the chair is to organize an effective discussion centered on the department's current status and practices and its views on how changes in perspective and technology are impacting its work. The chair's objective should be to help the department move forward effectively and enthusiastically.

Pedagogy

If the curriculum embodies the instructional content, pedagogy is the means by which that content is conveyed. At one level, university pedagogy has not changed in any fundamental way since the establishment of the first recognized university in Bologna in the eleventh century. The primary method was the professorial lecture, itself a derivation from the ecclesiastical sermon. Ask a student today how faculty teach and the most likely response is that they lecture. It is difficult to know if one should gasp in awe at this remarkable line of continuity or recoil in horror at the lack of adaptability to a world that in most respects is dramatically different from that of medieval Europe. However, if the lecture is alive and well, perhaps it is because it continues to be useful in some pedagogical applications. Furthermore, in the United States in particular, there has been an orgy of experimentation with other teaching methods so that it is unusual today for students to be denied experience of other methods. The future promises even more fundamental innovations as teaching moves onto the Web and as we change our frame of reference from teaching to learning.

The discussion that follows aims to give a brief overview of a number of the pedagogical options being used. The enumeration is not encyclopedic. Nor could it remain up-to-date for long, for instructors all over the country are continually making small and large changes in the way they teach. And the more we emphasize learning outcomes the more experiments we can expect to hear about. The purpose of the ensuing material is first to alert chairs to major categories of pedagogical techniques beyond the lecture that are being used. Applicability to your department is something to be decided through collective dialog, perhaps supported by individual experimentation. The latter, however, will not be collectively useful unless its results are systematically shared within the department.

The second purpose is to urge chairs that a discussion of pedagogy is a critical issue for any department. It is not enough that individual faculty work on improving their pedagogy. It is important that faculty learn from each other and encourage each other through the inevitable experimental failures. Furthermore, it is not possible to develop a sound curriculum without discussing how you will teach! Depending upon the confluence of the nature of a discipline and the philosophy of faculty, certain pedagogical forms will be more appropriate than others. For core introductory courses a common understanding on pedagogy is as important as consensus on content. For "service" courses taught for majors in other departments, you need to understand the educational philosophy of your client department. A good way to find out what that philosophy might be is for you as chair to invite faculty from that "client" department to discuss these issues with members of your department. Once you know that, you may find that it is preferable to rely on pedagogical techniques different from those your department would apply if teaching the same subject to its majors.

Nor can your department escape addressing the use of new technologies. The p.c. and e-mail are all but universal. The possibilities of the World Wide Web and distance learning are new options ready to be addressed at the department level. No department would—nor should it—attempt to utilize all the pedagogical alternatives listed ahead. What departments *do* need to do is to look at their curricula in combination with the options in the pedagogical smorgasbord to choose the means most appropriate to its discipline. Development will remain haphazard unless you help your department focus collectively on this matter as something of importance.

Experience-Based Learning

The North American penchant for practicality, probably encouraged by our frontier heritage, found conceptual dignity with John Dewey. Learning by doing has become a respected form of pedagogy and one that appeals to students. One example of this kind of applied learning is the case method. Applied as the core teaching method at the Harvard University Business School, the approach presented students with real business cases in which complex decisions needed to made. The cases gave students a chance to dry run the kinds of decisions they would need to make once they left the ivy walls of Cambridge. Case studies are now widely used in a variety of settings and disciplines.

Another form of applied learning is provided through faculty-student research collaborations. Initially this was a basic building block in graduate pedagogy. Now that approach is being used ever more extensively for undergraduate students. The appeal of the method is that it gives students the opportunity to experience firsthand the kind of work that their professors pursue. At the graduate level, the method provides faculty with labor (either free or modestly compensated) for their research. The arrangement has an inherent danger of exploitation, for as graduate students advance it can become difficult to untangle who really deserves recognition for the work done and the new knowledge generated.

The student internship, a concept that can be traced back to the medieval guild apprenticeships, is yet another form of applied learning. Five or six hundred years ago craftsmen learned their trades by attaching themselves to a master. Artists worked in much the same way, as we know today when we read museum labels that identify works of art as produced in the studio of a great master. These guild apprenticeships survived to our own day in the fields of law and medicine. Currently, however, the concept of internships is finding much broader application. Students are now offered opportunities to serve as interns while they are undergraduates. The motivation is varied. For students there is the appeal of doing—that is, accomplishing—something. There is also the appeal of having a "work" experience on their resumes when they go for their first job interviews. At the institutional end of the arrangement is the appeal of finding something intellectually justifiable that appeals to the students, demand for relevance in their education.

Laboratory and studio work are also forms of applied teaching. For any undergraduate student aspiring to become a scientist, experience in a laboratory is essential. Unfortunately, in large public institutions the opportunity for undergraduate students to carry out actual experiments is limited to nonexistent. Small independent colleges are often better able to give undergraduate students that kind of applied experience. At the graduate level, however, large institutions are where students will find the advanced equipment. Artists, like scientists, must have the opportunity to "do." Thus, studio experience in the fine arts, theater, dance, and music are inherent to the pedagogy of those disciplines.

International study can also be considered to be a form of applied pedagogy. Here we are talking about North American students studying abroad. The numbers of U.S. students going abroad remains much smaller than the number coming into the country from beyond our borders. [2] However, there are signs here and there that some departments are seeing overseas study as desirable *for their majors*. An example of that trend is provided by the University of Southern California, which now requires its M.B.A. students to "complete a study tour in China, Japan, or Mexico." In the spring of 1997

> some in the Mexico group looked at the implications of a proposed expansion in Tijuana of Samsung, the Korean electronics company. The group in China, meanwhile, helped develop an export strategy for a Nanjing corporation. And in Tokyo students worked on an expansion strategy for Morgan Stanley, Japan. (*Chronicle* 1997, A52)

Yet another form of applied learning is the skill of participant observation. This is a basic technique in anthropology that can be applied to a wide variety of social studies. The skill that must be perfected is the ability to observe a situation objectively without becoming a participant in that situation. The technique can be considered applied learning insofar as it involves observing real, ongoing social phenomena. A reporter at his or her best should embody those very characteristics. Participant observation can be pursued as a solitary endeavor or as part of a team study.

Partnered Teaching and Learning
It has been a fundamental assumption in U.S. higher education that students should learn independently, and our frontier cult of rugged individualism

certainly lent appeal to that assumption. Within the academy the fact that plagiarism is considered the most heinous of crimes derives from that same assumption that the ideal student thinks for himself or herself and shines through his or her individual effort. While those standards will remain central, we can also acknowledge that partnered learning is also a viable form of pedagogy.[3] Two phenomena are important to the development of learning in collaboration with others. One strand is the realization that in the work world beyond the academy students will find themselves working as members of teams to solve problems. Hundreds of engineers may work on the design of complex machinery. The Space Control Center in Houston is a familiar view of a task team at work. Businesses in looking for new hires are eager to find candidates who are adept at working in task teams. Even more compelling is the appearance of new organizational systems that Sally Helgesen has dubbed "web organizations."[4]

The other strand exists at the student end. As new populations have moved into higher education, some have brought with them profoundly different ideas about work and learning. One of the more interesting discoveries was that made by Uri Treisman in teaching calculus at University of California, Berkeley. To his surprise he found that if he encouraged Latino/Latina and African-American students to pursue their work in structured groups, individual performance sky-rocketed. Instead of preparing homework individually, students were encouraged to work in small groups. Together they solved problems, which resulted in sound individual learning.[5] A related technique that has been used in large university classes is forming work teams within a course. Members of the team are responsible for each other and their work is a team product in which one succeeds only if all succeed. This, too, has been a successful methodology.[6]

Another form of partnered learning can be found in school-college collaborations. A 1990 survey indicated that 1,200 school-college partnerships were in operation.[7] The focus of such collaborations varies with the interests and needs of the institutions who undertake these arrangements. Among the concerns that have been addressed through collaborative arrangements are educational access, intervention with at-risk students, services for gifted and talented students, school restructuring, teacher mentoring, etc.[8] The issues you explore with your department colleagues might include evaluating the benefits that could accrue to the department by building a base of external contacts with local school systems. These benefits can range from expanding the recruiting pool of your department (and institution) to improvements you can contribute to the quality of life in your community. Before venturing into an external collaboration, your task as chair will be to ensure that the premises for such outreach are clear to all involved, and supported by them. Linkages are possible regardless of discipline, although the form and content will be shaped by your department's discipline and the needs of the linkage schools.

Assessing the Learning Process

One of the most interesting changes in perspective has been the shift in emphasis from the effectiveness of teaching to the results of learning. This shift has entailed a change in focus from the activities of the faculty to those of students. Two techniques have emerged as particularly useful in that assessment process. One is the use of portfolios and the other is the application of a technique called classroom assessment.

Portfolios have long been used in the fine arts. They provided the means by which artists documented their work, a process that modern technology has facilitated. For example, in the fine arts, artists now present much of their *oeuvre* as slides. Technology has made it possible for musicians to create their own "portfolios" by offering examples of their musicianship on audiotape, while actors and dancers can demonstrate their performances on videotape. Part of the appeal of the portfolio is that it permits the presenters to show the development of their work over time. More recently the portfolio has been adapted and adopted by other students and faculty. Both have used the portfolio as both a demonstration of growth and a proof of competence. For example, students may be asked to demonstrate writing competence by producing a portfolio of their best college papers, rather than being asked to sit for an examination. Faculty have presented their teaching of a course through a portfolio demonstration that spans their teaching philosophy, syllabus, discussion of teaching methodology, and examples of student product. Portfolios are a highly adaptable artifact, applicable in any department, both to students and faculty.[9]

Classroom assessment can be pursued in a very simple and basic manner or used to probe sophisticated conceptual concerns. The goal remains the same, namely, to examine the effectiveness of teaching by looking at the results of a technique upon the learning of the students. The process, however, changes the relationship between student and teacher and invites immediate change in teaching strategies while a course is in progress. The classic entry exercise to the process of classroom research is what practitioners call the "one-minute paper." At the end of a class period students are asked to write the answers to two questions: (1) What was the most important point made in today's lecture (class etc.); and (2) What point remains unclear for you? The responses give the instructor immediate feedback on the success of that class. If there is a wide range of responses (and especially if a substantial number of those are discordant with the professor's intentions) about "the most important point," the instructor knows immediately that the presentation was not clear to the audience. Knowing that gives an opportunity to correct the misapprehension before the instructor proceeds to other points that may depend on previous material. Because the process of classroom assessment must be explained to students, they become partners in the teaching-learning process. This changes students' perceptions of their roles as learners, and it alters the dynamic between student and instructor. Rather than remaining recipients of wisdom, students become a resource to their teachers. Because the process not only invites but also effectively requires professors to adjust their teaching in mid-course, instruction becomes a dynamic process (Angelo and Cross 1993).

New Delivery Systems

Technology, specifically computers and video, is another element of pedagogical change. The computer "revolution" has been longer and slower than optimists predicted in the 1970s. But the results are now beginning to roll through campuses. Those changes include the widespread use of e-mail and the phenomenon of the World Wide Web. Although as O'Banion (1997, 69) observes, "technology has been applied to extend the old model of education rather than to reengineer a new model,"[10] it is clear that the long-term probability is that technology will result in a reconfiguration of the relationship between teacher and student that will effect profound changes in the process of teaching. The availability of e-mail means that professors can "speak" both collectively and individually to their students at one and the same time. A general e-mail to the class can be dispatched to all students at once. The recipients can receive that communication when they choose. Furthermore, students can respond individually to the professor about any aspect of the message to the group. Individual "conversations" between student and professor are also possible. Problems with an assignment, difficulty in finding a reference, or a hang-up in writing a paper can be communicated from student to professor without the constraints of time.

The availability of extensive data resources through the Web also changes the professor-student relationship. The professor can no longer stand as The Authority on a given subject. Energetic students can locate data independently. Professors no longer hold an information monopoly. Where professors remain an irreplaceable resource to students is in their experience of a field, their breadth of vision, their practice in asking key questions of the data, in the art of synthesis, and their skill in perceiving the implications and significance of data. The role of professor will shift to that of opening the door to a field of inquiry and as advisor and coach to the student.

The explosion of the World Wide Web is swiftly introducing changes in the process of teaching. Some universities are requiring that all courses utilize a Web site.[11] Professors need assistance in preparing such sites. If they plan to put course materials—beyond the syllabus and general information—on a Web site, the need for collaboration becomes even more urgent. Preparation for teaching a course must become a collaborative activity in which professors work with colleagues as well as with technicians. This reality will make obsolete the cherished concept that the classroom is a private sanctum ruled exclusively by the professor. Teaching is becoming an ever more public and collective process (Oblinger and Rush 1997). A dramatic application of technology to education is the initiative on the part of the Western Governors University, which launched its first programs in 16 states and the island of Guam at the start of 1998. Distance education is also being used extensively by proprietary institutions such as the University of Phoenix.[12] In fact, it is clear that proprietary institutions will offer significant competition to public and independent universities in the future.[13]

Advising

Advising may appear on the roster of faculty duties, but it is a professional activity that is often not systematically evaluated. And it is a topic that has not found the central place it deserves in the departmental agenda. It is an activity that needs to be second only to teaching itself. While the act of teaching is geared to provide students with structured intellectual content, advising is the forum in which faculty can help students shape their individual careers and lives. Like the curriculum, advising needs to take cognizance of the particular stage of a student's enrollment and the life goals s/he is pursuing. Advising is a topic that can be separated into three categories: the novice "undecided" student; the undergraduate major; and the graduate student.

"Undecided" Students

The "undecided" student is the one most likely to be lost in the cracks of any institution. Departments tend to see the "undecided" student as beyond the purview of their responsibility. It is not until an undergraduate declares a major that departments are interested in offering counsel and advice, a duty usually fulfilled by assigning the student a "faculty advisor." But concerns with the issue of retention require a change in formerly dismissive views of the "undecided" student. For independent institutions the goad is fiscal. Recruitment is expensive and every departure represents a financial loss. Independent colleges are apt to be acutely aware that a major variable in student retention is the extent to which successful bonding takes place between new students and the institution. In public institutions legislative scrutiny that demands statistics on student completion rates leads to a concern with the issue of retention. In either case, departments cannot remain aloof if institutions are to improve their retention and/or graduation rates.

How your department can contribute will depend in part on the practices of your institution. Independent schools often have devised elaborate orientation procedures that aim to provide a bridge from high school to college and from home to institution. Your department may be asked to participate in these activities and the good grace with which this is done will be affected by your attitude toward this obligation. Some institutions form cadres of faculty to act as "freshmen" advisors. Others have a phalanx of specialists to perform the task. Departments need to think about their connections with "undecided" students, because within that group can lie the lifeblood of the institution as well as potential majors for the department.

Majors

Advising majors is an accepted departmental faculty duty. However, it is a process that is usually left to the inventiveness of individual faculty. Departments are not apt to discuss the process as a collective activity. An unexamined premise is that advising should be a one-on-one process. There is no doubt that students want, expect, and deserve individual attention. However, much can also be accomplished by working with students in groups. Again, the role of chair is that of leader of a dialog. The department should ask what general tasks could be effectively addressed in small groups. For example, what is the structure of your undergraduate major? Does it offer some subspecialties? These are topics that can be fruitfully addressed in a meeting of faculty and new majors. Are there activities that face advanced majors that can be discussed in a group context? Topics such as senior capstone projects, applications to graduate schools, or preparation for internships would fall in that category. Small groups of students can be encouraged to attend pertinent public events, meeting afterwards to discuss faculty and student reactions.

The department should also be knowledgeable about its majors. As chair you should keep the department informed about fluctuations in the numbers of majors. If there are dips, all members of the department need to be conscious of that fact and it should become a collective task to find answers to the phenomenon. More importantly, the department needs to strategize together to change that dynamic, assuming it is a source of concern. The department should also know what happens to its graduates. Are most going immediately into the work world? If so, that should affect curriculum (as indicated in an earlier section of this chapter) and it needs to inform the advising process. If a significant number are planning to apply to graduate school, the department should adjust its advising practices accordingly.

And then there are the alumni. As indicated in chapter 9 where fundraising is discussed, alumni are a critical source of future support both for the institution and the department. The department should consider how best it can maintain contact with those alumni. The department may even wish to extend its formal advising process by providing counsel to graduates. This can be done independently or within the context of reunions. The former approach may be more appropriate in public institutions where graduates often remain in the geographic vicinity. The latter is feasible in the context of independent institutions for whom alumni reunions are important social events. Another resource someone will surely find a way to use is the Internet.

Graduate Students

Much of graduate student advising takes place on a quasi-apprenticeship basis. Prospective Ph.D. students are linked with advisors who become their mentors through the long process of preparation for comprehensive examinations and take on the task of supervising the dissertations. Our university culture, which exalts the autonomy of individual faculty, may not serve graduate students responsibly. There is the student whose advisor moved to another institution when the dissertation was half done. There is the candidate who could not pull together a committee for the dissertation review because a member was on sabbatical or attending an international meeting. It is time for departments to assume some collective responsibility for assisting graduate students in completing their work in a timely manner. Delayed degrees are costly to the student and can even jeopardize employment. The only way this will happen is if chairs bring up for regular department discussion the progress of individual graduate students. Departments need to understand that the progress of graduate students is in part a function of the support and direction given from the department.

It is time also for departments to look at the question of the length of time to a degree. In the face of a hollow job market in the 1970s and 1980s, some institutions sought to assist their graduate students by prolonging their time as students, providing them with a continuing intellectual home as they waited for academic employment opportunities. The result has been a prolongation of the process of completing doctoral degrees. This expansion of the period of apprenticeship now imposes financial burdens as well as complicating the lives of students with an ever more onerous period as academic postulants. Only departments can reverse this process.

CONCLUSION

Heretofore, the process of teaching has remained a largely individual activity. Technology is certainly imposing change on the teaching process, but it is not the only drive toward change. The premises of education have been altered. Formal education centered around literacy is no longer limited to a specialized elite. Literacy has become a fundamental functional requirement for all citizens. The fact that education has become more a right than a privilege is helping to reshape the relationship between teacher and student. Teaching is gradually becoming more public in character, and that means that there is a growing imperative to bring the subject of teaching to the forefront of the collective departmental dialog. Furthermore, teaching is more than the activity defined within the classroom walls. We need to work for maximum success for students. Departments must, therefore, keep their curricula under review, ensuring that students do not just enroll in disassociated classes but that they experience a curriculum made up of individual course experiences that reenforce and build on each other. It means that departments need to think together about issues of pedagogy, consciously building the skills of each faculty member and seeking out those methods that bring greatest success to each student. It means seeing student advising as a central feature of the teaching process. Effecting these changes in a department will require conscious, consistent leadership from chairs. However, one of the central responsibilities of a department chair is building the pedagogical success of faculty as individuals and of the department collectivity. Department success in its teaching mission derives from collective success in designing and delivering curricula and in the effectiveness of the individual advising and mentoring that takes place between faculty and students. It is the chair who ensures that a department will develop a reflective agenda and exert the self-discipline to monitor and improve teaching performance as an ongoing task.

NOTES

1. In some institutions class lists will include students' academic majors. That can tell you whether students are your majors or not. If they are not your majors, the institutional curriculum may tell you if they are taking your department's course as a support to their major, as a college-wide requirement, or for personal interest. Departments may choose to verify such information by doing a quick survey of the students themselves in selected courses.
2. Figures published in *The Chronicle of Higher Education* (Desruisseaux 1996, A65, A67) from the Institute for International Education note that 84,403 students from the U.S. went overseas, whereas 453,787 (five times as many) came to the United States.
3. Not treated in this chapter, but nonetheless very important, is the whole movement for collaborative and cooperative learning. A useful entry point to that topic and its literature is Barbara J. Millis (1995).
4. Helgesen (1995) describes the theoretical characteristics of a non-hierarchical organizational form and then reviews five enterprises ranging from Intel, a newspaper, a hospital, a wholesaler, and a commercial company that function in the web style.
5. *The Chronicle of Higher Education* (Wheeler 1992) published a descriptive article on Treisman's experiment conducted at Berkeley, and its subsequent spread to other colleges, which by 1992 numbered some 125. Treisman's work won him a MacArthur Foundation fellowship.
6. Cooperative learning and team learning have been used both at the secondary school level and in colleges. In the latter it has been applied across many disciplines, including the natural sciences and business courses.
7. See Stoel et al. (1992) and Dodge (1993).
8. See Greenberg (1991) and Policy Studies Associates, Inc. (1996).

9. Seldin (1993) is perhaps the best known proponent of the use of the teaching portfolio.
10. The transformative impact of technology on education is effectively addressed in several essays in *The Learning Revolution* by Oblinger and Rush (1997, 69). See in particular the four entries in part I: "Understanding the Challenge."
11. The University of California at Los Angeles announced in the summer of 1997 that "it will provide a Web page for every course in its liberal arts college" (*Chronicle* 1997).
12. *The Chronicle of Higher Education* (1997, A32) published an extensive article on the for-profit University of Phoenix, which enrolls 40,000 students across 10 states.
13. *The Chronicle of Higher Education* (1997, A47) announced the merger of Corinthian Colleges, Inc., "a string of 18 proprietary institutions," with Phillips Colleges, Inc. "another chain of 18 for profit colleges" to create "the nation's largest privately held higher education company."

REFERENCES

Angelo, Thomas, and Patricia K. Cross. 1993. *Classroom assessment techniques: A handbook for college teachers.* San Francisco: Jossey-Bass.
Cross first pioneered the concept of doing research on classroom teaching, with that research to be carried out by teachers. Angelo, in collaboration with Cross, has produced a detailed handbook on classroom assessment techniques, ranging from the simple to the conceptually sophisticated. For a department interested in examining its success in teaching, the handbook is an excellent guide.

Breivik, Patricia Senn. 1998. *Student learning in the information age.* Phoenix: Oryx.
This volume provides a useful overview for grasping the scope of change wrought by the "information age." Although the information age is much affected by the availability of resources such as the Web, Breivik's book pushes beyond technology to look at the effect on the process of learning, the particular impacts on disciplines, and the challenges at the human and institutional level.

The Chronicle of Higher Education. 1997. International Section (23 May): A52.

Desruisseaux, Paul. 1996. A record number of foreign students enrolled at U.S. colleges last year: Even so educators worry that the rate of increase has slowed dramatically. *The Chronicle of Higher Education* (6 December): A64–A68.

Dodge, Bernard J. 1993. School-university partnerships and educational technology. ERIC Digest. Educational Resources Information Center, 1-800 LET-ERIC.
This report provides an overview summary of school-university partnerships up to the early 1990s.

Gaff, Jerry G., and James L. Ratcliff, and Associates. 1996. *Handbook of the undergraduate curriculum: A comprehensive guide to purposes, structures, practices and change.* San Francisco: Jossey-Bass.
This volume offers an exhaustive review of curriculum design for undergraduates, covering topics from the history of curriculum to its aims, reforms, administration, and issues in producing change.

Greenberg, Arthur R. 1991. High school-college partnerships: Conceptual models, programs, and issues. ASHE-ERIC Higher Education Report no. 5.
This is a good place to initiate a review of the kinds of partnerships that have been developed.

Grunert, Judith. 1997. *The course syllabus: A learning centered approach.* Bolton, Mass.: Anker.
This slim monograph addresses the nuts-and-bolts issues of putting together a learning-centered course.

Helgesen, Sally. 1995. *The Web of inclusion: A new architecture for building great organizations.* New York: Currency/Doubleday.
Helgesen describes the theoretical characteristics of a non-hierarchical organizational form and then reviews five enterprises ranging from Intel, a newspaper, a hospital, a wholesaler, and a commercial company that function in the web style.

Millis, Barbara J. 1995. Introducing faculty to cooperative learning. *Teaching improvement practices: Successful strategies for higher education.* Bolton, Mass.: Anker, 127–54.
This essay differentiates between collaborative and cooperative teaching, noting that the latter "is a highly structured subset of collaborative learning" (129). The comprehensive bibliography furnishes the resources for further research on the topics of collaborative and cooperative learning.

O'Banion, Terry. 1997. *A learning college for the 21st century.* Phoenix: Oryx.
O'Banion looks at how learning colleges can develop and furnishes examples from community colleges that have succeeded in making this paradigm shift. Although O'Banion's examples are drawn entirely from the community college sector, the overall principles are transferable to other kinds of institutions including four-year colleges.

Oblinger, Diana G., and Sean C. Rush, eds. 1997. *The learning revolution: The challenge of information technology in the academy.* Bolton, Mass.: Anker.
Applying technology to the educational process is a complex matter. This volume is a valuable introduction and guide. The opening essays give four insightful views of the nature of the challenge. Part 2 provides a series of vignettes of institutions that have responded variously to the challenge. Part 3 projects possible future developments.

Policy Studies Associates, Inc. 1996. Learning to collaborate: Lessons from school-college partnerships in the excellence in education program. Washington: Policy Studies Associates, Inc.
This publication provides a review of 26 collaborative projects funded by the John S. and James L. Knight Foundation. These are categorized into three groups: "cooperative, symbiotic, and organic." This description offers another set of criteria for forming collaborative school-college projects.

Seldin, Peter. 1993. *Successful use of teaching portfolios.* Bolton, Mass.: Anker.

This monograph is a useful guide to any department that wants to launch itself into the application of teaching portfolios to the improvement of teaching. Nine case studies provide the means for seeing the range of approaches that can be taken.

Stoel, Carol, Wendy Togneri, and Patricia Brown. 1992. *What works: School/college partnerships to improve poor and minority student achievement.* Washington: American Association for Higher Education.

These projects have in common their focus on improving the achievement of minority students in nine states.

Wheeler, David. 1992. Teaching calculus to minorities helps them stay in college. *The Chronicle of Higher Education* (17 June): A15.

CHAPTER 9

Resource Management for Chairs

THE NEW CONTEXT

There was a time when resource management was thought of as the oversight of the department's operating budget, with the major skill required being the ability to gauge how and when to push the dean or vice president for academic affairs to expand the department's resources. Put crudely, budgeting was a begging or cajoling function. To be sure, the chair needed to practice those skills with exceptional perseverance during the annual budget struggle, but however that exercise concluded, the chair had no compunction about seeking a subvention any time in the year when a need arose. In that delightful, but short-lived, past, resources available to higher education were plentiful. Enrollments were expanding and state and federal sources stood ready to invest in society's favorite project: higher education (and research). The souring process began in the 1970s when the declining job markets for new Ph.D.s became an early sign of trouble. Institutions quickly felt the pressure when states began a process of stop-and-go appropriations, which alternated between largesse and recisions.

Today, higher education no longer stands as the favored social project. The exploding demand for health care has brought another petitioner to the budget table. Barely acknowledged by the general public, which continues to vote for strict enforcement of prison terms, the costs of incarceration have ballooned. In California they have outstripped total expenditures for education. Transportation infrastructure has become another pressing social need.

The national highway system, built 40 years ago, is showing signs of age. This process of deterioration can hardly be ignored since our economy has developed on the premise of being able to move both people and freight vast distances reliably, and in short periods of time. Tax-payer revolts, which have been particularly spectacular in California and Oregon, have shrunk the funding pipeline. Private foundations, which have very generously supported higher education in the past, are being besieged with expanding sector demands as is the public purse. Philanthropic subventions to higher education are additionally stressed by the appearance of public as well as private institutions as funding applicants. Wherever one turns, it is harder and harder to find dollars for buildings, new programs, scholarships, or educational experimentation. There has been internal institutional response as well. Among the more dramatic is the move in some institutions to "responsibility-centered budgeting," known as RCB. [1] In this approach more budget responsibility (and control) is pushed down to the point of activity, which in many cases is the department. Institutions are also working to improve their grasp of unit costs for delivering their services accompanied by an effort to link that information to planning and budgeting. [2]

The effects of these changes are discernible in the lives of chairs. First, budgeting responsibilities can no longer be a "begging function." The chair must be able to *manage an assigned budget.* Second, the chair needs to *understand the department budget in the context of the institution*, particularly when it comes to the construction of the annual institutional budget. Third, the chair must cultivate a broader vision and *think in terms of resource management.* To see the department operating budget as the limit of working resources can curtail the activities of the department unnecessarily. Fourth, for many chairs, they must join the institutional cadre that *looks actively for external sources* both of funds and other resources. Fifth, some chairs are finding their responsibilities have changed as the institutional approach shifts from using the budget for purposes of control to using it as a vehicle for accountability. Under the control model central administration retained control of major blocks of funds that could include all personnel, plant, and equipment dollars as well as contingency funds. Department chairs monitored modest allocations for office supplies and copying. If chairs controlled any travel funds, these would generally be insignificant, which meant that faculty might have to petition a dean for assistance for travel to professional meetings. Currently, some institutions are adjusting to an accountability-based model where chairs receive a lump of money for which they are then accountable. Chairs determine the categories into which blocks are to be carved. However, at the end of the year the chairs must account for the monies spent and justify decisions made. The accountability form of budgeting certainly gives chairs greater power and authority. It also means that they have to accept responsibility—that is, public scrutiny—to an extent not expected of them before.

MANAGING THE DEPARTMENT BUDGET

As a new chair you may meet the department budget in one of several forms depending on the time in the academic fiscal cycle that you assume your duties. The budget could appear as a "close out" report, as the projected budget for the upcoming year, or simply a report on the current month (see the glossary of common budget terms at the end of this chapter for a definition of close out). Depending on the procedures used in your institution, you may be introduced to the budget in print form or on-line. Regardless of the form of presentation, the first elementary question to ask is: "Can I read this easily and comfortably? Do I understand what it is telling me?" (Be assured that there are many chairs—and not only new ones—who do not understand their institution's budget reports whether as printouts or on-line reports.) If your answer is negative, the first imperative is to find someone to help you become comfortable and well informed about *your* department's budget. If yours is a large department and/or you are operating in a sizable institution, you may have the luxury of having a budget assistant—be it the department secretary or a person with a designated job description as budget manager. Should you have such assistance available, count yourself blessed. However, it remains vitally important that you understand your department's budget and be active in setting and maintaining its management goals. The budget, after all, is the statement of your department's intentions. Those intentions are modified, revised, and realized as monies are spent. Without consistent fiscal management you and your department cannot expect to reach the goals you have agreed to set.

Managing Budgets

Monitoring Expenditures
An ongoing responsibility of any chair is to remain aware of the state of the budget at any given moment in the academic year. How you do this will depend upon whether your institution relies on monthly printouts or has made available on-line access to the budget. The difference in the information you have to work with parallels the difference between a monthly bank statement of your personal checking account and your check register. The monthly bank statement enables you to verify the accuracy of your check register. However, any monthly bank statement gives you only "lagging" information. It can never tell you what checks you have written that have yet to be redeemed. An institutional monthly report is similar to that monthly bank statement. It tells

you what monies have been officially spent from your department budget. It says nothing about the commitments your department has made that will in the course of time be presented for payment from the university. An on-line system offers you information similar to that provided by your personal check register. In other words, it gives you current rather than historical information.

Whatever the manner of presentation, there are some standard data that you would do well to monitor regularly. You can assume that your budget will be displayed to tell you what your total budget was/is/will be for each given "line item." (See the glossary for a definition of "line item.") That means you can tell how much has been spent for each line item. It will also tell you either what percent of the year's budget in that category has been expended, or, in some institutions, you will be told what percent of the budget remains unexpended in each category. However you track the department's expenditures, the important points to keep in mind are as follows:

- Make a point of reviewing the status of your budget on a regular basis. There is an advantage to the monthly printed budget, for its arrival is a reminder to review where the department stands fiscally. If you receive a printed monthly report, make a point of reviewing it within 24 hours of its arrival Speed is important, because the monthly budget printout represents history, rather than current financial reality for the department. There is always a lag, rarely less than two weeks, between the moment of closing the monthly report and delivering the print summary to departments. Thus, if there is a budget hemorrhage and you delay spotting it, you are like the unlucky homeowner who has left the garden water running through a freeze. You may not see the damage until the thaw comes, but at that point your problems can become catastrophic. One means of diminishing the effects of this reporting lag is to keep a rough record of current running expenditures in the office. The more centralized the functions of the department, the more accurate such a log will be. Even without an accountant's precision, such a running log can save headaches and embarrassment.

  With an on-line system, you will need to establish the discipline of reviewing the fiscal condition of the department regularly. If you fail to do so the same kinds of headaches can afflict you as with paper printouts. The on-line system may efficiently log the department's expenditures, but unless you pay attention to the effects on the budget balance you can find the department headed for a deficit just as easily as with a lagging print report system. Information, like money, is without effect until used.

- Take a look at the rate of expenditure for each line item. If this is the first month of your department's fiscal operation and you find that 20 percent of the copying budget has been expended, you could well run out in that category before year's end. On the other hand, if you know that your department has a special project at the beginning of the term that requires a great deal of copying, that figure may not be a concern. What you need to know is what is "normal" for your department both in terms of total expenditure and for the rate of expenditure at that point in the year.
- If you find figures that strike you as unusual, check first to see that they are accurate. For example, using copying as a case study, it could be that the 20 percent is abnormal. However, inquiry leads you to know that these charges did not emanate from your department. Once you have your facts, determine what action you need to take. Using the copying case again, if the charges do not emanate from your department, you will need to identify the person or persons who can correct the charge. This will probably be someone in the accounting office. If, on the other hand, the charge is abnormal and is generated by a particular departmental activity or by a specific individual, you will want to think through your strategy for handling the matter. If the bulge is caused by a departmental activity, this needs to be discussed with the department. If the problem is caused by a specific individual, you may choose to focus your attention exclusively on the person in question. However, keep in mind that your goal needs to be to halt the hemorrhage. Reflection may lead you to conclude that though this particular problem was created by the activities of one individual, similar behaviors can (do) occur during the year generated by other department colleagues. This would then be an issue to discuss with the department. An appropriate goal would be to create departmental mechanisms that will forestall future hemorrhaging of the copying account. Keep in mind that verbal acquiescence may not forestall the behaviors causing the fiscal grief. You may need to think concretely about how charges are made, who is authorized to make them and what changes in procedure might be needed to ensure that further abuses do not occur. Once you decide on your course of action, you will need to monitor what happens to see that the prescribed procedures are in fact being followed.

Fiscal Year Operating Budgets

The fiscal year (FY) budget will tell you what operating monies you have available for the department for the fiscal year, which in universities runs from July 1 to June 30 (see the glossary for a definition of "fiscal year"). The document in itself is of limited benefit. Fiscal year budgets almost always will tell you what was allocated in the previous year for each line item, as well as what is being allocated for the coming fiscal year. However, without some sense of history you will not know what the implications are for the fiscal year you are managing. A good place to begin getting a fix on your department's fiscal history is to compare the close-out budget with the new fiscal year budget. By working with these two "documents"—be they print or electronic— you will see whether your department overran significantly in particular lines. If it did, it behooves you to find out why. If you have the misfortune of being in an institution that habitually and consciously under-funds departments, expecting chairs to seek special subventions during the year, such overruns may be impossible to avoid. That kind of budgeting will require you to cultivate the "begging" function. As a chair you are more likely to function in an institution that makes serious allocations that you are expected to live within. In that event, major gaps between original allocation and close out need to be analyzed with care. Once you have a grasp of the budget and its implications for the year, it is appropriate to review your findings with the department. Your department's history may indicate the need to make some policy decisions to manage within fiscal reality.

Budget Transfers
Beyond knowing something of your department's fiscal history, managing the assigned budget also requires you to know the basics of the accounting rules applied in your institution, particularly those governing line transfers. Do *not* assume that these rules will correspond to what you see as "common sense." For example, the budget will reach you listing a variety of items from supplies to copying to equipment. It may also include personnel monies ranging from secretarial salaries, to student workers' salaries, to part-time salaries, to sabbatical salaries. It is vital to learn what kind of line transfers are possible. In an ideal world all dollars are fungible. That is, if you have a surplus in one "pocket" or budget line, you can use it to relieve the stress in another line. However, in some institutions it is not possible to transfer any kind of salary monies to the purchase of goods, e.g., equipment or supplies. On the other hand, you will probably be able to move sabbatical savings to part-time replacements. Knowing when and *how* you can move monies can give an important range of flexibility during the fiscal year.

For example, a department that is paying annual leasing fees from its expense category for a duplicating machine may find buying the machine cheaper in the long run, thereby precluding the yearly outlay of expense monies. Purchases of equipment, however, must be paid for out of the equipment expenditure category. If the department's equipment expense fund is low, the only way the purchase can be made is by transferring funds from the expense category, provided that such a transfer is permitted. By knowing in advance how much flexibility for transfer exists, you will know the best strategy for obtaining the equipment in question.

Another kind of transfer that may be possible is to trade monies with another department. For example, if your department finds it has more than it plans to use in its student worker budget but is desperate for additional dollars for supplies, you may be able to swap with a chair who has the reverse imbalance. In this kind of swap the institutional dollars stay in the same line category, but they are internally reassigned to a different department. Consult your accounting department on the mechanics of making such a transfer.

This discussion of budget transfers provides a good illustration of a fundamental truth about any budget, namely, that it is a dynamic instrument. It should be regarded as your road map for the fiscal year. However, during the journey circumstances will change. Actual expenditures in any category will look different at the end of the year than they did at the beginning. While you do want to keep within the overall parameters of the budget, you should not turn it into a straightjacket. You should expect to review the flow of expenditures on a monthly basis and you should plan to review the status of the budget with your colleagues several times during the year. You can count on unanticipated events that will invite realignment or a need to exert fiscal restraint as the year progresses. If the department's history indicates chronic difficulties in a category, that suggests a need to redraw the next fiscal plan. This of course assumes that problems are not being caused by profligate behavior.

Perhaps the best way to approach budget management is with an open mind and a creative imagination. Identify the department's fiscal goals and then see where money could come from within the existing budget to sustain those goals. Master the budget management rules of your institution and see what fiscal shifts are possible, either within your budget or by "trading" with another department with complementary needs. Be aware that your department's budget is a component of a larger whole, and look for ways in which collaboration can alleviate your department's stresses. It will help to be aware of whether your institution is operating with a philosophy of budget as a mechanism of control or with principles of responsibility centered budgeting. The demands on you as chair will differ in each model.

Preparing a Budget for the New Fiscal Year
As a new chair you are likely to be in the position of managing a budget you had little or no part in constructing. The same will not be true for subsequent years of your tenure. While tracking the department's budget is a basic skill any chair must master, the budget itself is but the fuel for the department's policies. You can think of the department's operating budget as the gasoline

allocation for the year. It may give you a rough idea of how many miles you can go, but it says nothing about the destination. Nor does it give you any profile of the terrain, which can have a major effect on the mileage you will get per gallon. Two factors will influence that journey. The first are the institutional budgeting rules, which tell you which routes are open and which are closed. The second are the values and traditions and goals of your department. The importance of understanding the budgeting rules of your institution has been discussed. In constructing the new budget it may be possible to build toward some modest flexibility by using categories carefully in the light of the accounting rules you need to follow.

The second influence on you as you construct a new budget needs to be the values, traditions, and goals of the department. At this level, you should bring the budget up for discussion within the department. The equipment purchase proposed earlier is a good example. If monies need to be transferred from operating funds to effect the purchase of the equipment currently leased, one question for the department is what will be the impact of that operations "loss?" Do the members of the department need to agree together to curtail certain expenditures for the year to accumulate the funds for the proposed transfer? In some departments these discussions have not occurred previously. That does not mean you should avoid them. To the contrary, such discussions may be an excellent vehicle for helping your department build a shared understanding of its goals.

The Department Budget within the Institutional Context

The position of the department in the context of the larger institution will affect what you can accomplish as chair. As a budget manager, you need to maintain a clear-eyed understanding of where your department fits within institutional priorities. All departments have historical roots within an institution. If your department has *only* historical roots, its future is probably not bright. Assessing the real position of your department within the institution is a moment when the department needs to exercise a disciplined rather than a romantic or self-justifying vision. It is this disciplined vision that needs to underpin the construction of the department budget when you present it in the institutional budget cycle. As chair, one of your important responsibilities is to help your colleagues understand clearly and realistically where the department stands institutionally and where the institution stands within a larger public context. To come forward with what others perceive as fantastical and even irresponsible requests will only undermine the perceived reputation of the department. Like the boy who cried "wolf," the department may then find its reasonable and important requests ignored.

All departments should have a firm idea of the institutional purposes and goals they are expected to meet. Different departments meet different institutional needs and commitments. Following are examples of five types of departments whose activities include performing specific functions to meet the institution's commitments.

1. Departments that exist solely because of the university's commitment to an academic discipline. Examples are classics and humanities departments, which generally do not attract large numbers of students or generate large amounts of contract and grant monies. These departments often have stable enrollments and may not rank high in the institution's priorities for resource allocations. Nevertheless, they have traditionally been identified as indispensable components of the liberal arts, and their contribution to the university is felt to be important. In documenting their budget requests, it is particularly important for such departments to demonstrate the quality of their programs and the nature of their contribution to the institution's mission. For this kind of department it is particularly important to demonstrate the *quality of results achieved* since enrollment figures will not serve well in implying impressive accomplishment.

2. Departments that offer large numbers of service courses. Many English and mathematics departments fall in this category. The budget requests of these departments should use official enrollment figures as a basis for demonstrating the need for personnel and instructional support funds. Although these departments might also have good graduate programs, their requests should emphasize service to other departments and relate needs to anticipated enrollment increases. Keep in mind that you need to point out the implications of the statistics you present in terms of the results the department is achieving. Furthermore, those achievements should be linked to the goals of the institution.

3. Departments that are heavily involved in community needs. Examples are education departments with large numbers of in-service teaching training activities. Budget requests from such departments need to show the effective use of resources in the preceding year and indicate how resources will be applied to achieve the goals of the institution and department in the coming fiscal year.

4. Departments that are able to obtain outside contracts and grants to support expanding research programs. Departments of natural and physical sciences are the most likely to fall in this category. Budget requests should show how the outside funding augments internal allocations, and how in combination these funds make it possible to forward the purposes of both the institution and department.

5. Departments that are closely tied to a profession. Schools of law, nursing, and social work are examples. Budget requests of these departments

or schools should clearly demonstrate the linkage between societal and professional demands and the mission of university programs. Budget requests may emphasize the added instructional costs necessary to accommodate changing certification requirements and professional regulations, but they should also demonstrate how the program measures the quality of its public service. In other words, budget and results should be linked.

While placing your department within the context of institutional goals, it is also appropriate to take stock of your department's ambitions for itself. These, too, should shape the formulation of the annual departmental budget. A department that already has or is striving for a national reputation will want to emphasize its gains or losses during the current year and note the effect its national exposure has had on the university. Federal and state grant awards, prestigious publications, and improvement in student quality are developments that should be included as background in the budget request. If the department perceives itself as regionally oriented and has no serious intention of competing in the national arena, it should present information that shows its local influence. If the department is basically a service department, the budget request should include information about current faculty loads, as well as a statement of the positive effect that additional resources would have on generating credit hours.

The construction of the department budget will be affected by the institution's formulas. It is important to master those and to present the material asked for in a manner that makes your department's request easy for your dean or VPAA to compare with that of other departments. A table should be provided to serve as a summary that communicates the essence of the budget request. It will further serve as a visual aid in budget discussions with the dean. In addition to the budget itself, it is also important to assemble good supporting material. If the institutional formula does not facilitate this, consider submitting support materials as an appendix. That material can also be used in verbal presentations to emphasize the goals and accomplishments of your department. This part of the budget presentation is very appropriate to bring before the department for discussion. It can help solidify the department around mutual goals, and it gives you an opportunity to test your budget presentation before what is (should be) a supportive audience.

As you prepare the budget for presentation to your dean or budget committee, remember that while a budget is transmitted in quantitative form its purpose is to achieve qualitative goals. Hence as you report the kind of statistical material suggested ahead, remember that the purpose of those numerical facts is to demonstrate what your program has accomplished in the preceding year (or years) and the goals it seeks to reach in the coming fiscal year. Like any form of communication, budgets have a particular "vocabulary," and it worthwhile in your presentation to draw on what your institution has defined as "official" so that precious discussion time is not wasted in disagreements over facts and figures. University fact books, published financial reports, and information that has been widely distributed should serve, as much as possible, as the sources of the data presented. Each institution has an office of institutional research, which is responsible for providing accurate information to external agencies. Therefore, if published information is unavailable, that office should be consulted for data or for verification of the accuracy of unpublished data.

Several indicators of the department's workload and its relative standing within the university should be compiled and kept current. These indicators include *department trends* and comparative data. A recommended way of showing the department trends is to compile the following types of data for each of the last three years and to project figures for the next year:

1. number of credit hours produced by the department
2. number of students majoring in the department's discipline
3. number of service courses offered
4. average class size of service courses
5. number of faculty members and percentage distribution of faculty effort in instruction, research, public service, and other areas
6. number of teaching and research graduate assisstants
7. number of nonacademic staff persons, such as secretaries and technicians
8. effect of federal and state funds

You may also wish to present comparative data. These may focus on change experienced in the department as a result of pursuing its budget strategies in the preceding year. Or the data may focus on comparisons between the department and general institutional data. It may be more difficult to obtain information that will permit comparisons with accomplishments of parallel departments in other institutions, but where available these may also be useful. The important point to keep in mind is that you want to demonstrate how your department has applied its budget in the past to achieve its goals and why it sees its proposals for the coming fiscal year to be appropriate to its ongoing mission. The presentation of comparative data is most effective when presented as ratios or statistical averages. The purpose, as always, is to demonstrate accomplishment—hopefully superior to whatever benchmark you choose to use. Some of the kinds of information you might wish to present are:

- Percentage change in credit hours for the department compared with percentage change for the university
- Faculty-student ratios compared with those of similar departments
- Average faculty instructional loads compared with those of similar department
- Faculty-support staff ratios compared with those of similar department

The budget request should review, as concisely as possible, the various programs within the department, stressing the program's age, its mission, its relative academic and professional standing, and its strengths and weaknesses. The presentation should be clear, logical, and brief.

The request should include a summary of how the department is organized. Faculty members' names should be associated with department functions wherever possible. Special achievements of faculty members that have helped advance the goals of the program should be cited. It is important to indicate how or why an achievement benefited the department's mission.

After providing the background information, the chair should present the department's precise needs for the coming year. This section of the budget request should incorporate appropriate strategies. Once the background information has been clearly presented, then programs and indications of desired activities may subsequently be referred to by title.

In a world in which resources are limited it is important to be both honest and realistic. For example, if partial funding can provide some reasonable progress toward the department's stated goals, this information should be stated, accompanied by a phased schedule for obtaining the remainder of the resources needed in future budget years. If internal reallocations can be used to accomplish in whole or in part some desired objective, that possibility should be stated. If it is clear that resources to cover all of a department's customary activities cannot be secured, it behooves the department to look at the option of discontinuing some activity. Certainly, if the department's goal is to undertake new programs or activities, it may be necessary for some programs and activities to be discontinued. Credibility for both chair and department is dramatically reduced by maintaining that everything the department is currently doing is absolutely essential. The department is also in jeopardy when you insist that programs are minimally and inadequately funded so that any reallocation or reduction in funding would absolutely cripple the department, ensure that the reputation of the department would be devastated, defeat the department's efforts to improve itself, or (most assuredly) destroy the morale of its faculty. Any dean or provost can see this argument for what is it, and knows that any department can survive reasonably intact with some degree of budget reallocation or reduction.

Managing Departmental Resources

There is no doubt that the annual budget is a basic departmental resource. However, to limit one's inventory of resources to that instrument is to curtail the flexibility of the department. An important exercise for chairs is to survey and list other available resources and assess how they might be used to advance the goals of the department. People and time are among the most important of the department's "hidden" resources. There are also some material resources that are often overlooked. And there are sources of funding beyond the university of which chairs need increasingly to be aware.

People

The Faculty. The faculty itself is a resource, beyond the expertise they dedicate to the classroom and to research. Faculty have a range of talents and interests that can be brought to bear on the work of the department. Any chair should seek to delegate as many department tasks as possible to others in the department. For example, if the department has determined that it wants to improve its advising of senior students, that goal can be pursued by delegating prime responsibility to a particular faculty member. Faculty also command a range of skills. For example, if one member has devised ways of using the Internet for instructional purposes, a chair can spread that expertise by providing the occasion for that "expert" to share that knowledge both formally and informally with colleagues. Or if the department has a new member in need of guidance and support in mastering the mores of the institution, the assigning of a senior colleague to act as mentor would be a suitable strategy. Broadening participation has the extra benefit of contributing to the building of a cohesive and effective department. It also helps establish a healthy departmental culture.

The Staff. While there can be no doubt of the importance of staff skills in a department, those skills can either be squandered or multiplied. With the advent of personal computers, there is less need for secretarial staff to perform the traditional typing and filing of years past. The question now is how that person power can be best applied to assist the department in realizing its goals. This is a matter that staff and department should discuss together. Secretaries should not be left adrift to determine work priorities. In a department functioning in this manner, two categories of persons determine what gets "done": those with the highest rank and those with the loudest voices. The best result you can expect in such a circumstance is that work will be handled in the order it is received, obviously having no relationship to urgency, deadlines, or departmental purposes. While the "buck" may stop at the chair's desk, the question of setting priorities for department work should be discussed among the faculty with the staff person present. Once the "rules" are agreed to and made public, you will still need to see that those "rules" are followed. The existence of public agreements, however, makes it possible for secretaries to refuse inappropriate requests. And "rules" give the chair a basis for intervening on something stronger than a personal sense of justice or propriety. Similar standards can be applied to any support staff positions, be it laboratory assistants or student workers.

The Students. Another department resource, and one frequently overlooked, are the students themselves. A department-wide discussion of students as resources may open some intriguing possibilities. For example, if the department has determined that it wishes to increase its number of majors, current students are an excellent source of information on student views of the department. Majors are also a source for attracting additional students. To make any of these possibilities productive requires that the department work purposefully with its students to pursue the designated goal. In this rapidly evolving world of technology, students may even be an important source of technical expertise. There are still faculty who hold new technologies at arm's length. There are others who have taken the plunge, for example, into e-mail, but who have done nothing more than that. We live in a world where, in some areas, students can tutor their professors. While this may happen serendipitously, there is no reason why as a chair, one cannot survey the department's student pool in search of connections that could be purposefully developed. Students can also be enlisted to tutor and support other students. Whether this is to be pursued in a formal paid-work sense or whether it can be pursued informally within the department is something to be worked out in response to particular circumstances. The important attitude is that one sees students as a part of the resource pool that can be drawn on to advance the department's mission.

Alumni. It is probably easiest to see the alumni as resources. A classic has been to regard them as sources for annual or special donations. Fund-raising for chairs will be addressed shortly. But alumni are useful well beyond their pocketbooks. Alumni can be important sources for internship placements for the department's students. Those internships can be local, regional, national, or even international, depending on the field, the students' desires and resources, and the locations of alumni. The general strength of alumni and their degree of interest in the department can have an impact on the position of the department within the larger institution. A dedicated alumni group is an invaluable resource to any department. Alumni can also be a conduit for new students, whether for undergraduate or graduate programs. Any student recommended to a department by an alumnus/a should be reviewed with care. Unless you have evidence that suggests poor judgment on the part of the alumnus/a, the recommendation should give you a sense that the talents of the student and the strengths of the department will link effectively.

Time

Individual Chair Time. A resource we tend to ignore is time, and ironically it is the one resource that can never be replaced. Ultimately, time is what each of us contracts to dedicate to the department and institution. Chairs experience great discomfort by the shrinking of their time for teaching, research, and family. With the escalation of tasks some of the shrinkage is unavoidable. Chairs, as with people in general, tend to feel driven by a multiplicity of demands. Deciding to become the driver instead of the driven is an important first step in regaining mastery of individual time. Possibly the most difficult time management problem for chairs is the fragmentation of their time combined with the constant appearance of unscheduled people and events.

Some boundaries can be created by designating tasks to specific time zones. For example, if completing a particular piece of work necessitates reserving to yourself an uninterrupted hour, you may need to implement a specific strategy. If you have decided to execute the task in your campus office, you may need to close the door—and establish a written or unwritten rule that "door-closed-means-do-not-disturb-short-of-a-fire-earthquake-or-nuclear-attack." Further, you will probably need the help of the department secretary to ensure that telephone calls are not sent through to you during this personal time. If a quiet hour on campus is not feasible, an alternative strategy is to remain at home on a regular basis to give yourself time to complete tasks that require reflection. That option, though, also requires you to "enforce" your decision. In this case it may be that under no circumstances do you answer the telephone. Just let the message machine pick up the news that you will deal with later. A longer range arrangement is to make a public commitment that you will not be interrupted by phone calls or drop-in visits at specified "work" times. Your colleagues and students will adapt, providing they know they can count on you to return their calls at a particular time, or that your door is always open on other specified occasions. These suggestions may sound bureaucratic and, hence, unappealing. However, if as chair you wish to have any relief from the sense of running endlessly and aimlessly in an increasingly frenetic manner, it is necessary to give up a degree of spontaneity in exchange for control and a sense of sanity.

In addition to creating some "time zones" for things like answering phone calls, welcoming drop-in visits, and pursuing reflective work, it is important to learn to delegate tasks to others. A good way to start creating the "delegation habit" is to ask yourself each time you are about to take an action, "Who else could possibly do this?" If you are someone who has immense difficulty shedding any responsibility, no matter how mundane, the better question could be, "If I were off in the North Woods fishing for the next month, who would take care of this?" One question or the other should produce the name of at least one person who could potentially relieve you of a task. The next step is to go ahead and ask that person to take care of the matter. There are, of course, tasks that are not only the chair's prerogative, but also the chair's responsibility to fulfill. Such tasks, obviously, should *not* be delegated. But there is much else that goes on in a department that can be done quite nicely by someone other than the chair. The goal should be to maximize that list.

Department Time. But more is at stake than individual chair time. We may not think of time as a group resource, but when we do some interesting things happen. It can be enlightening to look at all facets of the department in terms of the uses of time. For example, ask the secretary to give you a time log for a given week, which the two of you should then discuss. Is the secretary's time being wasted through the sequencing of tasks, through the inattention of individuals in terms of what they ask of the secretary, through unrealistic demands of students, or through poor planning either on the part of the secretary or by the department's policies—or habits? If the resource of time is being misspent, it behooves the chair to take action to rectify such profligacy.

Another dimension of time is the faculty's time. Although chairs may feel particularly martyred by "lack of time," faculty tend to share some of the same feelings of Alice-in-the-Looking-Glass, running hard just to stay in place. Endless committee meetings are the bane of academic existence. As chair, you have influence and even control over at least one group situation: the meetings of your department. The temptation may be to save everyone's time and have fewer meetings. However, this may not be a rational solution at all. More important is to ascertain the faculty's view of the usefulness of meetings that are held. Do they think the right questions are being addressed? If not, what is missing or what is included that is unproductive? Do they look forward to department meetings or do they dread them? Do people habitually skip meetings? How do faculty feel at the conclusion of the department meetings? Do faculty perceive the group interactions as constructive, or do they see departmental debate as debilitating and ineffective and even personally destructive?

If you decide to solicit faculty views on such questions, it should be done systematically in writing with a careful effort to record all voices. It is probably best to preserve anonymity as you solicit views. However, the aggregated responses are appropriate to discuss within the department. Armed with the responses, you will have useful material for initiating a substantive discussion with the department on its composite view of the department's utilization of time. If the department identifies important areas of dissatisfaction with its mode of doing business, it can initiate corrective action. It is the chair who then needs to guide the department so that it remains on course and carries out its aims. As this happens, department time will be better spent in advancing collective goals.

Student Time. Time is also a factor in student lives. Depending on the institution and the program, many students today are working adults—"adult" being defined as someone over 25 years old. Understandably, many of these are part-time students. Because of work obligations, these students may have great difficulty in adapting to an eight-to-five school schedule. And insofar as we are beginning to see students more as clients and less as postulants, we are faced with a need to redefine the academic day. Some institutions—especially community colleges—have made extensive adaptations to these needs. Other institutions, while educating adult students, are oblivious to the difficulties they experience in combining needed employment with the rigidities of class schedules.

Producing the department's class schedule is one of the chair's more tedious tasks. While the headaches of the paperwork involved cannot be evaded, that chore should be preceded by a departmental review of its scheduling *vis-a-vis* its student body. A residential, private college will have a very different answer to the scheduling issue than will an urban public institution. In the latter, it is worth asking one's students whether the schedule options presented work well for them or merely add to the burdens of earning a living while studying. It should be a departmental task to devise a schedule that works as well as possible for students. If, in the light of preferred work patterns, adjusting to student needs is a burden to faculty, it is important that department members share such burdens equitably.

Meeting student time needs requires the department to think in two dimensions. There is the daily time schedule in a given term, quarter, or semester. The department should explicitly review its schedule to see that required courses are not set into identical time slots, forcing students to plod slowly through a list of basic requirements over an extended period of enrollment. Scheduling should also reflect an understanding of the time patterns of students. Are morning classes impossible for many of the department's enrollees? Is it important to schedule some classes in the late afternoon or evening?

Beyond the daily schedule is the annual sequence of offerings. If some courses are rotated in the curriculum, it is important to see if the department is rotating required or heavily subscribed courses, perhaps forcing students to prolong their enrollment and slow the completion of their programs. The department should also ask itself whether other departments are depending on them for certain offerings, as well as looking to see if it, in turn, depends on other departments to serve its majors. In either case, the scheduling conversation should be broadened to include other departments.

Material Resources

Departments also often have control over physical resources such as space and equipment. By and large institutions tend to pursue a policy which says space is university space and can be assigned to accommodate interests of the institution. In fact, however, people become accustomed to "owning" certain spaces. This is particularly true in the sciences, but it affects the thinking of others as well. As all institutions face declining resources, departments led by astute chairs need to think less about "their" space but rather how space and or equipment that they command can be used to advance the interests of students and the institution as a whole. If this seems like a "Pollyanna" stand, it would be well to keep in mind that a department that becomes overly territorial may find its prized square footage reallocated from on high. The wise chair will prefer to lead the department in a preemptive initiative that may involve making the first overtures in proposing collaborative use of space that advances the interest of cognate departments as well as their own. It is also appropriate to think about the relationship between space and pedagogy. We know that labs need lab benches. But how much thought is given to the physical arrangements in traditional classrooms? Individual departments cannot expect to control all the varieties of space they may need for different forms of pedagogy, but if several departments with similar approaches work together it may be possible to devise a better fit between methods of teaching and architecture. It is also appropriate to give thought to creating a "departmental space" where students can meet with students, faculty with students, and faculty with faculty in an informal setting. Learning, after all, is accomplished not only through formal processes. Some of the most important insights come in face-to-face unscheduled conversations, and these can be encouraged by using space imaginatively.

Searching for External Resources

A new area of activity for department chairs is fund-raising. At first blush, chairs may say that is well beyond their knowledge or capacity. The fact is that chairs and faculty colleagues are often at the very source of fund-raising knowledge, for they have personal knowledge of the institution's alumni. Those students who retain a connection with their university do so either by maintaining connections with the friends they made during their enrollment or by retaining contact with a favorite professor. It is the latter student that is a potential conduit of knowledge, resources, and money for the department and the institution.

Many chairs think of fund-raising as grantsmanship. Grants are certainly an excellent source of extra funds for a department. However, they are far from being the only source and they are an increasingly difficult source to tap, especially at the federal level. While the chair can and should encourage colleagues to seek grants, the search for resources must go beyond that pool. If a department and its chair proceeds to look for funds from private donors, be they local businesses or alumni, it is important to consult *first* with the university development office. While entrepreneurship is to be applauded, uncoordinated efforts can cause havoc. Keep in mind that the university is probably already cultivating contact with that local business you see as the logical source of support for your department's research or teaching initiative. A development officer's worst nightmare is a call from that prospective donor who is on the verge of making a six-figure gift to the institution, who says, "Tell me about Dr. So-and-So who called me this morning asking for $20,000 to help furnish a new art studio. You promised my projected gift for new science labs would be anonymous and that there would be no other approaches from the university for the next three years!"

The same situation holds for alumni. Remember that "your" departmental graduate is a *university* alum as well. However, it is possible in this instance that the department may know more about their alumni than does the development office. Effective collaboration between development office and department can produce very effective results for the department and for the institution. Departments often know about the personal circumstances of their alumni in terms of their postgraduate success, factors that can bear on the alum's ability (and interest) in giving support either to the department or the institution.

How can a department keep track of its alumni? Too often this is a hit-or-miss system depending entirely on individual contacts between particular students and favorite professors. The department as a collective entity can seek to institutionalize that contact by creating a simple newsletter that receives information from graduates and shares news with them about the department's activities, faculty news, and the activities and successes of their fellow students.

CONCLUSION

Unless your personal interests and/or professional experience has provided you with a quantitative bent, budgeting may be one of your more stressful responsibilities as a chair. For better or worse, the burdens of fiscal responsibility are more likely to expand than diminish. With the realization that effective change can take place only at the departmental level, there is a trend within universities to transfer greater control (and responsibility) of fiscal affairs down to the department level. Although some facility with figures is certainly helpful, you can probably find help with the accounting functions involved. The responsibility only a chair can handle is leading the department to think more broadly, innovatively, and creatively about the subject of resources with the goal of maximizing the positive effects the department derives from *their use.*

GLOSSARY

close out: It has long been the accepted accounting practice in educational institutions to start with a new budget at the beginning of each fiscal year. Hence, at the end of each university fiscal year the budget is "closed." That is to say, monies are not carried over from year to year. (This practice is being amended in some institutions.) Surpluses "disappear" from department lines and are swallowed into the general university funds. Happily for chairs, the same has been true for department "debts" or overruns. About 30 days before the annual budget shifts from one fiscal year to the next, budget administrators go through a process known as "close out." During those last 30 days the objective is to make use of all "surpluses" that may remain. It is the time during which most departments buy supplies for the next year, for example. If sums are sufficiently substantial, some equipment purchases may be possible. It is generally a somewhat frantic procedure since all transactions must reach the accounting office, which is itself going through close-out maneuvers for the entire institution, before the last day of the budget year. If you do not succeed in that, you will have "encumbered"—that is, spent—money from the next fiscal year.

encumbered: To encumber means to commit monies for payment when invoices are submitted. For example, if you are ordering chemicals for laboratories for the year, you may decide to place an order for the supplies needed for the entire year with a particular supplier. However, you may arrange to have the order delivered in several lots during the year. At the time you place the initial year-long order, the supplier will give you an estimate that you will submit to the accounting office, which will in turn give you a "purchase order," known as a PO number. At the time of issuing the purchase order number, the accounting office will "encumber" the amount in your budget. That means it will appear to have been "spent." That saves you as chair from assuming you have more money available in your budget than you do. At year end, if you have not spent all the "encumbered" funds, you may have extra cash available.

fiscal year: Any calendar is an arbitrary arrangement. The calendar most of us live with is what we call the calendar year, which runs from January 1 through December 31. The federal government runs with a budget calendar that goes from October 1 through September 30. Colleges and universities use a July 1 through June 30 fiscal calendar, which approximates the academic calendar year. It is often referred to as FY followed by the year. For example FY98 would be the July 1, 1997, through June 30, 1998, fiscal year.

incremental budgeting: Many budgets are produced "incrementally." That is to say, you take the current year's budget, examine to see where additional funds may be needed, and then add them to the relevant cost lines. The hazard of incremental budgeting is that is produces ever-expanding budgets, a feature contradictory to current trends of downsizing and recession.

line item: Budget figures are listed by category, for example, supplies, copying, student help, etc. For each category you read across the budget sheet to see what you have available for this year, how much of it you have spent, etc. Hence, the designation "line," i.e., the supplies line, the copying line, the student help line, etc.

purchase order: This is the piece of paper produced in the accounting office that records the fact that you have money being held for a particular purchase. You in turn can give that PO number to your supplier to indicate that you do have the money to pay for a particular purchase and that when the material is delivered, the accompanying invoice will be honored with a payment.

responsibility-centered budgeting (RCB): This is the new catch-phrase in university management. It is the heart of the process of decentralizing budgets and it is intended to give rise to accountability budgeting. Instead of transferring minimal funds to departments to cover general operating expenses, a department (or school) may be given a block of funds with which it has to manage all its needs. Pursued to its extreme, the budget entity (department, division, etc.) will "pay" for everything it uses. This can include space, heat, light, phones, as well as the familiar operating expenses of paper clips and paper. It may include salary monies as well. While this kind of fiscal devolution gives much more power and authority to chairs—and departments—it comes with a price: that of public accountability for the way funds are spent. Another price is that there is nowhere to go in search of contingency funds when things go wrong or if the department simply outspends its allocation. Another change that can come with RCB is that surpluses may be carried over to the next fiscal year. But keep in mind that debts can also encumber your new fiscal year.

zero-based budgeting: If you are asked to produce a "zero-based budget" what is wanted is that you mentally erase all preceding budgets and reformulate your budget by reestimating and justifying every single proposed expenditure. The purpose of this exercise is to get budget officers to think anew about how they spend money. (See "incremental budgeting.")

NOTES

1. Indiana University is an institution using "responsibility center budgeting." A description of RCB and its impact on the Communication and Theater programs is provided in Robert C. Dick (1992).

2. One of the perplexing dilemmas is the lack of national figures for comparing costs of delivering discipline curricula. Individual institutions are working to assemble figures for their own use. For example, Theresa Smith (1991) reported on efforts at producing such figures at the University of Oklahoma. At the University of Wisconsin-Madison, Casey and Beck (1992) illustrated how the university sought to link teaching load policy with strategic planning and budgeting.

REFERENCES

Casey, Martha L., and Bruce D. Beck. 1992. Development of a teaching load policy. AIR 1992 Annual Forum Paper.

Dick, Robert C. 1992. Prospective impact of responsibility center budgeting on communication and theater programs: View from a state supported university. ERIC clearinghouse #CS 507980.

Smith, Theresa. 1991. Discipline cost indices and their applications. AIR 1991 Annual Forum Paper.

Whalen, Edward L. 1991. *Responsibility center budgeting*. Bloomington: University of Indiana Press.
    Although this volume was written for budget officers rather than chairs, it does provide a good reference on this new approach to budgeting.

CHAPTER 10

Strategic Planning in the Department

A ll organizations engage in some type of planning. Governments do it, private businesses do it, and universities and colleges need to do it. Departments today cannot survive and defend their existence to those who hold them accountable without possessing a sense of where they are now, where they want to be, and how they are going to get there, combined with the means to measure how well they are doing along the way. George Keller, drawing on the work of organizational scholars Michael Cohen and James March, commented on the challenge facing higher education leaders.

> The American college or university is a prototypic organized anarchy. It does not know what it is doing. Its goals are either vague or in dispute. Its technology is familiar but not understood. Its major participants wander in and out of the organization. These factors do not make a university a bad organization or a disorganized one but they do make it a problem to describe, understand, and lead. (Keller 1983, 27)

You, as chair, are the department's planning leader, whether you choose to recognize this fact or not. Although most chairs agree that goal setting and planning are important to a department and can provide it with stability and direction, not all departments have well-articulated planning documents to guide their actions. The extent to which such documents exist usually depends on the priority given to planning activities by the department chair.

In the context of higher education today strategic planning dares not be relegated to the status of an optional activity.

WHAT IS STRATEGIC ABOUT PLANNING?

In effect there are two kinds of planning. One is the planning that establishes goals and priorities. The other is the kind that operates on a reactive, incremental "plan-as-you-go" principle. Decisions and commitments are made almost daily—and every commitment made now will have consequences later. Ultimately the department will become the sum of those commitments and their consequences. Commitments made in response to unanticipated pressures or opportunities *may* have a strong positive effect on the future of the department *if* the commitments contribute to the realization of the department's mission and goals. On the other hand, commitments made without consideration of mission or goals can cause confusion, conflict, and turmoil within the department and between the department and the university at large.

With increasing external pressures it is all too tempting today to plan on an *ad hoc* basis. As chair, your challenge is to help the department maintain focus and continue to plan strategically rather than on an "as-you-go" basis. What makes planning strategic is that it explicitly defines in advance where you want to go, articulates how you will get there, and provides continuing evaluation of progress toward your objectives. If one of your goals as chair is to develop a coherent planning process with your department, the following inventory is a good place to start. Does the department have a written mission statement? Is it up-to-date? Is it referred to as the department makes its decisions? Is the department mission compatible with the institution's mission statement? When decisions are made that imply action, does the department explicitly articulate an implementation process along with a time line and method for assessing results and standards for measuring their effectiveness? More difficult to measure, but nonetheless potent in effect, are the beliefs, assumptions, and values by which the department operates. These elements should not be overlooked. In fact, a sound planning process should seek to make those unexpressed elements visible.

What Strategic Planning Is Not

Before you engage your department in developing an academic strategy, it may be important to understand what strategic planning is not (Keller 1983, 140–41).

Strategic Planning Is Not a Blueprint

Your objective is not to produce a bulky document to be followed line by line. This unfortunately has been the approach to planning in many institutions. The mega-document approach has produced many linear feet of planning papers that are never referenced as actions are taken. The document has become the goal. However, it is more effective to think of your strategic plan as a trail map that you consult frequently. Used in this manner, the department can adjust the pace and progress of its plan in response to changing external conditions as well as permitting revisions derived from results both achieved or unrealized.

Strategic Planning Is Not a Set of Platitudes

To say your department strives for excellence in teaching, research, and service is equivalent to saying you believe in life, liberty, and the pursuit of happiness. This pitfall can be especially potent in the department mission statement, which needs to be the foundation of the strategic plan. The mission statement is circulated publicly, appearing in such documents as the college catalog. Students, parents, legislators, and the general public are no longer prepared to accept at face value vague statements we make about higher education and the nobility of our work. High-flown statements unsupported by results will not sell.

Strategic Planning Is Not a Collection of Departmental Reports Compiled and Edited

A strategic plan is more than an aggregation of reports. The administrative demands of any institution result in departments producing many reports on its activities. Don't assume that this constitutes a plan. A strategic plan is a coherent, integrated statement that includes goals, plans for implementation, and means for assessing progress.

Strategic Planning Is Not the Personal Vision of the President, Dean, or Department Chair

While your department's strategic plan will reflect some of the vision you bring as chair, it must also reflect the faculty's vision. That means that the strategic plan must be built through broad consultation that emphasizes consensus.

Strategic Decision Making Is Not Done by Planners or Consultants

Strategic planning can be facilitated by a professional planner or consultant, but the planner does not plan; s/he merely facilitates the planning process. You and the faculty and staff decide on your department's goals and implementation strategies. And it is you and your colleagues who carry out the plan.

Strategic Planning Is Not a Substitution of Numbers for Important Intangibles

Data, forecasts, and models are used to enhance intuition, sharpen analysis, and shape judgments. Decisions, which are the conduit for turning goals into substantive realities, need to take into account important intangible values as well.

Strategic Planning Is Not a Form of Surrender to Market Conditions and Trends

Developing a strategy does not mean giving up your department identity to attract more students. What you do want to do is to connect your department's goals with the external realities that affect you. You want to find the means to achieve the department's goals within the context of the reality in which you function.

Strategic Planning Is Not Something Done on an Annual Retreat

Your department must engage in planning on a continual, ongoing basis and not as a one-time workshop or retreat. This means that planning needs to be part of the regular schedule for the department. If planning is picked up as an afterthought, the process becomes episodic and the department will lose its sense of continuity and its control over its own evolution. Perhaps one of the most difficult things to do is to connect strategic planning to the daily activities and decision making of the department. To do so requires constant vigilance and attention. As chair your function in this regard is to act as head coach, continually reminding the department about its agreed-upon goals and pushing its faculty to assess the impact of new decisions on the realization of those goals.

Strategic Planning Is Not a Way of Eliminating Risks

Just the opposite; strategic planning encourages responsible risk taking and fosters an entrepreneurial spirit. It prepares your department to try new ventures. It is the framework that makes it possible to change in an organized manner in response to alterations in the environment.

Strategic Planning Is Not an Attempt to Read Tea Leaves and Outwit the Future

Instead, strategic planning helps your department make this year's decisions more intelligently by projecting probable outcomes that can then be linked to department and institutional goals. Strategic planning is a continuous, flexible process taking into consideration the external forces that help shape the college, university, and department. Pursued consistently, strategic planning will free your department from passively adjusting to external events and transform it into an entity that chooses and shapes its own future.

What Strategic Planning Needs to Be

No two departments will approach strategic planning in exactly the same way. Certain common themes, however, do run through most successful academic strategies. Each theme will be shaped by the unique characteristics of your department, the purposes of your institution, and the particular external challenges that are most pressing to both department and institution (Wolverton 1994, 15–16).

Purpose

The purpose of strategic planning is to articulate the department's mission both for internal application within the department and as a means of describing its identity to students, the university at large, and relevant external audiences. Strategic planning is also intended to provide the link between goals and resource allocation, both as the department expends its resources and as it presents its budgetary requests within the context of the overall university budget.

Perspective

Any planning process takes place within a context that is particular to each entity. An important component of that context is historical. Institutions founded with a religious mission are apt to preserve elements of that past history even after they are secularized. State teachers' colleges and agricultural colleges will retain elements of that founding mission long after they have become comprehensive universities. Historical context may affect program components, the kinds of students attracted to the institution, and the beliefs and values of the institution. The same historical effects impact departments in ways that may coincide with or diverge from the institution's patterns. Current challenges also color context. For example, the shrinkage in public resources is a phenomenon that is affecting higher education in general. Its particular manifestations, though, vary by region, type of institution, and particular departments. The point is that planning does not take place in a vacuum. Nor can it be borrowed from a pattern book. It takes place within a specific context that will shape the range of planning options your department can realistically target.

Focus

The focus of strategic planning is both internal and external. It is internal in the sense that you and your department will be working to create the means of articulating your goals and implementing plans that are internal to the department. It must also be external in focus since your plans will not succeed unless they mesh successfully with institutional realities and ever more urgent external pressures.

Primary Interest
A department's primary interest in strategic planning is to enable it to apply resource allocation in a way that will advance departmental goals and ensure departmental well-being. This is in stark contrast to permitting resource availability to write the strategic plan.

Departmental Leadership
Leadership within a department is in some ways fluid, in part because many chairs serve for such brief periods of time. However, there are certain tasks that devolve to the "designated leader," who in the case of the department is the current chair. The transitory nature of chair leadership should not be confounded with lack of importance, influence, or authority. Department chairs play a crucial role in strategic planning. They rely on faculty involvement in decision making pertaining to department activities. They seek input from constituents in the external environment when that input has the potential of affecting departmental direction. Perhaps the chair's most important role is keeping any planning process going. As we all know, "fire fighting drives out planning." Or put another way, day-to-day activities crowd out the future. It is the chair who keeps the department's focus on strategic planning.

Doing Strategic Planning

What does all this mean to you as the department chair? Basically you need to work with your faculty and constituents to answer the four basic questions with which this chapter began:

1. Where is your department now? A useful tool in answering that question is what many strategic planners call a SWOT analysis—assessing one's internal *strengths* and *weaknesses* and external *opportunities* and *threats*.
2. Where does your department want to be? This is where your vision comes into play—how would you define your department's mission and goals for the future? Departments cannot exist without a vision—and goals to achieve it.
3. How are you going to get where you want to go? Goals and visions may be meaningful, but until implemented they remain abstract concepts. How you achieve your goals will depend on setting objectives and devising action plans you and your faculty can implement together.
4. Strategic planning is a dynamic process that requires the plan itself to evolve. Corrections and adjustments need to be made on a continuous basis. That means that as the department implements it must monitor direction (Are we on the right path?) and make judgments on effectiveness (Are we advancing toward our destination?) (Gmelch and Miskin 1993).

Where Is Your Department Now?

The acronym SWOT represents the essence of your environmental analysis of where your department is now—its strengths, weaknesses, opportunities, and threats. The SWOT analysis will tell the department chair just how difficult the achievement of the department's mission and goals is going to be. It allows you to identify key competitive advantages and disadvantages. The internal strengths of your department are those positive characteristics, which, when combined with the idiosyncrasies of the department's context, give it a strategic advantage in achieving its mission. For example, does your department function as a collaborative team (see chapter 7)? Does it have supportive alumni and constituents? Does it enjoy a reputation of excellence with its students and colleagues? In contrast, the department's weaknesses are the situations that constrain its ability to achieve its goals. For example, is the faculty's current research interest inconsistent with the goals of the department? Do many of the department's classes receive consistently poor teaching evaluations? Are faculty uninterested in teaching and advising their students? Most of the internal strengths and weaknesses are within the control of the department. What may be lacking is an understanding that there is collective responsibility for the department's strengths and weaknesses. Maintaining its strengths takes collaborative effort. Eliminating weaknesses requires not only collective energy, but the ability to focus on the substance of those weaknesses rather than on personalities and individual foibles. Leadership is needed both in maintaining points of strength and in correcting areas of weakness.

In contrast, external opportunities and threats are those forces over which you may have little or no control but that have the potential of affecting your department. Opportunities are those favorable conditions that will assist your department in achieving its goals, while threats, such as new competitors in the higher education market, may jeopardize your department's existence. Sometimes opportunities can be found in external threats. For example, while government budget reductions may first be viewed as a threat, a reconfiguration or amalgamation of two departments into one may provide additional strength where once there was weakness.

Though many methods of determining environmental trends have been tried, no commonly agreed-upon set of procedures for scanning the environment exists. Each institution needs to devise its own method of conducting this very important analysis (Keller 1983, 157). The bottom line is, use what works for your department. Either you or an external facilitator should take your department and selective constituents through an environmental scanning analysis (Morrison 1985, 31–37). This analysis will increase your awareness of and commitment to the future and provide critical information to help formulate strategic goals and objectives.

Where Does Your Department Want to Be?

Department Mission Statement. The mission statement is the foundation upon which the department's strategic plan is built. It tells you why you exist and what you aspire to be. It should clearly identify the ongoing purposes, functions, and aims of the department and should parallel, or at least not conflict with, the mission statement of the university. This statement is important because it sets the tone, as well as some parameters, according to which the department will operate. Thus, it is a broad guiding statement reflecting the purpose for which the department exists and the major functions it performs. It emphasizes the uniqueness, distinctiveness, and singularity of the department and represents the commitment of the department's resources to its purpose.

Higgerson outlines an effective series of strategies for shaping a departmental mission. A department chair steering such a process should:

1. Determine the key shared values—by soliciting viewpoints of department members on a number of central questions:
   • Who are we?
   • What is our purpose?
   • Where do we want to go in the future?
2. Involve all department members. Remember that consensus building is preferable to vote taking.
3. Keep discussion focused on the department and not on individuals.
4. Identify departmental strengths and weaknesses.
5. Know the institution's mission and environment.
6. Assess potential allies and markets.
7. Keep the mission statement vivid and viable. (Higgerson 1997)

The result should be a clear mission statement that answers three basic questions: (1) What functions does this department perform? (2) For whom does the department perform these functions? and (3) How does the department go about performing these functions? The statement does not include a time sequence or a time limit for the mission to be accomplished as this will be specified by the objectives and action plans.

Department Goals and Objectives. Once you have articulated your department's mission, you can move on to the second and third levels of specificity—goals and objectives. A goal is a statement of a desired accomplishment that will contribute to the realization of the department's mission. Both mission and goal statements are policy declarations. However, while the mission statement is continuous, the goal statement suggests a temporal framework. The mission statement proclaims who you are; the goal statement indicates a particular end you wish to achieve and implies a time line for realization. Depending on the goal, the time frame may be projected in weeks, months, or years, which is to say that goals can be either short- or long-term.

In addition to specifying a certain end, goal statements have other characteristics: They represent a logical extension of the mission statement, they are oriented toward specific results, they are explicit, and they are supported by a series of objectives. A goal, therefore, is a statement of intention to achieve a specified result that is compatible with and will contribute toward accomplishment of the mission or purpose of the department and institution. It is the end toward which one or more activities are aimed.

An objective is a statement of intention to achieve a specified result that, when realized, will contribute to the achievement of the goal. It is an expression of the desired, measurable end results for the department. To speak of objectives is to speak of the concrete, the observable, the measurable. Although missions and some goals may be ambiguous and imprecise, objectives should specify some observable product or result. They express, in finite terms (time, resources, quality, quantity), the results the department will achieve en route to fulfilling its mission. For example, "by the academic year 2000, 20 percent of our operating budget will be funded from sources outside the university"; or "within the next academic year 100 percent of the tenure track faculty will each publish two peer-reviewed articles."

In summary, well-stated goals and objectives have these characteristics:

- They are consistent with the missions or goals from which they are derived.
- They are oriented toward specific outcomes.
- They identify activities by which the outcome or result is to be achieved.
- They are measurable in some way.
- They suggest an expected qualitative or quantitative change or accomplishment.
- They stipulate a time by which the result will be achieved.

How Is the Department Going to Get There from Here?

Action Plans

Having goals and objectives without action is like "nailing jelly to a tree." The hierarchy of mission, goals, and objectives provides you with a sense of direction, but goals do not just happen—they require definitive action, organized faculty effort, and the allocation of resources. The careful consideration of how goals and objectives may best be reached is called action planning. Action plans state the specific and sequential activities needed to accomplish a given goal or objective. They include the description of strategies, tactics, and tasks that will be implemented. Furthermore, action plans identify who in the department is responsible for taking each action and within what time frame. They also need to provide a means for measuring both individual and department performance as a means of accountability.

The steps in action planning can be briefly outlined as follows:

1. Start with a clear statement of a desired goal.
2. Describe the department's strategy as it relates to the goal—i.e., what objectives need to be achieved to move the department from where it is now to where it wants to be?
3. List alternative courses of action that might be a means of achieving each of the objectives.
4. Analyze each alternative course of action, listing the tasks required. Look for anticipated consequences and prepare to cope with unanticipated consequences.
5. Rank the action steps in preferred order of implementation.
6. Set up a procedure for evaluating the success of the action plan.
7. Begin to implement the top-ranked course of action.
8. Be adaptable. Be prepared to shift to the next-highest-ranked course of action if serious problems arise.

Evaluating Results

Evaluation can be applied at two points. It can be used to facilitate decisions when the department needs to choose among several implementation options. Or evaluation can be applied to actions completed. Some departments use a simple technique to evaluate suggested action steps for achieving a desired goal. Each action step is rated in terms of its ability to meet the criteria of: (1) centrality of the action to the department's mission; (2) potential for achieving the goal; (3) cost; and (4) feasibility. The rating scale as to how well the action plan meets the criteria can be a simple one, such as "high," "medium," or "low." Or you may choose to use a rating scale of 1 to 10. A decision table can then be made to help choose among alternative courses of action. The same exercise needs to be applied to evaluate results achieved. This is all too often the missing step in academic planning. We can be quite creative in designing plans. We can be enthusiastic, and even diligent, in implementing these plans. In higher education we are often less than attentive in assessing the results we have achieved.

STRATEGIC PLANNING: THEORY INTO PRACTICE

A Hypothetical Case

At this point, a hypothetical case may be helpful in pointing out the relationships among the mission, goals, objectives, and action plans. The department, a small physics department, provides the following statement in the college catalog:

> The mission of the department is to provide undergraduate instruction in physics for physics majors and for elementary and secondary preservice teachers, and to fulfill some of the general education needs of the university in the physical sciences. In addition, the department shall contribute to new knowledge in physics and physics education and shall serve local and regional needs in this area through programs for in-service teachers.

The department's annual report shows that it has six faculty members, adequate office space, good facilities for instruction , and an annual budget of around $200,000. The department's assets include well-quipped teaching laboratories, two young faculty members who are especially enthusiastic and recognized as excellent teachers, and other faculty members who have strong capabilities in the field of theoretical physics. The report recognizes the department members generally lack expertise and proven performance in experimental physics.

As its hypothetical chair, assume that state law requires that faculty members teach a minimum of 12 hours per week or the equivalent, and that the state college system has set minimum class size at 12 students. From the environmental scan of "threats and opportunities" you have determined that the need for general education will remain constant for the next three to five years. Also the number of physics majors is expected to remain the same—i.e., about 40 students. The need for elementary and secondary science teachers is expected to rise and there is a continuing need to upgrade the training of general science and physics teachers in your state.

Although the statement of the department's status is brief, its application will require you to assemble the information base of your department for your strategic plan. For example, you have had your staff collect data about enrollment levels, number of majors, number of course offerings, faculty assignment patterns, levels of faculty research productivity, and patterns of financial expenditures over the past three years. From this data you have produced a "fact book" you have found useful for planning and goal setting, preparing annual reports, writing grant proposals, justifying budget requests, and simplifying many of your tasks as department chair.

At your urging, the physics faculty and you have developed the following goals: (1) to increase the current level of faculty research and publications; (2) to train elementary education teachers in physics science topics required in the public school curriculum; (3) to plan and implement a summer workshop for high school teachers; and (4) to improve the writing skills of undergraduate physics majors. Outlined below are the objectives and actions your department has identified for reaching the first goal.

Goal 1: To increase the current level of faculty research and publications.
　Objective 1: Increase the amount of faculty time assigned to research.
　　Action: Increase each faculty member's research assignment by 5 percent per year, to a level of at least 35 percent per faculty member.
　　Action: To compensate for increased research assignments, increase class size to reduce the number of classes to be taught.
　Objective 2: Seek and acquire funding for research projects from external sources.
　　Action: Conduct a proposal writing seminar in fall quarter.
　　Action: Supply clerical and technical assistance for proposal writing.
　　Action: Write grant proposals to potential agencies and donors.
　Objective 3: Publish six articles in referred journals over the next two years.
　　Action: Establish a biweekly research seminar for faculty members to discuss ideas and projects.
　　Action: Discuss and, if feasible, implement a reward structure for publications.
　　Action: Provide clerical and technical assistance for research projects.

Although the goal, objectives, and actions are presented here in outline form, the outlines themselves are a result of faculty discussion over weeks of dialog at special department strategic planning meetings. Action planning forms may be a useful practical aid, and these are available in most strategic planning guides. A sample action plan form is provided in figure 1.

In establishing its goals, the department first established its mission, then identified four key goals for the next three years. After establishing its goals, the faculty met to plan how these could best be implemented. Each goal was broken down into objectives—i.e., results to be obtained—which then became the focus of action plans. The objectives and action plans were formulated after the department faculty considered a variety of possible ways of achieving its goals.

The outline examines only the first objective, and obviously the same process needs to be repeated with the other three goals. The process becomes particularly interesting when you combine the goals, because the achievement of one may impinge on the success of another. Should that happen, you will need to circle back to clarify the importance of competing goals and find ways either to harmonize or prioritize them. Not every goal or objective or action plan can always be attained, but when a legitimate goal is not met, an active and strong department needs to review its activities and procedures and reconnect the ideal with reality. A strong department is a learning organization, which means that it learns from mistakes and does not repeat useless routines year after year.

TITLE: _____

SPECIFIC OBJECTIVE: _____

STEP NO.	ACTION STEP	RESPONSIBLE:	ASSIGNED TO:	START DATE:	DATE DUE:	DATE COMPLETED:

ACTION PLAN

FIGURE 1

Faculty Involvement in the Strategic Planning Process

When it comes to developing a strategic plan, the process sometimes is just as important as the product itself. Academic departments are made up of a diverse faculty varying in age, background, ethnicity, gender, personality, style, and ability. Whereas it might be easier to get a consistent and coherent strategic plan from a group of like-minded people, the diversity of the faculty is a greater asset than its homogeneity. Diverse faculty will have complementary skills and multiple perspectives. The problem you will face as department chair is how to develop a compatible strategic plan from faculty with different needs, styles, and interests. Constructing a department mold into which all faculty must fit will eventually stifle talent, creativity, and individuality. On the other hand, if you permit the decision-making process to become captive to the personalized agendas of single individuals or subgroups you will put the department in a state of suspended animation. Creating a balance between these tensions is at the heart of effective leadership.

As chair you will need to encourage the faculty to work as a team—a community of scholars (see chapter 7)—to develop the department's strategic plan. Strategic plans cannot be effectively implemented without the support of the majority (or better yet, consensus) of faculty. Your leadership style will influence the way your department arrives at its strategic plan. Some alternative approaches to strategic planning are:

- The chair prepares statements of department goals and objectives and circulates them to the faculty to stimulate discussion and input. The danger of this initiative is that department faculty may see strategic planning as "this is what the chair wants" or, worse yet, "this is that action plan handed us from the university." This approach will work if there is a high level of trust in the department, with faculty seeing such a paper as a tool for opening discussion. It will not be effective in a department riven by suspicion.
- The chair asks a faculty committee to discuss and recommend appropriate goals and objectives for formal review by the entire department faculty. This is a very traditional approach in universities. It is a method utilized by central administration when it wants to accomplish certain objectives that it cannot achieve without active support from faculty. The positive side of this approach is that it seeks to devolve responsibility and authority and it broadens participation. Particularly in mid-sized or large departments, this kind of delegation may be the only way to make a planning process work. Again, the level of trust within the department will affect the reception of such a mandate.

- The department forms a composite of the individual goals of the department faculty and makes this composite the basic department statement of goals and objectives. The department works as a committee-of-the-whole, drawing input from all faculty to create a coherent plan. This approach is practical in small departments. It will work most easily in circumstances where there is a solid level of trust among the participants, the ability to pursue the discussion of divergent views objectively, and the willingness to stick with and implement decisions once made. This approach has the virtue of further building cohesion and trust as the procedure is implemented.
- The department employs a consultant or a representative from another department or accrediting agency to engage the department in a strategic planning process. One might call this the "professionalized approach" to strategic planning. Its suitability will depend in large measure on the attitudes of faculty. Some departments are reluctant, if not hostile, to the idea that someone from "outside" can in fact "teach" them something about their professional work. They may assume that the academic enterprise is unique and that no outsider can possibly give useful guidance. In other departments faculty may find it reassuring to have an "expert" give them assistance in a process they see as technical and requiring particular skills. The major caveat is to be sure that the department wants professional assistance before you arrange for such a person to appear. The department should also understand that no consultant can "fix" things in one shot. What you are looking at is forming a relationship of some duration. Should you engage such a consultant, as chair you need to give that person your full public support. When difficulties arise, which they will, it is important that you make sure that the department does not turn the consultant into a whipping boy for its frustrations. Such behavior merely permits the department to distract itself from the real task at hand.

CONCLUSION

In the 1970s strategic planning was a popular topic for middle and upper level administrators. It was a less urgent matter for departments. Twenty to 30 years later we are realizing that strategic planning is vital to departmental success. The change in perception has been made urgent by the external stresses of shrinking resources and by the increasingly obtrusive oversight of external bodies, particularly state legislatures. Higher education can no longer expect the public to take on face value the statement that we know what we are doing and we are doing it well. We need to demonstrate the validity of such statements, and that validity reaches right down to the department. There is no doubt that the demands of teaching, scholarship, and community service are more than enough to keep both individual faculty and departments well occupied. But time must be made to develop and monitor the activities of departments. Their goals need to be clear and the activities selected need to support the stated goals. Whatever goals are adopted, the faculty must ultimately see them as their own. Without faculty "buy-in" any strategic plan will be no more than rhetoric, never reaching the reality of results. However, the likelihood of faculty finding the time to articulate a strategic plan is dim without the energetic leadership of you as department chair.

REFERENCES

Cope, R.G. 1978. *Strategic policy planning: A guide for college and university administrators.* Englewood, Colo.: Ireland.
   Cope provides an examination of traditional college and university planning.

Dolence, Michael G., Daniel James Rowley, and Herman D. Lujan. 1997. *Working toward strategic chance: A step-by-step guide to the planning process.* San Francisco: Jossey-Bass.
   For those who appreciate the assistance of a methodical handbook in approaching a new and complex task, this volume is what they are looking for.

Gmelch, Walter H., and Val D. Miskin. 1993. *Leadership skills for department chairs.* Bolton, Mass.: Anker.
   Gmelch and Miskin address three major challenges facing department chairs: (1) to develop an understanding and clarify the motives and roles of department chairs; (2) to understand the strategic planning process for creating a productive department; and (3) to develop key leadership skills required to be an effective department chair. Chapters 3 and 4 provide background and exercises for department planning and goal setting.

Higgerson, Mary Lou. 1997. Shaping Mission and Leading Change session at American Council on Education, June, Washington.

Keller, George. 1995. The vision thing in higher education. *Planning for Higher Education* 23 (summer): 8–14.
   As editor of *Planning for Higher Education,* Keller addresses the issue of how vital vision is to planners and educational leaders. His conclusion is that vision may originate with the department chair or central administrators, but whatever the source, each college and university should design a vision for itself.

———. 1983. *Academic strategy: The management revolution in American higher education.* Baltimore: Johns Hopkins University Press.

Keller predicts new patterns in higher education demographics, funding, diversity, technology, and management, and paves the way for academic leaders to respond to this revolution. The first part of the book describes what is happening in higher education and why. The second part prescribes strategic planning and suggests how colleges can introduce the process.

Morrison, James. 1985. Establishing an environmental scanning process. In *Leadership and Institutional Renewal*, edited by R.M. Davis. Jossey-Bass Higher Education Series, no. 49 (March): 31–37.

Morrison discusses how participation in a scanning process enables academic leaders to achieve a shared perspective on possible futures for the institution.

Taylor, Barbara E., and William F. Massy. 1996. *Strategic indicators for higher education*. Princeton, N.J.: Petersons.

Wolverton, Mimi. 1994. *A new alliance: Continuous quality and classroom effectiveness*. ASHE-ERIC Higher Education Report no. 6, George Washington University.

This monograph reviews the concept of total quality management (TQM)and examines the experience of seven organizations as they worked to improve effectiveness of the classroom through the integration of quality principles with the teaching and learning process.

PART
FOUR

. . . .

The Department and The University

CHAPTER 11

The Chair and the Dean

epartment chairs have a symbiotic relationship with their deans. Each is dependent on the other, and in a position to help or hinder the other's success. Department chairs who enjoy a constructive working relationship with their deans have established a relationship built on mutual trust and respect. Creating such a relationship requires the chair to understand the dean's perspective while recognizing the points of potential conflict between them. In exploring the work relationships that bring deans and chairs together, the goal in this chapter will be to identify some of the actions that chairs can take to establish and nurture a more effective working relationship with their deans.

ROLES AND RESPONSIBILITIES: DEANS AND CHAIRS

Deans

Deans occupy a middle management position within the institution's organizational structure. While they have responsibility for the success of all units within the college, they are not the front-line managers of these units. Deans work "in the middle ground" between the central administration that leads and coordinates the mission and direction of the institution and the department chairs who orchestrate the daily activities that make that mission manifest. As middle managers, deans need clarity from central administration on the broad directions of the institution; from chairs they need the implementation that will enable the institution to reach its goals. Thus, the dean's perspective is one of being the administrator in the middle who, to be successful, needs to ensure productive collaboration between the central administration and individual academic departments.

The dean's responsibilities and priorities derive from this middle management perspective. When working with chairs, one of the dean's functions is to interpret campus policy and practice. Deans need to have a strong grasp of the institutional mission and priorities, and in working with chairs their aim is to see that institutional and departmental goals and activities are appropriately linked. The central administration expects deans to uphold the priorities of the institution in their spending of the college budget whether that is exercised through direct control or manifested through the supervision of responsibility center budgeting. (See chapter 9.) On a more technical level, deans are responsible for making sure that departments and others in the college comply with campus policy and practice. This responsibility encompasses everything from policies on such matters as sexual harassment and promotion and tenure to campus procedures for handling student complaints, managing budgets, and hiring new faculty or staff. Often, how department chairs and, subsequently, faculty and staff understand and accept directives from central administration depends upon how the dean presents them.

When working with provosts or presidents, deans are the primary agents for communicating college needs and objectives to the central administration. Deans also order college priorities. Whereas the department chair represents a single discipline, deans represent a collection of disciplines housed within the same college or school. It is important for deans to see the connections between the work of departments and help those units to reinforce each other. Consequently deans must view the needs of individual departments as they relate to those of other departments as well as their relationship to the college mission and priorities. As they address central administration, deans need to transmit accurate and constructive perceptions of the individual academic departments and programs within their college or school. They need to demonstrate how specific departments and programs serve the institution's mission and goals. They need to alert central administration to departmental needs that warrant the institution's attention and response. Deans are responsible for presenting formal college requests for resources. In an era of fiscal constraint it is important for deans and chairs to remain aware of overarching institutional goals, finding ways to connect unit needs for resources with the mission of the institution. The time for turf wars has passed. That does not mean that discussions of resource allocation will be blissful moments of harmony. It does mean that deans have to be aware of the needs of other deans for institutional resources in the same way that individual department chairs need to be conscious of the demands of other chairs for college resources. All need to understand that particular interests may need to be subordinated to institutional goals.

As middle managers, deans must be aware of external audiences and issues that affect the campus. These external influences have become more complex and potent than they were even 20 years ago. Public assumptions about the role of higher education have moved steadily toward a view of education as a service. State and national governments look to higher education for economic benefits to citizens. Students want to know that they can find jobs. A whole new sector, the proprietary schools, is emerging to deliver education and training to individuals who have not yet found a place within existing institutional frameworks. However, the most obtrusive external influence, at least for public institutions, has been the articulation of detailed state priorities and productivity measures for higher education. Working from their understanding of such external forces and conditions, deans strive to build a college community that blends individual interests into a collective unit that best serves the institution's mission and priorities.

Lacking direct supervisory responsibility for faculty and staff, deans are very dependent on department chairs for their success. Unless chairs are effective advocates for their departments, the dean will lack important information needed to promote the college with external audiences, including the central administration. Unless department chairs are effective front-line managers, deans are likely to fail in achieving institutional goals. For example, since teaching is the primary business of our institutions (even research institutions have teaching as part of their mission), the delivery of quality instruction is likely to be cited as a top priority. Deans, however, are helpless in achieving this goal without chairs who are effective leaders of quality instruction and curricular revision. Savvy deans realize the importance of department chairs to their overall success and understand the need for effective working relationships with their chairs.

Chairs

Like deans, chairs also occupy the "middle ground," although in their case chairs have the department's faculty (and students) on the one hand and the dean on the other. However, a chair has a more complex set of responsibilities, which span both planning and implementation. Chapter 10 discusses the chair's planning responsibilities in greater detail. Meanwhile, in terms of implementation, chairs are responsible for department governance, which covers everything from running department meetings to tending the administrative business of the department; for instruction, which encompasses everything from curriculum development to the organization of class schedules; for faculty affairs, which runs the gamut from performance evaluation, to supporting faculty development, to smoothing out conflicts among faculty; for student affairs, which includes advising, counseling, and recruiting students; for external communications, through which the department maintains contact with extra-departmental constituencies within the university as well as nurturing (and creating) external linkages that are useful to the department. The chair is also the department's chief fiscal officer and general administrative head, responsible for maintaining the department's fiscal, capital, and human resources, overseeing the use of the department's equipment, and ensuring that basic department records are maintained. The latest addition to the list of chair responsibilities, at least in some institutions, is that of fund-raising.

Role Conflict

With different roles and responsibilities, it is understandable that chairs and deans may at times find themselves in conflict. There are three areas of interaction that are particularly vulnerable for generating tension between chairs and deans. These include differences that are essentially positional, differences concerning loyalty to a particular discipline, and differences engendered by contrasts in work contexts. In addition, the new demographic complexity of the workplace may add a fourth source of tension with its gaps in cultural perspective emerging from gender, race, and ethnicity.

First, as leaders of specific academic departments, chairs work to carry out a vision for a single discipline or academic unit. Deans, however, strive to orchestrate the work of several academic departments to serve an overall institutional purpose. In the event that a department mission requires attention and resources that compete with the aims of another department, or even of the college as a whole, chair and dean may experience conflict. For example, a broadcasting service housed in a communications college that operates a public television station may seek equipment funds through external grants. Grants for public broadcasting are likely to stipulate that these funds be used in pursuit of the institution's public broadcasting mission. A dean interested in having the broadcast equipment used for instruction will find this limitation too narrow and detrimental to the college mission to provide quality instruction to students who study television production. The positional tension between the dean's responsibility for quality instruction and the broadcasting service director's responsibility to public broadcasting creates the potential for conflict.

A second but related source of conflict between dean and chair accrues from the differing commitment that chairs and deans have to a specific discipline. Department chairs must possess a strong belief in their individual discipline whereas deans must understand, value, and support all of the disciplines within the college. While it is increasingly important for chairs to perceive the linkage among disciplines, they remain most strongly grounded in a particular specialty. Chairs are expected to speak knowledgeably and persuasively about their disciplines and the goals of their departments. On the other hand, deans who champion a particular discipline and place its welfare above that of other departments within the college are likely to be perceived as biased, if not unfair. A dean promoted from within the institution is more likely to be perceived as having an affiliation with his or her home discipline. To counteract that perception, a dean hired internally may seek to demonstrate that s/he doesn't favor his or her home department. For example, a dean might be particularly wary of pushing the requests of his or her home discipline for fear of appearing to play favorites. S/he might even be exceptionally circumspect in maintaining old departmental friendships for fear of being partisan. This can lead the dean's former colleagues to become disillusioned when they perceive their one-time friend forgetting the department's agenda and needs. For the chair who senses that a one-time associate is no longer committed to the department, this can be a stressful situation.

A third source of potential conflict can arise from the differing work context of chairs and deans. Chairs work directly with those who are affected by personnel decisions, revisions in the curriculum, and other policy and procedural changes. When chairs set out to implement campus policy and procedures they do so with a full understanding of the impact these will have on particular individuals and with a vivid knowledge of specific personalities and their anticipated reactions. Deans, who are more removed from daily activities, find it easier to remain objective in such matters as promotion and tenure decisions or merit pay increases. For the department chair these are not merely organizational decisions. They are also decisions affecting particular people with whom they interact on a daily basis.

A good example is to look at the differing impact of a negative tenure decision seen from the dean's vantage and from the chair's. The dean, of course, knows that a negative tenure decision will be upsetting to the recipient. The dean also knows that the rejected faculty member will probably want a conference to discuss the decision. Stressful as such an encounter may be, it is curtailed in time. The person appears for the allotted appointment and then will leave. The dean's day will go on. For the chair, on the other hand, the scene will be quite different. The chair will know of the negative decision, will know when and how the formal letter of rejection will reach the candidate, and may anticipate seeing the person soon thereafter. All this is likely to occur within the confines of the department and will quickly become generalized news. Every member of the department will have a strong opinion, some in support of the rejected candidate, others in support of the decision. The chair is likely to be bombarded on all sides with reactions. From the candidate the chair may have to endure an angry confrontation. From colleagues there will be a range of response from outrage to support. The worst of the situation for the chair is that the atmosphere of the department may remain highly charged for days, particularly if the candidate seeks to challenge the decision. This means that during every working moment the chair may be immersed in unpleasantness. The difference in context affects the perspectives of chair and dean. When conflicts emerge from these differing perspectives it can be managed productively if each party recognizes and respects the point of view of the other. This requires both parties to focus on the substance of problems rather than on rivalries of turf and power.

The fourth area fraught with the potential for conflict is the difference in management assumptions from which deans and chairs make their decisions. These may go beyond the gaps in position, discipline loyalty, and work context. With the increasing demographic diversification of the work context, gender, racial, and cultural differences may be added to the list of tensions. Although there will be differences in viewpoint even within a relatively homogeneous group, those differences are more powerful when they derive from divergent cultural assumptions. Working collaboratively is greatly complicated when the "cooperating" parties differ not only in their perception of what is important, but find it difficult to communicate comfortably because they differ on matters so fundamental as standards of courtesy. The challenge to all concerned is to expand their cultural comfort zones.

BUILDING DEAN-CHAIR COLLABORATION

Building an Effective Working Relationship with the Dean

Know Your Dean
Even when chair and dean fundamentally "like" and respect each other, the divergence of interest inherent in their different positions make some degree of conflict all but inevitable. That means that the building of a collaborative relationship has to be a conscious effort that is consistently pursued, preferably by both parties. A start on that path is for the chair to understand some of the dean's expectations. Deans need and expect a lot from department chairs. For starters, they assume that chairs are managerially competent. That means deans expect chairs to understand campus policy and procedures. This includes everything from knowing what forms to use when executing routine budget matters to knowing the specific criteria in the institution's promotion and tenure document. Deans expect chairs to be efficient in paper management. This includes the submission of appropriate paperwork by the designated deadline.

Deans assume that chairs understand the nature of the dean's position institutionally and the perspective and responsibility that accompanies that position. From the dean's view, it is this understanding of the dean's role that should enable chairs to respond positively to requests from the dean. Deans expect chairs to understand that the dean's obligation is to act in the best interest of college and institution. In recent years, the increased pressure for institutional accountability from external groups has resulted in more top-down planning at many institutions. Deans expect chairs to respond supportively to requests for such accountability measures as student learning outcomes assessment. Deans also expect chairs to implement such requests, obtaining a positive outcome while generating a minimal amount of backlash. Deans rely on department chairs to be effective sources of motivation for faculty and staff in meeting these external demands. While the specific demands vary from campus to campus, in general faculty live with an ever-evolving (and often expanding) job description. On very few campuses do faculty engage only in teaching and research activities. More and more, they are expected to help with student recruitment and retention, fund-raising, alumni relations, and a long list of other such activities that at one time were managed centrally.

Deans expect chairs to keep them appropriately informed about problems within their respective units and, most importantly, forewarning them of any potential crises. Deans appear poorly in the eyes of the provost if they must report problems that might have been prevented or managed more effectively. Yet deans cannot possibly succeed in meeting this expectation unless individual department chairs keep them informed of developing problems.

Deans also hold very clear expectations for department chairs as leaders of their academic departments and expect them to shape the vision of the department. It goes without saying that the department vision should be one that complements the college and institutional mission. In addition to being the intellectual visionary for the academic department, chairs are expected by deans to be creative managers and problem solvers. Particularly in recent years with dwindling fiscal resources, chairs are expected to do more with less. They're expected to preserve, indeed improve, program quality while spending fewer dollars. Similarly, chairs are expected to understand and present new directives or mandates from central administration without inciting revolts from faculty and staff. Better yet, chairs are looked to to mobilize positive responses to new challenges.

These multiple expectations held by deans require department chairs to possess strong interpersonal communication skills. Chairs must be able to work effectively with faculty, staff, and students as well as a long list of external audiences including area businesses, granting agencies, accreditation agencies, and other special interest groups. They need strong communication advocacy skills to sell the department mission and resource needs to others. Strong communication skills are also required to manage department conflict, engage the department members in productive dialog, and lead the department in needed change. Deans expect chairs to be effective in solving department problems. Experienced deans recognize that they are not in a

position to do the chair's job, but they are in a position to suffer the consequences in the event that the department chair is unable to solve department
problems and manage the academic unit effectively.

In addition, deans seek individuals with whom they are comfortable
working. They are apt to prefer to hire/appoint department chairs who possess
personalities and interpersonal styles that are compatible with their own
management styles. This does not need to imply homogeneity of background.
It does mean that there may be a preference for working with individuals who
share similar attitudes and values. There is no doubt that these preferences
can constrict the range of people a dean is comfortable working with. If you
perceive this as an issue for you and your dean, overcoming those barriers will
take conscious and persistent effort.

How as a chair can you respond effectively to these varied expectations? A
good place to begin is by giving some thought to your dean's management style
to learn how best to interact and communicate with that person. For example,
some deans prefer formally scheduled meetings to informal discussions. By
adapting one's approach to the dean's preferred style of doing business, you
can maximize the positive attention you get from the dean. Similarly, it's
helpful to know what type of data or evidence is most persuasive with the
dean. Some deans tend to trust numbers more than narratives. When this is
the case, chairs who are able to make their case using numbers will do more to
persuade the dean than if they rely on narrative or anecdotal information.
This does not mean that you should change the purpose for any request.
Rather, it means that the request is more likely to be heard and understood if
you use a language that is familiar and credible to the dean.

The Issue of Chair Credibility

The first and most important step in developing a productive working relationship with your dean is for you to establish and maintain your credibility as
chair. Higgerson (1996, 172) explains that the department chair's credibility is
composed of three specific components: "the perception of the chair's knowledge; the perception of the chair's motive or intentions; and the perception of
the chair's trustworthiness." Credibility is a perceived or assigned attribute.
Hence for department chairs to remain credible with the dean, the dean must
perceive them as possessing these three attributes. Being perceived as credible
is always advantageous. Highly credible chairs find that others are more
cooperative and less resistant to their suggestions for change. High credibility
also gives one more freedom for being innovative and for taking risks. Higgerson
(1996, 207) points out that "a person's credibility determines his or her
latitude for making mistakes." In other words, the dean is more likely to
dismiss a mistake as atypical behavior if the dean perceives the chair as highly
credible. A chair with low credibility, however, is likely to reaffirm the dean's
unfavorable perception with even the smallest mistake. The assessment of

one's credibility evolves in the same way that our perceptions of individuals can change over time. Consequently, chairs must work continuously to maintain their credibility.

An important factor in maintaining your credibility with the dean is open and productive communication, through which chairs are able to demonstrate their understanding of college and university policy and procedures. It is the content and form of the chair's communication with the dean that is the basis from which deans assess the chair's knowledge, motives, intentions, and trustworthiness. Open and productive communication implies a useful exchange of information that allows both chair and dean to fulfill their respective responsibilities more effectively.

If communication is important, what should be communicated and how? At a minimum, make sure you alert your dean to potential problems or brewing issues that could become crises. By doing so, you enable your dean to work collaboratively on the resolution or prevention of unpleasant situations or events. Don't forget to keep deans informed of positive information about the department, as well. Good news will be particularly appreciated by a dean, much of whose professional time may be monopolized by problems large and small. Deans may need to be educated about the discipline and the resources the department needs to teach that discipline. A well-informed dean is empowered to serve as an effective advocate on behalf of the department within the institutional dialog. Experienced deans recognize the importance of information, both positive and negative.

An example may serve as illustration. Assume that as chair you are head of an art department. You know that one of your art professors in teaching a graphics course is using chemicals whose vapors can be harmful if improperly vented. You are aware that the ventilating fan in that studio has broken down. As chair you have filed a repair request with the physical plant, but the repair has yet to be made. You have determined what your next interventions will be.They include giving instructions to the faculty member not to proceed with the print-making process until the repair is made and making an appointment with the head of the physical plant to get the problem solved immediately. You may choose to inform your dean of these actions. In so doing you are demonstrating your competence in dealing with an issue; you have preempted the possibility that someone else will appear at the dean's door with a complaint on this issue (and the inference that you are failing to take responsibility); and you have alerted the dean to the possibility that you may need help if your efforts do not produce the desired result.

Communication and Collaboration
Credibility is built through effective, responsible communication. Effective collaboration also builds credibility. While the previous example served to demonstrate how you might choose to keep your dean informed concerning a

specific matter, it is useful to have in mind some categories of business where it is particularly important to keep that line of communication strong. In so doing, keep in mind that you are not compromising your autonomy; rather you are strengthening your effectiveness and helping to build a collaborative institutional culture. Pinkus (1994, 11) identifies five critical areas about which it is important to keep your dean informed:

Chairs Must Instruct the Dean about Their Disciplines. Unless the dean comes from the same discipline, a chair should not assume that the dean is well informed about the nature of the discipline. Hence you have an educational task to perform. It is a task that requires some thought, for you should identify specific aspects of the discipline about which you think the dean should be knowledgeable. It is desirable to undertake this educational process while the department's affairs are running smoothly and routinely. Trying to carry out this educational process at a moment of crisis is both difficult and hazardous. By supplying the dean with timely and relevant information about the discipline, you enable the dean to champion the department's achievements and back its resource needs. By establishing a foundation of understanding of the discipline while department affairs are running routinely, you build the platform from which to work with the dean in moments of crisis.

Convince the Dean That the Department Is Producing. Obviously this cannot be a fictionalized account. If the department is not effectively serving the institutional mission, this is a matter that needs to be worked on within the department. However, assuming that your department is, indeed, mindful of the support it gives the institution's mission, it is important to remind the dean of how that is being done. Again, you are establishing the foundation for seeking the dean's support at times when the department needs it.

Keep the Dean Well Informed. Keeping the dean informed of the department's achievements is not a sign of immodesty. Rather, it is good public relations. It is equally important to keep the dean informed of problems in the department, particularly if they are the kinds of events that may reach his or her ears from other sources. A dean's worst nightmare is being blindsided by an irate constituent about a problem of which s/he is ignorant. In reporting a problem to the dean, it is desirable to be able to relate how you are handling the matter. Or, if this is a mega-problem requiring consultation, it is wise to have a recommendation to present.

Clarify and Document Requests and Proposals. There are times when you will have formal requests to bring forward. Those requests will have a kinder reception if they are properly presented. Everyone is busy, and the last thing a dean wants to cope with is the need to get your request into the proper format for formal action.

Support the Dean's Efforts. Our institutions have honed a we-they approach classically described as the split between faculty and administration. This cleavage, much of it artificially created, is not in the best interest of our institutions. A chair who regards the dean as "the enemy" serves to harden those institutional divisions. Although there will be differences in point of view and although there may be heated disagreement, in an ultimate sense, deans, chairs, and faculty are all in the same boat, be it leaky or sound. It behooves chairs to support the dean's efforts. Instances of disagreement should not be equated to damning any and all initiatives from the dean—or of damning the dean as an individual.

The primary advantage of building an effective collaborative relationship with the dean is that it establishes a backdrop of mutual trust and credibility from which chairs and deans can work collaboratively for the welfare of the department and the institution. Most important, issues of disagreement are resolved more satisfactorily when both chair and dean begin with a collaborative alliance defined by mutual trust and respect. Without such a relationship, it is virtually impossible for deans to count on the work of department chairs. Similarly, without an effective collaborative relationship, it is impossible for chairs to bank on the dean serving as an effective advocate for the department. Without that collaborative relationship there is little productivity or satisfaction for either in their respective roles, and when chairs and deans do not have an effective working relationship, both are likely to look inept. The symbiotic nature of the relationship between deans and chairs makes an effective working relationship between them imperative to the success of each as well as to the effectiveness of their collaborative results. When chairs help their dean by supplying essential information, forewarning about potential problems, and managing in a way that preserves college priorities, they help the dean succeed. At the same time, these actions typically empower and enable the dean to help the academic department succeed. Effort invested in building an effective working relationship with the dean accrues the double benefit of directly helping the department and ensuring your success as chair.

Communication and collaboration needs to extend beyond the dean to include his or her staff. In some instances, deans will delegate significant decision-making authority to staff. The dean, for example, may have an associate dean who handles all personnel matters. The dean may make it clear that the associate dean responsible for personnel is the person who will review all paperwork and make decisions or at least recommendations regarding new hires, promotion and tenure decisions, merit pay increases, and other personnel matters. When deans delegate authority to staff members, it is important that chairs expand their communication to encompass any member of the dean's staff who handles activities that connect to the department.

Form and Content

Earlier in the chapter we suggested adjusting the presentation of materials to the dean's management style. However, you also need to consider the relationship between form and content which exists independently of your and the dean's style preferences. Communications can take a number of forms: formal or informal, written or oral. When you communicate with the dean, consider the connection between the content of your message, any relevant circumstances, and the most effective method for presenting the issue. If, for example, you want to sound out an idea you anticipate the dean may not like, it may be best to present the suggestion informally in a face-to-face conversation. Such an approach will allow you maximum opportunity to read the dean's verbal and nonverbal reaction to the suggestion. The dean's response will be harder to interpret in a telephone conversation during which you do not have access to any facial expressions or gestures. Similarly, e-mail communication, though fast and sometimes efficient, denies the sender and receiver much information about an individual's true reaction to an issue. On the other hand, there will be times when you will want to put a request in writing and submit it formally to the dean. A dean who has been unresponsive to informal warnings of needed safety renovations, for example, may need to see the dangers spelled out in a formal memorandum. In such an instance, the memorandum also serves the purpose of documenting that you did apprise the dean of the safety hazard.

The method used to forward information or a request to the dean says something about the content of the message. For example, issues that chairs raise only in an informal context are less likely to be perceived by the dean as serious or pressing. To be maximally effective in communicating with the dean and the dean's staff, chairs need to select the communication mode that complements and enhances the communication purpose. Deans are likely to appreciate a phone call that informs them of an urgent new development. Should a chair elect to send such information through a written memorandum or hold it until the next regularly scheduled meeting, the dean is likely to conclude that the chair cannot assess priorities or failed to live up to the expectation that the dean be kept informed. Should chairs select an inappropriate or ineffective method for communicating their messages to the dean, they lower their credibility with the dean.

It is important to remember that matters are not settled merely by sending written communications to the dean. Even when chairs forward information using a formal memorandum or report, it is important to follow up the initial communication to assess its effectiveness. Higgerson (1996, 206) describes the value of feedback in learning whether or not chairs succeeded in communicating effectively. Chairs can solicit feedback in the event that deans do not offer it voluntarily. You can do this by scheduling a follow-up meeting to answer any remaining questions that the dean may have. It may also be done in future conversations by referencing the particular document and assessing the dean's response. You need continually to assess the effectiveness of your communications with the dean. This includes determining if the dean interpreted and processed the information as intended.

Information is more likely to be interpreted as intended if the chair can structure the initial message in a language that is familiar to the dean. For example, if the dean is worried about student recruitment, a funding request to support a special summer program may best be advocated by describing the benefits to student recruitment. Individuals read and interpret incoming information from their perspective and experience, and for deans this means they interpret incoming information from the perspective of their role as a middle manager. To the extent you are able to communicate that department goals are compatible with college goals and that satisfying department needs will advance the college mission, the more likely the dean will be a favorable receiver of the information.

CONCLUSION

Deans depend upon department chairs to conduct the daily business associated with running an academic department. As front-line managers, chairs are responsible for implementing campus policy and procedures, motivating faculty and staff to work toward college and institutional goals, and upholding the quality of the department programs. Deans may have supervisory responsibility for the performance of these important tasks, but only department chairs can actually deliver results. Consequently, deans are dependent upon the effective performance of department chairs. At the same time, chairs must rely on deans to understand and advocate the needs of the academic unit. Unless the devolution of responsibility is well advanced, chairs have only secondary control over resources and they often have only indirect effect on setting institutional policy.

The interdependent nature of chairs' and deans' responsibilities makes it absolutely essential that chairs and deans learn to collaborate effectively. Chairs will enhance their chances of success to the extent they are able to establish their credibility with their deans and to the extent they build a successful collaboration with that administrator. Differences in position, perspective, and responsibilities can cause conflict. But open communication and understanding of each other's point of view can provide the means for bridging differences and can provide the basis for a collaboration that fosters success for both parties.

REFERENCES

Bennett, J.B. 1990. The dean and the department chair: Toward greater collaboration. *Educational Record* 71, no. 1 (winter): 24–26.
> Bennett discusses similarities in the roles held by department chair and dean.
> The author presents five specific strategies for collaboration between chair and
> dean in the areas of program development, communication, motivation, budget,
> and evaluation.

Harper, J. 1994. Survival tips for new department chairs. *ADFL Bulletin* 25, no. 3
(spring): 94–98.
> Writing from 24 years of experience as a department chair, the author offers
> advice for new chairs. The advice includes strategies for how to work with the
> dean, how to gain support from people outside the department, and how to
> belong to a network of administrators. Many of the tips intended for new chairs
> apply to all department chairs who wish to improve their working relationships
> with the dean.

Higgerson, M. L. 1996. *Communication skills for department chairs.* Bolton, Mass.:
Anker.
> In chapter 7 of this text, Higgerson discusses the communication barriers that
> can disrupt effective communication between department chair and dean.
> Higgerson discusses specific strategies for establishing and maintaining credibil-
> ity with the dean, keeping communication with the dean open and productive,
> and cultivating a team relationship with the dean.

Mee, G. 1996. *Chairs' and deans' commitment to continuous improvement: Measuring
departmental effectiveness through program review.* ERIC Document Reproduction
Service no. ED 394 551. Proceedings of the 5th Annual International Conference of the National Community College Chair Academy, February, Phoenix.
> The author describes a model for program review that allows department chairs
> and deans to work together in pursuit of continuous improvement. The pre-
> scribed process includes four steps: (1) clarify program goals and objectives; (2)
> describe such program inputs as requirements, faculty credentials, and institu-
> tional resources; (3) assess program outcomes based on objectives; and (4) state
> future plans for the program.

Pincus, M. S. 1994. Dealing with the dean. *ADFL Bulletin* 25, no. 3 (spring): 11–16.
> The author offers prescriptive advice to department chairs on how to more
> effectively "deal" with the dean. The advice includes tips on knowing who the
> dean is and the dean's goals for the college, learning to understand and speak the
> dean's language, knowing numbers that serve as key data points in measuring
> department success, and learning how to make the department and the dean
> look good.

Welch, G. 1996. *Seasoned chairs and deans can learn new tricks.* ERIC Document Reproduction Service No. ED 394 589. Proceedings of the 5th Annual International Conference of the National Community College Chair Academy, February, Phoenix.

Welch discusses the reasons for dean and department chair burnout and suggests some steps that might be taken for renewal. The article begins with a discussion of the department chair's role and responsibilities. Chair renewal is presented as a three-step process: reflective reexamination, examination of the institution's commitment to chairs, and time for making serious decisions.

CHAPTER 12

Legal Issues for Chairs

NEW TERRAIN

Thirty years ago no one would have considered including a discussion of legal issues in a text written for department chairs. In fact few institutions had in-house legal departments. A law firm on-call to assist for the intermittent occasions when they needed legal advice or services used to be sufficient legal coverage for most institutions. Legal issues that did arise seldom spread beyond the confines of the president's office.

The landscape could not be more different today. Perhaps it was inevitable that a country such as the United States with its legalistic biases would use the law as one of its principal mechanisms in responding to rapid social change. Much of human behavior and interaction used to be molded exclusively by custom or what some saw as human nature. No one thought about language and its uses—except for the unusual circumstance of libel. But that sin was not one of the afflictions of the academy. The term "gender issues" would have elicited no more than a puzzled stare. Today there is a recognized field of higher education law, with practitioners who are kept busy dealing with an array of human interactions that a preceding generation would not have dreamed would be solved through legal means.[1]

These changes have made everyone in the academy far more conscious of their interactions with peers, subordinates, and superiors. However, enhanced consciousness in a chair is not sufficient. This chapter will begin by outlining some basic principles to keep in mind before turning to some of the legal categories that could generate problems that might involve you as a chair.

The first basic principle to keep in mind is that as an employee of the institution the chair nominally acts as agent for the principal; his or her acts, when committed within the scope of employment, are attributable to the college or university. There are two sequelae that flow from this principle. The first is that as chair, your actions are no longer merely individual. You are acting for the institution and, intentionally or not, you are committing the institution. To translate that into operational terms, it means that if you make a performance commitment to a member of your department, you speak not just for yourself, but for the institution. Unless you are speaking of something over which you have complete authority and control, you potentially commit your institution to a course of action that those who are supposed to make the decision may not wish to take. Should that happen, you have created a conflict between an individual and the institution. The best you can hope for is that the gap merely engenders anger and disappointment. At worst you can look forward to an unpleasant legal battle that will invade your time and destroy your credibility.

The other sequela of the principle of the chair nominally acting as agent is that one of your major responsibilities is carrying out your institution's procedures. In the event that you fail to act in a timely manner as designated in those institutional procedures, you implicate your institution. You can effectively place your institution in a position of having breached a contract.

A second principle is to be aware of the nature of the institution in which you work. Applicable legal standards vary depending on the institutional type involved, particularly where an institution is exclusively private or pervasively religious in character in contrast to state-supported public institutions and land grant colleges. Another important variable is whether yours is an institution with a collective bargaining agreement. If it is, your role will be defined by that agreement and the procedures you need to use when conflicts arise will be prescribed in that agreement. If yours is a public institution without a collective bargaining unit, state law may affect your actions. Private institutions have the greatest latitude in their choices, but they, too, must adhere to civil and constitutional law.

The third basic principle is to be sure you have a working knowledge of the main institutional policy documents that affect faculty, students, and staff. These documents may include items such as the faculty handbook, search and hiring guidelines, affirmative action statements, policies governing consensual relations, procedures for handling student complaints, labor requirements for staff members, etc. The reason it is so important to be familiar with those policies and diligent in following institutional procedures that carry out such policies is that whenever conflicts are settled in a legal arena, our civil courts will take cognizance of the internal governance documents of the institution. Courts will want to know what the governing principles are in the institution, and unless it finds them to be illegal or unconstitutional, the court will use those internal procedures as the basis of its judgment. Thus, as part of your preparation for shouldering the responsibilities of the chair position, it would be sensible to gather these basic documents, read through them, and keep them readily available for reference for the moment when a problem lands in your office. You should also know something of federal requirements that constrain your institution. For example, the Family Educational Rights and Privacy Act—often referred to as the "Buckley amendment"—restricts the release of student record information. There are also regulations that affect research on human subjects and that specify procedures for investigating scientific or research misconduct.

Ultimately, you should feel reassured to realize that the existence of institutional review mechanisms are an important buffer when you are making difficult decisions that affect other people's lives. It is those institutional procedures that are the means of preventing what could otherwise be a personal face-off of the kind that are grist for TV cowboy movies. It is a wise chair who emphasizes the central role of academic policy implementation in his or her actions and who takes care to harmonize decision making with the educational objectives of the department and the institution. The chair who always assumes the correctness of his or her decision making forgets that "assumption is the mother of all foul-ups."

A fourth principle to keep in mind is the need to alert other key players whenever a decision you are about to make has the potential of resulting in a legal altercation. Whenever that occurs, the institution is implicated. Therefore, others need to know what you are about to do. Practically, this means that you should inform your chief academic officer. The two of you may decide that the college's legal office should also be alerted.

While the application of these four principles can help you manage conflict that could spill into the legal realm, none have the power to make all such problems vanish. The issue becomes that of highlighting the kinds of conflict you may meet as a chair that have the highest potential of creating legal conflicts. The types of liability most likely to involve the performance of a department chair would include allegations of arbitrary and capricious action, breach of contract, denial of constitutional rights, discriminatory practice, and unintentional or intentional breach of a common-law duty that results in injury to the individual.

LEGAL HEADLANDS

Arbitrary and Capricious Action

Where might one be at risk for arbitrary action? The benevolent chair who has granted exceptions to a rule or policy suddenly finds that the enforcement of the policy can conceivably be legally enjoined as arbitrary. Courts will insist upon a rationale for the disparity in treatment, and it behooves the chair to clarify every exception to a rule of policy, adopting the exception whenever later cases present the same or conspicuously similar circumstances. Nowhere is the allegation of arbitrary or capricious treatment more likely to appear than in cases involving students. Usually, the denial of the degree or dismissal for academic deficiencies engenders the litigation.

In an illustrative case, a law student whose cumulative grade point fell below required standards for graduation was informed that he could continue for a fourth year, but that regardless of whether he improved his overall average, he would not be given the degree. He refused to accept the conditions, but was permitted to enroll and managed to bring his cumulative average up to the requisite graduation standard in his fourth year. Despite his improvement, he was denied the degree.

While the court recognized that the law school had absolute discretion to deny the request for readmission to a fourth year, it took cognizance of the institution's previous practice of allowing other probationary students to enroll and correct deficiencies during a fourth year. In some cases these students had met requirements and been awarded the law degree. The imposition of a condition that the student could not be granted the degree even if he satisfied degree requirements was deemed by the court as arbitrary and a manifest abuse of discretion.

In addition to the need to adhere to a consistent pattern of decision making, it is also important that you assist the department's faculty in upholding the same kind of consistency. You can help build departmental consistency by legitimating the discussion of fraught issues within the department. An example might be that of a student contesting a grade. It is the chair who can help transform that kind of a disagreement from the level of an individual altercation to one that is relevant to the whole department. This is not a matter of meddling with a faculty member's prerogative as instructor. The fact is that whatever solution one instructor arrives at with a given student will be picked up and used by other students facing disagreements with other instructors. The department with clear policies upheld by all its faculty members will probably have fewer such disputes and will certainly have less trouble with them if and when they do arise. As chair you are the person who can raise such conflict from the individual and particular to the collective and general.

Breach of Contract

Written contracts are artifacts that permeate American life, including that of academic departments. The department chair is seldom considered to be a principal party to a contract involving faculty, staff, or students and does not normally act as an agent for the institution in the negotiation of a contract agreement. However, the chair is often responsible for the administration of a contract and must faithfully execute the obligations the institution has agreed to assume. The acts of the chair may also influence the determination of whether a contact can be implied between the institution and another party. As chair you have the potential of being involved with contractual agreements with students, faculty, and staff.

In terms of students, courts may consider college bulletins, program guides, and brochures as contracts that create mutual obligations between institution and student. For example, where department or college programs constitute a contractual inducement to enroll, and students can be said to have reasonably relied upon these contractual terms in undertaking a field of study, students may sue to enforce specific compliance with the proposed program or seek an award of monetary damages for their reliance on the contract. Similarly, oral and written representations related to degree and program requirements, often the result of inaccurate or improper advisement, have been the basis for suits in which students seek award of the degree or program modifications consistent with the alleged contractual obligation.

What this points to is the importance of your leadership as chair to see that your department as a collective body and your faculty as individuals understand the implications of their decisions, actions, and advice. For example, revision of the department's curriculum may be a very positive initiative. However, as chair, you need to keep your department aware of the possible effects of changes on students in-progress-toward-a-degree under the "old" system. It may be necessary to grandfather such students. Or you and the department may deem it advisable to provide for a transition between systems.

A more fraught matter is making sure that individual faculty in their capacity as advisors give students accurate information. Advice that results in students being denied a degree or having their education prolonged can be the basis of suits, which are costly to the institution and embarrassing to your department.

In employment contracts, whether collectively or individually negotiated, specified obligations are generally interpreted with greater emphasis on strict construction by courts. For example, a department chair who failed to take appropriate action under tenure denial of a contract was held to have violated the contractual obligation of a private college in Tennessee. The contract of employment specified that once a faculty member was given a contract to teach for the fourth consecutive year the institution must give notice within

10 days after the beginning of the second semester of the fourth year if a decision had been made not to grant tenure. The court noted that the institution had an affirmative duty under the contract provision to provide timely notice if the faculty member was not be continued. Since the department chair did not provide notice of tenure denial until three months after the start of the second semester, contractual notice had not been provided and the faculty member could be considered to have acquired tenure.

How do these contractual standards affect your actions as a chair? There are basically two things to watch for. First, be careful not to make offers or commitments that you do not have the authority to sustain. For example, in conducting a search for a new faculty member, as a chair you do not usually control the salary line. That is to say, a document bearing your signature would not have the authority to produce a paycheck from the institution. That means that in the search process, you should defer all discussions of the salary offer to the person with the legal authority to create an employment contract. In most institutions that will be the dean or vice president for academic affairs (VPAA). Unpleasant results could unfold should you overstep in this area. If you mention a figure higher than what the VPAA offers, you will certainly have a disappointed candidate. The likely outcome is that the person will refuse the offer. If, on the other hand, the candidate ends up accepting, it would be miraculous if that person did not harbor resentment and a feeling of having been "cheated." Should you talk in terms of a sum lower than what the VPAA offers, the candidate may read into that discrepancy a lower interest in his or her skills on your part and that of the department. That is not a good foundation for happy collegial relations. A good standard of conduct is to keep silent on matters that you do not control.

If in one realm, silence can be deemed golden, in the realm of review procedures the silence of procrastination can only be judged disastrous. The case example given before is a good illustration. As chair you cannot afford to miss faculty review deadlines. Should you do that you will precipitate problems within the department, between yourself and the dean/provost/VPAA, between you and the faculty member, and between the faculty member and the institution. There is also a high probability that a lapse in this area could cost the institution time and money for litigation and even the necessity of paying financial penalties. Failure to act may even saddle your department and institution with an unwanted colleague, an expensive result for the institution in monetary terms and a burden to the department in human terms.

Denial of Constitutional Rights

It may come as a surprise to read that as chair there are aspects of your work that are circumscribed by the Constitution. Public colleges and universities are obligated to respect the federal constitutional prohibition of certain governmental actions affecting students and employees. The doctrine of state action has extended this obligation to ostensibly private institutions who receive substantial federal or state funds for programs. The protections of federal constitutional law most often involve the guarantee of due process under the Fourteenth Amendment and the right to free speech and association secured by the First Amendment.

The Fourteenth Amendment: Due Process, Property Rights, and Liberty Interests

Under the Fourteenth Amendment, an individual's interest in property or liberty may be protected from arbitrary governmental action. In the public higher education setting, property interest would include the student's entitlement to continued enrollment and participation in the academic program after the payment of fees or notice of admission. An employee's property rights would be defined by his or her contractual status at the institution during the period of a contract or indefinitely for those who hold tenure status. Liberty is related to the individual's interest in protecting his or her reputation, particularly from any stigmatizing information that might foreclose other employment or educational opportunities. Typically, the student or employee must establish that a protected property or liberty interest has been denied to compel procedural or substantive constitutional protection.

Particularly as applied to public institutions of higher education, the denial of a liberty or property interest may require that the institution provide basic elements of due process. These elements may vary with the nature of the interest that is threatened, but fundamental due process will include a showing that procedural and substantive guarantees of due process have been extended. Procedural due process often includes notice of changes and timely opportunity for a hearing. Substantive due process relates to more subjective elements of fundamental fairness and reasonableness, usually tied to uniformity and lack of bias in the application of due process protections.

Due process issues affecting students can end up in courts of law when they involve misconduct by students. Courts have insisted on fundamental elements of due process in cases involving disciplinary due process, and usually insist that student disciplinary codes be followed when allegations of cheating, plagiarism, or falsification of information are involved. However, courts do not compel rigid standards of due process like those involved in criminal prosecutions, relying instead primarily on adequate notice of charges and an opportunity for a fair and impartial hearing of essential elements.

In an actual case, the court upheld the decision of an institution to revoke the doctoral degree of a former graduate student who was charged with fabricating data used in the dissertation. The court concluded that the department chair had acted appropriately in granting the former student notice of charges, an opportunity to review the evidence on which the charges were based, and the right to appear and respond to the charges. The fact that the graduate insisted on additional due process protections, and refused to attend the hearing when these were not granted, did not convince the reviewing court that the institution could be barred from rescinding the degree

The right of students to seek legal redress for acts that they feel injure them unfairly is certainly a reflection of important changes in our understanding of the relationship between student and professor, and student and institution. Students can no longer be regarded as humble petitioners at the Gates of Knowledge whom the Guardians can dismiss at will. As chair you are obliged to think of fairness toward students and not exclusively in terms of faculty prerogative. And you need to see that department faculty share those understandings. On the other hand, this does not mean that anything students want is appropriate. The department that withdrew the student's degree, as described before, acted appropriately in maintaining *departmental* standards. What is not supportable are actions based on individual whim. It is those distinctions that a department chair needs to clarify in departmental discussions.

Due process rights of faculty and staff are apt to focus on rights to employment. Under the Fourteenth Amendment, an employee's interest in public employment may be constitutionally protected. Procedural fairness must be observed whenever the public university threatens an employee's property rights or liberty interest. To compel due process protections, a faculty or staff member might show that a certain property interest is sufficient to justify court intervention. Typically, whether a legitimate claim of entitlement to continued employment exists will be defined in reference to employee contracts, negotiated agreements, institutional regulations, and state laws. Faculty in public institutions who are dismissed or otherwise denied property rights during the contractual term of employment are entitled to due process of law.

An example of how these property rights can play out is *Perry v. Sinderman*, a case in which the Supreme Court ruled that a teacher who had held his faculty position for four years in reliance upon a *de facto* tenure arrangement could establish a legitimate claim of entitlement worthy of due process protection.[2] The Court cautioned, though, that "If it is the law (of the state) that a teacher ... has no contractual or other claim to job tenure, the ... claim would be defeated."

The faculty member involved in the *Perry* case was able to establish *de facto* tenure by citing the institution's lack of a formal tenure system with oral and written representations by various deans and department chairs that satisfactory performance would be rewarded with continuing employment. The faculty member submitted the statements of his administrative superiors as proof that a contract existed, which granted him a long-term property right tantamount to tenure. Numerous appellate decisions have distinguished the *Perry* case by emphasizing that an established system with published standards and procedures for granting tenure would not allow for a *de facto* grant of tenure.

The *Perry* case serves to emphasize three basic points. The first is that institutional policies are vitally important. At one level, they may seem like constraints on your ability to take action. In fact, they are protections that you should welcome. Should you find yourself working in a situation where institutional policies are lacking or vague, it is not inappropriate to press for the establishment and/or clarification of such policies.

The second important point is that as chair it is critical to move in a timely manner when exercising your responsibilities The chair whose office becomes a "black hole" where problems seems to disappear, places not only the department, but also the institution, at risk. In the *Perry* case, lack of timely notice was one of the factors that caused the department and institution to end up with a permanent faculty member neither the school nor institution really wanted.

The third basic point is to differentiate between being a "nice" person and being a person with responsibilities and authority. You cannot afford to let your social training cause you to utter encouraging remarks to a faculty member you and your department do not really intend to retain. As chair, you *always* speak officially. What you may see as casual or friendly encouragement is particularly troublesome if your institution lacks clear decision-making procedures, because these "informal" remarks can be given an official turn, as they were in the *Perry* case. You are better protected if your institution has clear procedures, but you are not totally covered even then. If your verbal communications have been positive and encouraging and an employment decision is negative, you have created a problem of inconsistency. That kind of contradiction is fertile ground for legal action.

Another pesky matter you face as a chair is what lawyers call a "liberty interest." A liberty interest may be infringed when the results of administrative action impose a stigma or other disability on the employee that forecloses the individual's freedom to take advantage of other employment opportunities or otherwise injures good name, reputation, or standing in the community. To put that in plain English, you can destroy someone's "liberty interest" if you make public matters concerning his or her behavior that jeopardize the person's ability to find further employment. That issue can arise when you are dealing with the nonrenewal of a faculty member.

There is no legal obligation on the part of the department chair to give reasons for nonrenewal of contract unless there is a stipulation in state law, institutional regulations, or negotiated contract requiring that reasons be given. Although it is a general rule that timely notice be given if the employment contract is not to be renewed, the employee does not have a federal constitutional right to reasons for nonrenewal. Giving reason for a nonrenewal decision is permissible and appropriate provided the reasons are communicated to the employee in confidence and have to do with job-related concerns, such as inability to cooperate with colleagues, poor evaluations of teaching, declining enrollments, and budget constraints. Where problems can arise are if you communicate reasons for nonrenewal in a public manner. Should you do that, the person in question can assert that you have violated a "liberty interest," effectively compromising the person's ability to find further employment.

The manner in which issues of confidentiality and rights to employment can play out is illustrated in the case *Beitzell v. Jeffrey*.[3] In that case a faculty member who was denied tenure was made aware of several factors that influenced the denial of tenure. The faculty member's chair had submitted a memorandum to a grievance committee that described the professor's professional behavior as "irresponsible" and indicated that colleagues had expressed concern about the faculty member's drinking. The department committee had voted against a recommendation for tenure after a discussion that included references to the professor's lack of adequacy as a teacher and advisor and to his drinking. In all communications relative to the decision not to grant tenure, the department chair maintained a high level of confidentiality, disclosing the basis for the committee's decision to the professor, and forwarding his memorandum to the grievance committee only when the professor's attorney insisted that the memo became a public record in the grievance proceedings. The appellate court observed that the professor failed to show that the personal aspects of these discussions, including references to drinking habits, became public as a result of the actions of the department chair. Since the chair did not make the charges public, the university could not be said to have stigmatized the former employee in such a way as to interfere with his ability to take advantage of other employment opportunities.

The requirement that a stigma seriously damage the faculty member's ability to take advantage of other employment opportunities, coupled with the requirement of public disclosure of the reasons for the employment decision, has limited the number of cases in which faculty have successfully claimed a right to due process based on a denial of a liberty interest. A charge of inadequate teaching performance would appear to be insufficient to establish a stigma denying a liberty interest; rather, a showing that the institution made public charges that the employee had been guilty of dishonesty or immorality would seem to be required.

The extent of process that is due a faculty or staff member depends on a balancing of the public institution's interest in efficient operation of the system against the weight of the property of liberty interest of the individual. The seriousness and permanence of an adverse employment decision will influence the requirements for notice and/or hearing and the extent to which administrative appeal and review are necessary. Where the faculty member has established a property or liberty interest worthy of due process, minimal elements afforded to the employee would include the following:

1. The employee must be advised of the cause or causes for the adverse employment decision in sufficient detail to fairly enable the employee to show any error that may exist.
2. At a reasonable time after notice of cause, the employee must be accorded a meaningful opportunity to be heard in his or her own defense.
3. A hearing should be granted before a tribunal that both possesses academic expertise and has an apparent impartiality toward the charges.

Generally, the institution's formal grievance procedures established for administrative review of employment decisions accord the minimal elements of due process. The department chair is often charged with the responsibility of providing notice to the employee; informing the employee of the charges, procedures, and consequences of any action that might be taken; and outlining the route of appeal. Failure to provide timely notice to the employee has resulted in a court-ordered continuation of employment, specifically when the college or university has promulgated rules on notice of nonrenewal and the chair, as agent of the institution, fails to notify within the period established for notice of nonretention.[4] Similarly, a department chair's failure to discuss his renewal recommendations with a non-tenured faculty member, when college procedural rules specifically required such notice to the individual faculty member under consideration for renewal, has resulted in continuation of employment for the affected employee.[5] Both these results indicate the importance of adhering to procedural safeguards in employment situations, whether these procedures are developed by the institution, required by negotiated agreement, or extrapolated from state or federal law.

In cases where employment relationships are at stake it is of paramount importance that you follow institutional procedures with care. It is also both wise and appropriate to keep your dean or vice president of academic affairs informed of the actions you are taking. If you are facing a difficult case that might result in legal challenge, it may even be appropriate to consult with the institution's in-house legal counsel. The guiding consideration should be the answer to the following question: Do the actions I am about to take have the potential to involve the institution? If the answer is yes, those responsible for the institution should be kept informed.

Free Speech and Association
In the public sector, the First Amendment provides some protection to individuals in the exercise of speech and association. In colleges and universi-

ties, these protections are often linked to the notion of "academic freedom," but it is probably more accurate to characterize these rights as constitutional protections. Largely because U.S. courts have been reluctant to recognize an entitlement beyond the grant of free speech and association available to every citizen, few courts have recognized a right to "academic freedom" that transcends the protections already granted by the First Amendment.

Students, faculty, and staff all enjoy constitutional rights of free speech and association. For example, student rights of free speech and association were addressed by the Supreme Court in *Healy v. James*.[6] The case arose when a local student group was denied recognition by a state college president because of the group's avowed political activism. While the president sought to deny recognition on the basis that similar student groups had interrupted classes and fermented disruption on other campuses, the court took notice that the students had promised to abide by reasonable campus restrictions on advocacy and action and disassociated themselves from the national organization (Students for a Democratic Society). Adopting the view that the students' right to speech and association was of paramount constitutional importance, the Court required that the student group be recognized in the absence of strong evidentiary proof that the students acting in concert could reasonably be predicted to substantially disrupt or materially interfere with the operation of the institution.

Free speech has become a prickly issue as campuses have tried to deal with the tensions between a diverse student body and issues of free speech. The best that can be said at present is that we are not at the end of this story at either the human or legal level. Within the academy we have become more sensitive to the nature of speech and the fact that it can subtly create gender and racial discrimination. Efforts at establishing gender-neutral speech are even spilling into non-academic life. Problems have been created, however, as some campuses have attempted to codify permissible speech. As they have pursued this approach some students have objected to the infringement of their free speech rights. Our courts have come down on the side of those rights whenever the focus of an institution's disciplinary code is prohibited speech rather than conduct. However, that will not dissolve the dilemma for the academy, for its educational role will continue to embody the goal of enlightening students and modifying human behaviors.

In the case of faculty and staff the courts have elaborated a series of tests that balance the rights of the individual against the state's interest as employer. For example, the application of free-speech constitutional protections is illustrated in a case involving a non-tenured teacher whose contract was not renewed following her sixth year of teaching in a junior college. The official reason for nonrenewal, "declining enrollment and poor evaluation of her work," was appropriate enough, but the faculty member introduced evidence that the real reason for nonrenewal was retaliation for her vigorous support of her husband's candidacy for the college board of regents and her efforts to promote a faculty association. The court noted that the department chair admitted advising the teacher to have her husband withdraw from the election, voiced objection to her activity on behalf of the teachers' association, and recommended nonrenewal to discipline the teacher for trying to create ill will and lack of cooperation with the administration. This evidence supported a jury verdict awarding damages after finding that the teacher had not been rehired because of her exercise of constitutionally protected rights.[7]

Given extraordinary circumstances, even the constitutional exercise of free speech will be balanced against the interest of protecting the campus from substantially disruptive or materially interfering conduct. The difference between advocacy, which enjoys constitutional protection, and action, which may not be so protected, is difficult to assess. There are times when courts recognize the authority of the chair and the institution to act despite the potentially "chilling" effect on the exercise of free speech. Another case involved a tenured assistant professor, dismissed for playing a prominent role in unauthorized protest activities. The professor contended that his dismissal was in retaliation for his exercise of free speech and assembly, a right granted by the Constitution. The facts were that the professor tried to stop a motorcade bringing officials to a campus ceremony, led student demonstrators in raucous catcalls to disrupt the ceremonies, and encouraged demonstrators to leave their seats and enter the stadium field, thus creating a danger of violent confrontation. The court upheld a finding that the professor's actions went beyond advocacy of ideas and that he engaged in a course of conduct that interfered with and disrupted the regular operation of the school in a manner that left him outside the protection of the First Amendment.

These free speech issues are further complicated today by the question of what is permissible in cyberspace. Is free speech on the airwaves to be monitored to protect children? Is offensive speech permissible? Is hate speech protected? Can categories of individuals such as women or ethnic minorities be verbally attacked or insulted on the airwaves? The legal sorting of these questions is very much in process. Meanwhile, chairs need to carry on as best they can.

Discriminatory Practice

Congress has enacted several federal statutes designed to extend and elaborate the prohibition against invidious discrimination contained in the equal protection clause of the Fourteenth Amendment. This plethora of federal statutory entitlements prohibits discrimination on the basis of race, sex, religion, age, national origin, and handicap in programs receiving federal financial assistance.[8] The laws protect employees and "participants in, or beneficiaries of" programs that receive federal financial assistance. Methods available for enforcement of these laws include federal agency reporting and regulatory standards, compliance reviews, affirmative action agreements, institutional self-regulation, and suits by private parties. The crucial issue for resolution of most allegations of discrimination remains a showing that the defendant was motivated by a discriminatory animus, and the discriminatory animus must be shown to have been overt.

Most cases alleging discrimination against students have involved the admission policies of the institution. While courts have struck down admissions quotas based upon race, some have indicated that race may be used as one of several factors that may be considered in ensuring an institution's legitimate interest in a diverse student body The decision of the United States Supreme Court (1978) in Bakke vs. Regents of the University of California struck down a medical school admissions program which allocated a number of admission slots to minority and disadvantaged students through application to a separate minority admissions council.[9] While declaring the university's policy discriminatory, the Court did suggest a rationale for an alternative strategy for the admission of minority and disadvantaged students, by the opinion of one justice, that race could be one of a number of factors to be considered in an admissions policy applied uniformly to all applicants. However, there was no clear majority in Bakke that joined in this view.

The issue surrounding affirmative action and its application to university admissions was again before the courts in 1996 in the case of Hopwood v. State of Texas, involving the University of Texas law school, in which the U.S. Court of Appeals granted preferences to minority applicants.[10] In its ruling, the court said that the use of race to achieve a diverse student body could not be a state interest compelling enough to meet the constitutional standard of strict scrutiny where racial classifications are involved. The court noted that the opinion in Bakke suggesting a compelling state interest in diversity was not controlling legal precedent, and that the subsequent decision by the Supreme Court did not indicate support for such a rationale. The U.S. Supreme Court subsequently declined to accept the Hopwood case for review. While the direct impact of the decision is limited to the jurisdiction of one federal circuit, it raised serious questions regarding the legality of any admissions program that uses educational diversity to justify granting racial preferences.

Further doubts concerning race-based preferences were precipitated in California, where in November, 1996, voters overturned the application of affirmative action preferences in the state. The U.S. Court of Appeals for the 9th Circuit upheld the legality of the measure, known as Proposition 209, and the U.S. Supreme Court declined to review the case. These developments suggest that the legal standard to justify race-based preferences is a very difficult one to meet and that in most cases race-neutral factors should be utilized in making admissions and hiring decisions to ensure that programs will conform to constitutional equal protection requirements. Affirmative action programs should continue to include measures to ensure the institution does not discriminate on the basis of race, ethnicity, or gender in employment or admissions decisions. Where there is identified underrepresentation of minorities or women, affirmative measures should be taken to attempt to increase their representation, which may include active recruiting efforts; but admission or employment decisions should be based on relevant factors other than the applicant's race, ethnicity, or gender. While achieving educational diversity is a legitimate institutional objective, it is not likely to be found to be legal justification for granting race-based preferences, and should be based on other, race-neutral factors.

The Americans with Disabilities Act (ADA) now also prohibits discrimination against individuals with disabilities. Universities are required by federal law to provide a reasonable accommodation for a student or employee with a disability and chairs should be very sensitive to these issues. In a decision involving admission of persons with disabilities, *Southeastern Community College v. Davis*, the Supreme Court did not require that a hearing-impaired student be admitted to a clinically oriented educational program in nursing.[11] The Court's rationale emphasized that Section 504 of the Rehabilitation Act of 1973 did not require the admission of a handicapped applicant where it could not be demonstrated that the applicant was otherwise qualified in spite of the disability, and the handicapping condition would require substantial modification of the college.

Cases charging discrimination against faculty have been brought under various federal laws, including the equal protection clause of the Fourteenth Amendment, Title VII of the Civil Rights Act of 1964,[12] Title IX of the Educational Amendments of 1972,[13] and the Equal Pay Act. Sex-role stereotyping has become a frequently cited basis for proof of discriminatory animus in employment decisions. An example is the case of a female faculty member who repeatedly sought consideration for additional teaching assignments that would have meant supplemental salary. Although male faculty received such assignments at periodic intervals, female faculty did not. In response to her request for an explanation, the department chair candidly explained that the assignments were reserved for male faculty who were married and needed extra income to support a wife and family. This presumption will not withstand judicial scrutiny and does not meet the test for a legitimate, nondiscriminatory reason which would justify disparities in the treatment of male and female faculty.

The college or university must demonstrate that its employment decision (whether related to hiring, promotion, award of tenure or benefits, demotion, or termination) is based upon legitimate factors and not on explicit or implicit considerations prohibited by Title VII. Such a proposition does not rule out peer review, nor does it hold that consideration of teaching, research, and service (essentially subjective criteria) are inappropriate to the employment decision. What is important is that there be no differential treatment in the employment decision-making process based on legally prohibited consider-ations. Uniformity of procedures and criteria for evaluation are essential. The articulation of a rationale for employment decisions that bears a reasonable relationship to departmental, college, and institutional objectives is extremely important. The articulated basis for adverse employment decisions should relate to legitimate, performance-related reasons, which might include nega-tive student evaluations, unwillingness to assume responsibility for teaching or service assignments, refusal to accept student advisees, and the like.

Although sexual harassment is a form of discrimination, enough case law has been created in this area to form a recognizable category. The prohibitions against sexual harassment are to be found in Title VII and Title IX. These titles have been accompanied by regulatory provisions prohibiting two forms of harassment: bargain transactions and hostile environment. Bargain transac-tions (also known as *quid pro quo* favors) include verbal or physical conduct of a sexual nature, whereby submission to the request or advance is either an explicit or implicit condition of employment or is used as a basis for decisions affecting the student's or employee's status. Hostile-environment sexual ha-rassment involves conduct that has the purpose or effect of unreasonably interfering with a person's work performance, or of creating an intimidating, hostile, or offensive sexually charged environment. Unpermitted touching, sexual advances, demands for sexual favors, sexually stereotyped insults, and demeaning propositions are among the forms of behavior that, particularly if shown to be continuous or repeated, would establish sexual harassment.

Common Law Duty: Negligent Torts, Duty of Reasonable Prudence

The last area to call to your attention is that of negligent torts. A department chair provides services to several constituencies (students, staff, faculty) that imply obligations beyond those recognized under contract or constitutional mandate. The provision of service implies a duty to act with reasonably prudent care in foreseeing possible dangers to the individual and in mitigating any potential risk of injury. Not all chairs will be affected to the same degree by these obligations. It is of particular importance to consider whether the departmental activities for which you are responsible entail any physical dangers to students, faculty, or staff. If they do, you need to

- assign appropriate supervisory staff,
- promulgate reasonable safety rules, and
- give due notice of possible dangers.

Here are some examples of situations where as chair you have responsibilities for the safety of students, faculty, and staff. A risk of injury might not be anticipated in a history class, but it could reasonably be foreseen if a chemistry lab program were overenrolled and inadequately staffed. Under such circumstances, the failure to assign employees with the requisite training to provide proper instruction and adequate supervision might ultimately be construed as a breach of reasonably prudent care by the chair. In the chemistry lab, the existence of foreseeable dangers requires the chair to verify that safety rules are posted, that notice of possible dangers is made, and that counter-measures have been planned. As part of those precautions, it is incumbent upon the chair to see that proper safety equipment is present and in operating order. As chair, you are also responsible for ensuring that staff are properly trained and that they are carrying out their responsibilities according to the department's (or institution's) safety guidelines.

Science laboratories is an obvious arena for concern with negligent torts. But whatever the discipline for which you are responsible, it is worth reviewing the possibility that there may be safety concerns that lie within your realm of responsibility. For example, in art and photography studios various chemicals are used, some of which can be dangerous. Is there adequate ventilation in rooms where there are such risks? Is there someone present in rooms with potential chemical risks who knows what to do if there is an accident? In theater departments stage rigging can be a source of danger. Has rigging been inspected? Are there safety devices on equipment used to build sets? Departments may do field work. Are there potential hazards in that work? If so, have precautions been taken and are there defined emergency procedures in case of mishap? While these examples may not fit your particular department, what is important is that you review the activities of *your* department to see where cases of negligent tort might arise.

CONCLUSION

The prospect of legal battles are a source of anxiety for chairs, perhaps in part because for most it is alien and mysterious terrain. While there is no doubt that a chair can precipitate serious legal problems for his or her institution, the more important point to realize is that in performing the duties of chair responsibly the chances of legal quarrels is minimized. It is true that as chair you are not a free agent. You do speak for the institution. When you speak, you need to remember that you speak in effect *ex cathedra*. Your scope for off-the-cuff remarks is constrained. You do need to be aware of deadlines, particularly those that affect issues of employment. Your failure to act in a timely manner is not just an annoyance; it is a potential liability. It is true that you need to have a basic understanding of institutional policy, much of which may be wrapped in soporific prose (or legalese). You do need to maintain a good working relationship with your dean and at fraught moments you may need to develop good teamwork with that individual.

It is worth remembering that courts are first and foremost the guardians of process. A number of substantive legal questions have been addressed in this chapter, but it is the procedural defect in an institution's policy or its implementation that most often creates the basis for litigation. In this regard, the role of chair is particularly critical. Courts will often abstain from hearing a case if the aggrieved party has failed to utilize the institution's procedures for redressing an alleged wrong. Courts will intervene when the chair has failed to follow appropriate procedural standards or has without justification created an injury for which there is no institutional appeal. In most institutions, the department chair is uniquely situated to resolve procedural problems and reduce the likelihood of litigation. By encouraging the adoption of procedures that provide notice, impartial hearing, and timely administrative appeal, the chair can facilitate institutional arrangements that provide for self-regulation and mitigate the potential effect of arbitrary action. In a conscientious and earnest effort to inform others of and comply with the institution's procedural standards, the chair demonstrates good faith and fair dealing.

Procedural obligations may seem an onerous burden, and the reassurance that diligent application of institutional procedures will keep you and your department out of court furnish cold comfort. But keep in mind that these responsibilities are balanced by the positive opportunity you have as an educator. As chair, one of your leadership opportunities is to help shape human relationships and create an effective working body in your department that includes faculty, students, and staff. As noted at the beginning of the chapter, a significant portion of the legal disputes in higher education actually involve matters of human behavior. While issues that come up in employment contracts or under torts may require diligent performance of prescribed tasks, there are other important issues in the free speech and discrimination areas that open to the chair the possibility of being an educator. For example, as a chair, you are likely to face free speech issues at the most fundamental human level. There your levers are less legal than behavioral. Does your department treat students, staff, and faculty with respect? How does the department deal with differences of viewpoint? Are those differences permitted to degenerate into personal insult, or do faculty, staff, and students work at defining issues and listening to different approaches to problem solving? Your strongest contribution on these complex matters may lie in both modeling and encouraging balanced, consistent respectful responses. Standards for dialog can and should be discussed within the department. The same standards should be observed in individual exchanges and among all members of the department. They are suitable for conversation among peers and among different categories of individuals.

Gender relations is another area in which behavioral leadership is critical. Fought out in the legal arena, gender friction has created a whole field of law on sexual harassment. One of the difficulties with sexual harassment is that it involves behaviors that have historically appeared "normal." There is a real need for leadership from the chair, first in focusing the department's attention on old "norms," and second on clarifying that not only are old behaviors socially out of date—they are prohibited by law. The internationalization of our faculties only adds to the complexity of the task. The very concept of sexual harassment may sound incomprehensible to faculty arriving from cultures in which participation of women in public life borders on the nonexistent. The essence, then, of your legal responsibilities lies more in the domain of educator than of lawyer.

NOTES

1. Fernando C. Gomez, in "The Evolution of the University Attorney," Proceedings of the American Association for the Advancement of Science, Pacific Division, San Francisco (1996), suggest that litigation has become a way of life in higher education due to "changes in statutory and decisional law; America's propensity for litigation to redress grievances, real or perceived; and advances in technology."
2. 408 U.S. 593 (1972).
3. Beitzell v. Jeffrey, 643 F.2d 870 (1st Cir. 1981).
4. Jacobs v. College of William and Mary, 495 F. Supp. 183 (E.D. Va. 1980).
5. Nzomo v. Vermont State Colleges, 385 A. 2d 1099 (Vt. 1978).
6. 408 U.S. 169 (1972).
7. Goss v. San Jacinto Junior College, 588 F. 2d 96 (5th Cir. 1979).
8. See, for example, 42 U.S.C.; 2000e (Title VII). 29 U.S.C.; 794 (Rehabilitation Act of 1973), 29 U.S.C.; 623 (Age Discrimination in Employment), 29 U.S.C.; 206 (d) (Equal Pay Act).
9. 438 U.S. 265 (1978).
10. Hopwood v. State of Texas, 78 F. 3d 932 (5th Cir., 1996).
11. Southeastern Community College v. Davis, 442 U.S. 397 (1979).
12. 42 U.S.C.; 2000e.
13. 42 U.S.C.; 1681.

REFERENCES

Cole, Elsa Kircher, ed. 1990. Sexual harassment on campus: A legal compendium. National Association of College and University Attorneys.
This compendium is most useful if one is looking either to revise or develop de novo a sexual harassment policy statement, since the publication includes a discussion of policy guidelines and offers seven college/university policy statements as examples.

Kaplin, William A., and Barbara A. Lee. 1995. *The law of higher education: A comprehensive guide to legal implications of administrative decision making,* 3rd ed. San Francisco: Jossey-Bass.
Written for university administrators and attorneys, this volume provides a thorough analysis and discussion of legal issues affecting campuses.

Paludi, Michele A. 1990. *Ivory power: Sexual harassment on campus.* New York: State University of New York Press.
While this volume does take note of policy and legal issues, much of the content, which is an aggregate of individual articles, is devoted to conceptual issues and discussion of the impact of sexual harassment on the victim.

Poch, R. 1993. *Academic freedom in American higher education: Rights, responsibilities and limitations.* ASHE-ERIC Higher Education Reports, Report 4.
This monograph provides historical background, including a discussion of the 1940 AAUP statement on which our definitions of academic freedom rest. It also reviews the three currently contentious issues, namely, freedom of artistic express, issues of political correctness, and problems precipitated in church-related institutions.

Sandler, Bernice R., and Robert J. Shoop. 1997. *Sexual harassment on campus: A guide for administrators, faculty and students.* Boston: Allyn & Bacon.
As the title implies, this is a guide for non-legal professionals. Treatment is thorough and practical, covering everything from definitions of what constitutes sexual harassment, to the characteristics of good policy, to guidance on informal, and formal resolution of complaints.

Weeks, Kent M. 1996. *Managing departments: Chairpersons and the law.* Nashville: College Legal Information, Inc.
Produced as a loose-leaf notebook, the publication covers 14 topics chairs handle that could generate legal action. The topics range from academic freedom, interviewing, and reference checks to the college catalog and disclosure of student records. Each chapter gives a brief overview of the topic and describes cases to demonstrate the legal applications. Most important to chairs is the section on each topic for reasonable preventive measures. This handbook has the advantage of being comprehensive, succinct, and easy to use.

CHAPTER 13

Evaluating the Department

THE CONTEXT OF DEPARTMENTAL EVALUATION

Individuals and Groups

Two attitudes underlie much of the behavior manifest in department life today. One is the notion of individual autonomy; the other is the conviction that the pinnacle of intellectual life is to do ground-breaking research. The theme of individual autonomy emerged as a dominant theme in western culture during the European Renaissance. Transplanted to North America, individualism became the foundation of the kind of entrepreneurial initiative and rugged independence required for survival on the frontier. Thus, historical reality and intellectual heritage formed a matched partnership. The other strand applies specifically to the academic setting and is a more recent arrival. The theme of research as the ultimate goal of intellectual life was a concept imported from the German universities of the nineteenth century. For decades American university students pursued their doctoral studies in German institutions, which were regarded as "the best." For those completing their studies in the United States, German became the language required of American Ph.D. students. German standards were first transferred to the United States by The Johns Hopkins University in Baltimore. The idea, however, did not take long to blossom in other North American universities, a trend that was greatly strengthened during World War II when national survival depended not just on the dogged determination of millions of infantrymen, but also on the intellectual acumen of American scientists who were often partnered with European refugees. Universities became the intellectual bastions of the war effort that they supported through their research efforts.

Today's colleges and universities have inherited the values of individualism and the reverence for research. Within the academy we view the teacher/ scholar as a brilliant individual whose professional privacy is sacrosanct. Academic freedom has come in practice to mean that we teach individually and autonomously. The notion that a colleague could—or should—observe one's teaching and offer counsel on improvements is a concept that is not readily embraced in the American academy. The fallout has been that departments are reluctant to discuss pedagogy and are uncomfortable with the prospect of looking objectively at departmental performance. As for research, it has become the quintessential definition of quality for undergraduate colleges, comprehensive universities, as well as for research universities. Although Ernest Boyer in his noteworthy monograph *Scholarship Reconsidered* has had major impact on the dialog at many a professional meeting, his influence is less discernible at the institutional level where young faculty, regardless of institutional type, continue scrambling to write scholarly papers and promotion and tenure committees are scrutinizing reviewees for evidence of scholarly product, i.e., "the scholarship of discovery" (Boyer 1990).

However, higher education is now experiencing powerful cross currents that are tugging at our application of individualism and our universalistic pursuit of original research. That pressure is coming from the public domain in the form of demands for accountability that can be answered only by moving one's cone of vision from individual to collective performance. Because this is a pressure dramatically at odds with fundamental values of the academy, it is a cause of great discomfort. At the same time it is a pressure that is irresistible, since the demand derives from another firmly held American belief in public accountability. That theme was played out in our political history, the earliest and perhaps most dramatic example being what we refer to as Bacon's rebellion. In 1676 Nathaniel Bacon led an uprising that brought together demands for accountability from local officials by the lesser folk of the colony. The American democratic tradition has come to rest on the concept that our political servants are accountable to us, the citizens, with no one—not even a president—exempt from judicious and/or judicial scrutiny. That same principle of accountability is being applied to postsecondary institutions by state legislatures from which come the bulk of funds for many of our universities. The fact that public institutions now graduate the majority of our postsecondary degree holders—not true 40 years ago—only makes the pressure more telling.[1]

Legislators are asking for comparison and evaluation via "performance indicators." The bad news for postsecondary institutions is that in an increasing number of states budget allocations are being tied to those performance indicators. For example, the South Carolina General Assembly notified the state's institutions that their allocations would be based on performance, not enrollment or facility needs. A report in *The Chronicle of Higher Education* (1997a, A26) indicated other projected adoption of this approach in many states. "New York's Rockefeller Institute of Government interviewed the chief financial officer in every state's higher education system and found that most of them expect, within five years, to see some share of their public colleges' budgets tied to how well the institutions perform" (*Chronicle* 1997b, A23). Nor is the thinking limited to the United States. Australian universities were notified in 1993 that a portion of their budgets would be tied to performance (University of Technology)[2]. By 1997 the practice was adopted in India by the University Grants Commission, which "decided that one-third of its $100,000 in development funds would be .... linked to performance" (*Chronicle* 1997c).

The result is that academe needs to redefine its perspective. As Michael Hooker, Chancellor of the University of North Carolina, Chapel Hill, observed in an interview with James L. Morrison at the UNC Program on Educational Leadership, "Legislatures will be less concerned with who produces results or how they are produced than with proof" (*On the Horizon* 1997, 2). That does not mean that academe can no longer assert its belief in the importance of the individual or that scholarly research has become unimportant. What it does mean is that we have reached a point where individual autonomy needs to be balanced with collective good. The academy has practiced its version of individual autonomy in a manner that has tended to make individuals into isolates and, in fact, within the academy we now lament the breakdown of community. If we are to reestablish that sense of community we will need to see that individuals are part of complicated social networks in which their behaviors can enhance, undermine, or even destroy collective effort. In this chapter we examine the changes that occur when one looks at a department from a collective viewpoint rather than limiting assessment efforts to measuring individual performance. We will also discuss how collective success of faculty can be evaluated and how that collective success can enhance individual as well as departmental performance.

Assessment is certainly not a new activity in higher education. Students have always been assessed, most commonly through examinations. It is not until the 1960s, however, that it became common to assess faculty performance. The measuring instrument devised was the student evaluation form. While some models have been elaborated in the scholarly literature, institutions have generally either created their own or adapted from published models (Centra 1993). The result has been that student evaluations are commonly used throughout the country. Where used, the questionnaires are often standardized to apply across disciplines, and the results are included among the criteria for individual faculty review. However, assessment today is a much more complex subject.[3] Publicly imposed demands are requiring us to look at collective effort; that is to say, the product of the department as a shared enterprise. The effect of this change in emphasis is to require us to account for the results (outcomes) of our teaching both at the individual *and* collective level. For a department chair, these changes are requiring nothing less than a redefinition of perspective in terms of both focus and process. The change in focus needs to be from an exclusive preoccupation with individual performance to one that examines collective performance. As the focus is changed, the data that will be used for assessment will change, as well as the procedures utilized for judgment. It is important to realize that it is not just the chair's perspective that needs to change. As a chair, you will need to help your colleagues debate and understand the emerging changes prompted by collective assessment. Ultimately, as chair, you will need to lead and participate in your department's creation of a view of itself that links its assessment of individual performance with measurements of its collective results.

The Issues of Size and Habit

Whenever one attempts to evaluate a department, the focus is necessarily on the success of collective activity. An individual cannot be a department. On the other hand, there is no accepted definition of department size either as a minimum or a maximum. Size, however, will have an effect on how you, as chair, approach the task of assessing your department. At the American Council on Education workshops for chairs, many attendees work with small departments with 10 or fewer faculty. They habitually constitute a quarter to a third of the enrollment. Representatives of large departments of 40 or more are unusual in the workshops. Most department chairs attending those workshops have mid-sized departments of from 11 to 30 faculty. Small departments can function routinely as committees of whole. Mid-sized departments may find it more effective to work through a committee structure, holding department-wide meetings less frequently and using them to ratify committee work or as a forum for policy discussions. For large departments, committees are a necessity in accomplishing the department's work. If traditional organization is working well for the department, maintaining that form and level of organization will suffice. If you conclude that departmental work is not proceeding either effectively or efficiently, it is appropriate to look for structural remedies.

Habit is a wonderful enhancer of efficiency as it saves us the time of repetitive decision making. The down side is that habit can keep us stuck in ineffective routines. An important task for you as chair is to reach some conscious conclusions about the effectiveness of your department's habits. Improvement is almost always possible. In some cases you dare not let it remain optional. Producing change within a collective context, however, is far from an easy task. Not only may you need to buck entrenched habits, but you may also need to initiate that much-feared phenomenon—change. Since departments tend to work by consensus, giving orders is not an option. Any chair will have to be adept in negotiating and building consensus. The word "consensus" may be concise, but practicing it is anything but. Building consensus takes skill not just on the part of the chair, but on the part of each and every member of the department. The chair's greatest lever of influence in that process is in setting the tone and atmosphere in which the department conducts its business. Not just the chair, but all members of the department need to perfect their listening skills so that all viewpoints can be not just listened to, but heard. The process of dialog must emphasize facts and rational decision making. The personalizing of issues and grandstanding are behaviors that need to be eliminated. When those behaviors appear, the chair has the authority of position to declare them out of order.

THE WORK OF ASSESSMENT

Assessing the Department as a Collective Entity

How you will lead the process of assessing the department as a collective entity deserves careful thought. Insofar as the impetus to this activity may be coming from outside—for example, from demands of a state legislature—it is easy for a department to drift into a resentful stance. It is helpful if the department can shift its focus in a way that will restore its mastery over its own activities. It can do so if it is prepared to be consistently methodical in looking at facts. Institutions have collected vast banks of data for years. Some are used for internal administrative purposes and some are funneled into required studies for accreditation, governing boards, and federal agencies. Departments have tended to be a bit haphazard about their basic data, collecting it only when required externally. They have been less inclined to follow pertinent data systematically *over time* for the purpose of their own internal improvement. Collecting data is a practice, however, that can bring important internal benefits to the department. What you do as chair and how you begin need to be shaped by the current "data status" of your department. The entire department or a subcommittee, if your department is large enough, can participate in reviewing the information currently available concerning the department. Look at what that data can tell you about your department's performance, and then ask what you do *not* know that you really need to know to function most effectively. In all instances, ask what the implications of knowing will be on the *actions* of the department. It is not appropriate to turn the department into a census bureau for the mere joy of collecting information.

Every time the department agrees that a set of data is important to it, the question then becomes how it can be retrieved. Does the information already exist in university files or will the department need to collect the information *de novo*? An invitation to confer with the department sent to the institution's registrar, planner, or institutional researcher may be in order. If the department discovers major lacunae, how you choose to fill the gaps should be carefully explored. Time, both individual and collective, is a precious commodity and should not be squandered. You may find it possible to engage students in assembling some kinds of data as part of class projects, or by devising a progressive process you may be able to expand your knowledge about the department without derailing ongoing basic activities. At all times, it is important to keep in mind that the goal is to enhance departmental decision making. Too much is at stake today to proceed on hunches and impressions.

Collecting Data: What and Why

Enrollment Patterns
The following basic information is important for any department as it makes decisions. The department needs a good grasp of its enrollment patterns. That means knowing how many students are taught by term or semester and by level of enrollment. And that information needs to be available longitudinally. Quality does not equate with raw numbers. For example, a department with large enrollments does not have greater qualitative virtues than one with small enrollments. It is, however, important to know whether your department's enrollment patterns are in a steady state, growing, or shrinking. Furthermore, you need to know whether the demographic makeup of your enrollment is undergoing change over time. These "facts" are relevant to your department. They affect the perception of your department within the institution and they make a difference in administrative reactions to the department's requests for resources. These same demographic facts should affect internal decisions about curriculum, pedagogy, scheduling, and advising. These linkages between demography and department actions have been examined in chapter 8.

Graduation and Retention Rates
Departments today also need to be able to document the success of their students more thoroughly than in the past. For example, state legislatures are now in the habit of asking for graduation and retention rates. There is a clear assumption on their part that the institution that retains and graduates its students is doing a better job than one that sees many of its students "disappear." There is also an assumption, now being publicly articulated, that baccalaureate students *should* graduate in a specified span of time, even though the old-time standard of a four-year baccalaureate has been abandoned. In Texas, for example, the standard has been established as six years. Legislatures in some states are even going so far as to link budgets to perfor-

mance, using funding to reward or punish institutions for achieving certain goals.[4] In Texas fiscal pressure will soon be brought on students. As of 1999 students in Texas will be limited to a specified number of credit hours per degree program available at in-state tuition rates. If students exceed the credit limit, they will be charged out-of-state fees, which are, of course, much higher than in-state fees. None of these measures can be carried out until institutions produce figures for retention or graduation, and that cannot be done without involving departments. The temptation to pin the donkey's tail to a particular beast will be irresistible and woe to the department that has failed to pay attention to its enrollment data. There may be very good reasons for students taking longer to graduate; there may be sound reasons for students to shift undergraduate majors—with the effect of prolonging the completion of a program; there may be sound reasons for students to transfer their enrollment to another institution. However, these explanations cannot be convincingly documented except at the departmental level. Furthermore, it is as important for departments to understand these phenomena as it is for state governments.

Student Outcomes Data
Student outcomes data has also become a focus of attention. In higher education we have an easier time describing what we would like students to be able to do than we have in advancing the evidence that we have achieved our pedagogical goals. We know we want students to read accurately, think logically, communicate effectively, and contribute positively to our society. We also know that the ultimate test comes as they work and conduct their lives after graduating. What we have difficulty with is the means of measuring student success and linking it convincingly to our efforts as teachers and scholars. There are some quantitative measures that a department can marshal internally. These include data on enrollment patterns, retention, and graduation rates; success in licensure exams; etc. However, much of what we want to know requires establishing and maintaining contact with alumni. For example, your department may know how many students apply successfully to graduate school, but does it also know in any systematic, non-anecdotal way, how successful they are in those programs? Do you know how long it takes graduates to find employment, and do you know what kind of jobs they take? How does their work connect with the curricula in their majors? Five years post-graduation, what kinds of positions do they hold? Private colleges are generally more proactive in tracking alumni data. But public institutions are learning that alumni contact is important for them, too. And often the most effective point of contact is through departments, since that is the institutional location where students are known on an individual basis. This may seem like an overwhelming list of information to track. In fact, in many institutions the office of institutional studies or assessment office may be

tracking much of this data already. The search for data can lead to the development of productive collaboration with other university units the department may have dismissed earlier as part of the administrative bureaucracy.

Other levels of student outcome data can elicit important dialog within the department. For example, what is the success rate of your students in your introductory course? As a department, are you assuming that this is a course in which you are weeding out the unfit, or is the introductory course your chief "marketing tool" for attracting majors? This is a policy question that should be of vital interest to the department collectively. And the answer has implications for your pedagogical methods. If, indeed, your department wants the entry course to be the means of recruiting majors, but a quarter of the enrollees are dropping out before the end of the course and another quarter are performing poorly, there is clearly a gap between intention and execution. If the department insists that the result is predicated on the ineptitude of the students, a "fact" with no cure, there is no hope for reaching the department's goal. If as chair you can initiate a meaningful dialog on what could be done to alter the result with the students, then there is a real opportunity for changing behavior in the department and connecting intent and result.

Resources: Physical and Fiscal
The informational inventory of the department should encompass some other basic areas as well. Resources are, of course, important. However, anecdotal complaints of cuts are not useful. The department should collectively have an understanding of its resources in terms of space, equipment, personnel, and budget. As with all data, any of this information gains greater meaning if it is collected over a number of years. Only when traced over time can you see if the department is standing still, losing resources, or gaining. At this point in time, diminution of resources is the more likely scenario. If that is the case, what one needs to know is how the department has coped with that kind of change. Has it found ways to substitute or share resources? Has it found ways of economizing? What have been the result of those economies? Have any of the adjustments actually enhanced efficiency of resource use?

Benchmarking
Departments today also need to pay attention to their standing within and beyond the institution. The commonly used tool for this purpose is benchmarking, which effectively means comparing your department's performance with that of parallel entities. Within a college or university, this means comparing the department's performance with that of other departments. This is something that academic etiquette does not encourage. However, rest assured that institutional administrators will engage in that practice as they prepare budgets and make policy decisions. The kinds of data that will be

weighed and measured include faculty teaching loads, retention, and graduation rates, and cost per student credit unit. The "norm" does vary by type of
department. The hard sciences, for example, are assumed to be more costly per
student credit unit than the humanities. "Normal" faculty loads are known to
vary by discipline. That means that any given department needs to know three
things about itself: where does the department fit in the general university
context; how does it compare to cognate departments in the university; and
how does it compare with the same department in other institutions?

For example, a hard science department looking at itself within its institution should find out the average cost-per-student credit unit in the institution
at large. Then it should pin down its costs as compared to other science
departments in the institution. That comparative information should be
available through the institutional research or planning office. Lastly, you will
want to ferret out your department's costs as compared with the costs in
another comparable university teaching the same discipline. This will be
harder to come by. However, if members of the department have maintained
close relations with colleagues at other institutions, they can be the avenue for
locating such data. It is important that the department determine which
institutions it sees as its peers. Because of the pattern of distribution of U.S.
institutions, peer schools will probably not be within the locale of your
department and they may not even be in the same state. It is important that
your department see the comparative department as a true peer. Once such
data are assembled, you can help the department look objectively (non-
defensively) at the data. By looking dispassionately, the department expands
its scope of action beyond the reflexive. It can make conscious decisions that
stand a better chance of achieving desired goals than will persistence in old
grooved behaviors. Your department can also be far more agile in working in
support of its interests within your institution.

THE WORK OF ASSESSMENT

Faculty Assessment within a Collective Context

Summative versus Formative Evaluation

If your department becomes engaged in assessing its activities from a collective
point of view, you can expect changes in the way you look at individual
performance. This will lead to the articulation of standards by which you can
measure collective success. The activities you will want to measure will
continue to be teaching, scholarship (or creative activity), and community
service. At present our emphasis is on summative measures—those measures
that give us an accounting of the "final" result. One could equate summative
evaluation with the act of picking up a cash register receipt after you have

completed a purchase. The receipt states what you "did" and gives the final accounting of the value of your activity. Formative evaluations are specifically focused, and their aim is to guide activities that are in process. To pick up the shopping metaphor, a formative approach would have you carrying a calculator and entering each purchasing decision as you make it. If you found yourself spending too rapidly you might return some items to the shelf, deducting their cost from your running total. Whatever the methodology we use in assessing faculty—and those range from applying student evaluations, collecting and reviewing colleague comments, utilizing professional portfolios, and scheduling classroom visitations—each can be pursued from a summative or formative perspective. Whatever the method, however, our present approach to individual assessment of faculty is predominantly summative. What happens if we apply these methods for formative purposes?

The most common instrument used for assessing faculty teaching is the student course evaluation form (Arreola 1995). These are classic summative instruments. They are usually standardized within an institution and may be required evidence in making personnel decisions. For example, the unit of measure for teaching is the course and the standard practice calls for handing out evaluations course by course approximately two weeks before the final examination. While a promotion and tenure committee may look at a series of courses to see whether student reactions are fairly consistent over time and between different sizes and levels of courses taught by a given professor; their reading is summative, not formative. In other words, the focus remains on particular, discrete results. As far as the measurements themselves, the standard faculty assessment that relies on student evaluations is administered once at term's end. These are classic summative measures, which presume to give a "final" result but in fact give a still photo of one moment in time. Although such snapshots are useful, they should hardly be relied on as the sole indicator of pedagogical success. Summative evaluation is important. Final decisions do need to be made in a department and institution. Faculty contracts need to be renewed or extended. Promotion applications need to be processed. Tenure decisions must be made. All of these activities demand summative decision making and all need to have summative evaluation data available.

On the other hand, the growing clamor on the part of the public for accountability in terms of our results with students can be more effectively documented with formative processes. While retention and graduation rates derive from summative data, the demand for improvement can be met only through a formative approach. If one's intent is to produce certain kinds of change, formative information must be collected and behavioral change must be pursued. At present, we may be more comfortable with summative approaches, since those have been polished for several decades. However, our knowledge and resources for formative evaluation are steadily expanding. As a chair, you do have a leadership function in opening the discussion that will introduce formative methods of evaluation to your department, if they are not already in use. If they are already being employed, your leadership is important in encouraging improvement in the methods used and in supporting their application.

Student Evaluations

The point may gain clarity if we look at the difference in the questions that would be asked in student evaluations of faculty if your interest were in formative as opposed to summative data. Formative evaluation has a different purpose, namely, to elicit feedback that can be applied immediately to adjust and improve a current activity. Its timing, therefore, must be different. While summative evaluations are administered at the end as a final summing up of accomplishment, formative evaluations are utilized multiple times while a course is in progress. The data is then used by the instructor to make in-course adjustments.

The kinds of questions asked also differ. Summative questions are of necessity global in nature. Although we continue to hear debate about the universal applicability of faculty evaluation instruments, most institutions have been able to construct summative instruments they can apply to a broad spectrum of disciplines and course levels. Formative evaluation questions, on the other hand, need to be specifically applicable to a discipline and even to a specific course. This is necessary since the objective is to give feedback to instructors about what they are doing in a particular course and at a desig-nated moment in that course. The assumption is that on the basis of the information generated, the teaching process will be adjusted while the course is in process. This means that teaching becomes a dynamic process in which teacher and student are partnered to make the instructor as effective as possible.

Finally, the standard of measurement is different. Summative evaluations provide measures of comparisons. These may be between instructors in a department or they may be among instructors in the institution as a whole. Summative evaluations can provide a kind of "bell curve" that measures a particular instructor's effectiveness within a larger context. The standard of measure in the case of formative evaluation is the instructor's pedagogical intentions. For example, are students demonstrating the kind of mastery the instructor has established as a course goal? Is it the intent of the instructor that all students achieve a specified basic mastery? Is that goal being met?

Because the purposes of summative and formative evaluation differ, the instruments used must also differ. Summative evaluations rely on generic questionnaires. The instrument administered in chemistry looks the same as the one in English. Formative evaluations, by contrast, use a variety of instruments. These can include questionnaires devised to reveal results at a particular moment in a course. Higher education has begun to develop some useful instruments through the classroom assessment movement, so it is not necessary for departments and instructors to shoulder the burden of devising new systems *de novo* (Angelo and Cross 1993). Effectively we have begun to create a "wheel," which means individuals do not have to be solo inventors. Teaching portfolios are another instrument that has gained great popularity in recent years, and is useful for pursuing formative evaluation (Seldin 1997).

Colleague Comment

Current practice also relies on colleague comment. Like teaching evaluations, these can be designed to take either a summative or formative approach. If the department needs to make a summative decision that will include colleague comment, it is important that the department (or institution) establish the standards for those comments. It is important that there be specific directions for the categories of data that are to be examined as well as consistent criteria for measuring that data. Whatever remarks are made need to be document-able. Summative decisions may originate in a department, but they are inevitably linked to the total institution. Hence, colleagues' summative com-ments must acknowledge institutional goals and indicate how the individual's performance relate to those goals. Lastly, colleague comments intended to serve a summative function need to "benchmark" those remarks to support judgments on the link between the individual's and the institution's goals.

Developing standards for colleague remarks that are to be formative in nature will take a different approach. Rather than relying on summative data, the colleague will furnish descriptive feedback. That feedback will be specific not only to the individual being assessed, it will be specific to a particular activity of that individual. Rather than relying on consistent criteria appli-cable to a broad range of persons, the colleague will be providing specific observations related to the individual's activities. While it is imperative that summative comments be documentable to individuals beyond the person being assessed, formative feedback needs to be demonstrable to the individual. As for the standard against which success will be measured, when a summative approach is used the standard will be the institution's goals. On the other hand, if the process is formative in nature, the standard will be the teaching goals of the instructor. When we look for benchmarks, the summative ap-proach will scan for university standards, while the formative approach will focus on discipline standards.

The Professional Portfolio

The professional portfolio is an assessment tool that is gaining in popularity. In application it is more frequently used for formative evaluation. However, it can also be used for summative purposes and it can provide important insights to summative evaluation. Rather than the classic student evaluations that remain discrete pieces of information related to single courses, a summative portfolio would lay out an individual's teaching history over time, indicating the number of courses taught, the instructional level, and the enrollment. The portfolio would include student test scores and any quantifiable student achievement. It could include teaching materials such as course syllabi, assignments, and tests. A summative portfolio can provide a more dynamic picture of an instructor's teaching.

However, the more common use of professional portfolios is for formative development. In that case the portfolio will record teaching methods and results over time. It will also include a discussion of the pedagogical approach used and its rationale. The student materials will focus on exemplary student product rather than on test scores. When looking at teaching materials, the formative portfolio will show the link between teaching goals and the syllabus and between teaching goals and evaluation strategies. The portfolio will also include a discussion of teaching strategies. Finally, there will be an attempt to evaluate success in all these areas over time. What was changed, how it was changed, and why it was changed will be important.

Classroom Visitation
While not yet common in the United States, classroom visitation is being used as part of the assessment process in some institutions. Like all other forms of assessment, it can be pursued from a summative or formative perspective. If classroom visits are going to be used for summative purposes, it is important that the observational questions be standardized, that the timing of visits be explicitly programmed, and that there be a clear understanding among all concerned of the institution's benchmarks. Used summatively, those observations need to be standardized and will become a contribution to "final decisions" about employment. Classroom visits that have a formative purpose will rely on individualized observations. Observer and observed will talk in advance about the instructor's intentions. The observation schedule will be arranged individually and may include several visits. The standards will be dictated by the instructor's pedagogical goals. Under a formative approach, classroom visits will become part of the ongoing process of adjustment in teaching as a course progresses.

EVALUATING TEACHING, RESEARCH, AND SERVICE AS DEPARTMENTAL ACTIVITIES
Courses versus Curriculum
Broadening the evaluation approach to individual faculty can be a first step in developing a system for evaluating departmental success. However, even more extensive change will occur if you change the focus from the individual to the

department. For example, as long as assessment focuses on individual faculty, courses are reviewed as a function of individual activity. The success of the course is measured by the success of its instructor. Once courses are seen as part of a department curriculum, different questions take center stage and the participants in the dialog change. Once one sees courses as the components of a departmental curriculum, it becomes not only possible but imperative that the department as a whole be party to the discussion of what courses should be taught, how they might be taught, and who should teach them. How might you guide such a dialog?

A good place to begin is to dust off your department's mission statement as one of the standards by which the components of the curriculum will be measured. Another standard that is appropriate to lay on the table are the definitions that form your department's discipline. While your department's mission statement may be quite broad—and even transposable to another department's—the discipline definitions will relate specifically to your department's work. The third corner of your triangle of standards can be your "clients." Who are your students? Are they undergraduate and/or graduate students? Are they full-time day students or working adults? Are they going on for graduate work or entering the work world immediately upon graduation?

With this triangle of standards available, you can help your department look at its curriculum. And the perspective should be different from the one you would use looking at an individual instructor. Entering courses into the curriculum moves from being a matter of offering courses that are of greatest interest to the instructor to courses that contribute to a pattern of offerings that supports the department's mission; that helps students become conversant with the discipline, its intellectual interests, and current preoccupations; and that speaks to the needs of your institution's particular student population. You and your colleagues will also need to be sure that you manage your curriculum to meet the time needs of your department's students, in terms of either arranging course sequences across the calendar or scheduling teaching times to maximize student enrollment.

With these shifts in emphasis, you will be looking differently at an individual faculty member's performance. It will now be important to see how the individual contributes to the department's curriculum and its mission. You will want to develop some criteria for assessing how the individual faculty member is keeping current with new developments in the discipline. That issue is separate from and goes beyond the familiar criterion of scholarly activity. Scholarly activity may help an individual remain current. However, if that scholarly work is in a small area of subspecialization, the individual may not necessarily be keeping up with broader changes across the discipline. In looking at individual faculty it will be important to see how well they work with the particular kinds of students your department enrolls. New student populations may pose unfamiliar challenges. A department will master these challenges effectively only through the aggregate success of its individual faculty.

The Issue of Scholarship

As noted at the beginning of this chapter, scholarship is the second common component in faculty evaluation. At first blush you might think that this is truly a matter of individual interest. In fact this may be one of the most vital points at which you can help connect individual development and departmental interests. Research requires time and resources. In most instances it also requires an ongoing intellectual dialog. Major research universities will form their research programs around and under the leadership of key individuals who are generally recruited to add to the stature of the institution. They are expected to design and implement their research agenda. However, most institutions in the United States do not and cannot proceed in this manner. Furthermore, if Ernest Boyer's admonitions have value, it is in urging institutions to take a broader view of research. The paths he has drawn to our attention, as indicated earlier in the chapter, are the scholarship of integration, application, and pedagogy.[5] The interesting aspect of all these is that they lend themselves ideally to a collaborative discussion within the department. For example, if your department decides to focus on applied research, it stands to gain if projects pursued by individual faculty can be linked. This can be done through outright collaboration. Or it can be done by seeing explicitly the connections between one project and another. Applied research is also likely to bring the department into contact with outside agencies, both public and private, in projects in which it may be logical to involve more than one faculty member and even students. Applied research is definitely an area in which the department can set some overarching goals, and these in turn can become anchors for individual projects. In this area a chair can take on the role of impresario, introducing key people to each other and encouraging collaborative projects.

Research on pedagogy is also best pursued as a departmental endeavor. Some of the particular forms of pedagogical research are reviewed in chapter 8. The point here is that it is appropriate for a department to take interest in improving its teaching effectiveness. A single instructor can undertake some experimentation within his or her courses. But impact at the department level is better realized through systematic collective effort. By working as a department the individual performance of instructors can be enhanced at the same time that the overall performance of the department can be strengthened. Such a department-wide effort requires chair leadership. As chair, you can make such a dialog legitimate and guide its progress.

The Obligation of Community Service

The third leg of the tripod of most faculty evaluation systems is community service. For better or worse, the standards for what constitutes recognizable service are seldom defined and individual faculty are left to fulfill this obligation in an atomized, uncoordinated manner. A department that is willing to define a common program can reap much greater benefits than it can ever hope to gain from haphazard individual choices. Again, this can become a matter in which individual interest and talent can be linked with departmental goals, thereby strengthening the department as a community. How might you go about this task? One piece of the conversation in the department can be a discussion of the university's committee structure, with a collective determination of where the department most urgently needs to have its voice heard. It can then become a matter of department debate to determine who specifically would have the necessary knowledge and willingness to serve. A parallel discussion can be pursued concerning external agencies with which it might be logical for the department to build connections. Some departments, by the very nature of their disciplinary work, may already have important external connections. In that case, your interest as chair should be to ensure that these activities are not left indefinitely on autopilot. Circumstances and opportunities change. Departments will remain successful only if they also remain responsive to current realities. In other cases, you may need to initiate those external connections. This may be particularly important for a department that does not have an established tradition of external linkages. Whatever the path chosen by the department, as chair you will need to see that decisions are implemented and initiatives appropriately sustained.

Shifting the focus of assessment from individuals to the department as a collectivity does not mean throwing out the kind of individual evaluation to which we have become accustomed. Review of individual teaching success across courses will remain important. Individual faculty research projects will remain relevant to individual evaluation. Community service will not cease to be an important component of faculty work. What is needed, however, is a richer view of what individuals are doing. We need to see ourselves not exclusively as single actors but in our connections to colleagues and our role in forming a coherent and effective department.

ASSESSING THE ORGANIZATIONAL SUCCESS OF THE DEPARTMENT

The final segment of departmental life that you should review is the organization and operations of the department itself. The department is the faculty's campus home. Like families, departments range from being pleasant and productive social organizations to being dysfunctional. If you have the bad luck as a chair to become the designated leader of a dysfunctional department, you should not expect to work instant miracles. However, you cannot wash your hands of the responsibility of initiating a process that may eventually lead to an effective unit, even though that time may not come to pass on your watch. Count yourself among the blessed if you are heir to an effective department with high morale. The probability is that you will find yourself heading a department that does its job reasonably well and that has a dedicated and supportive faculty spiced by individuals whom you will politely describe as "difficult people." Whatever the climate of your department, it comes with a past history, established patterns of interaction, and well-grooved patterns of decision making. Before you undertake any change agenda, a reasonable step is to give your department a general "physical exam." Your reflections on the following matters will give you a handle on the state of your department and point to directions in which you may want to guide change. Obviously the size and demographic profile of your department will make a difference in its organizational structure. The larger the department, the more difficult it will be to create or sustain a department that functions as a cohesive unit. When a department reaches a size of 40 or more members, you have progressed from the small or moderate size department to the "large," and you will probably need to conduct much of the department's business through the use of committees. However, the following issues merit review.

Reflect on the frequency and regularity of department meetings. While there is considerable range for both these factors, the most usual pattern is a semi-monthly meeting. Frequency may be less important than the organization and ambiance of those meetings. Attitudes are apt to vary by discipline. Faculty of humanities departments are often inclined to meet regularly and frequently. Their scheduled meetings often occur every two weeks and in some cases every week. Business faculty may opt to meet only when they have "business" to transact. Unfortunately, it is more norm than exception for department meetings to border on the dysfunctional. It is not unusual for faculty, if you can corner them alone, to admit that the departmental faculty meeting is something they dread. They will cite the wasting of time in useless dialog devoid of decision making. They will complain about negative colleagues. Should you be unlucky enough to have such a department, changes in the frequency of meetings will not cure the problem. Interventions beyond regulating the calendar will be in order.

Even in well-functioning departments it is revealing to look at the organization and procedures followed in your department meetings. Do you have a formal agenda? If so, who is responsible for drawing that up? In a department that has difficulty coming to closure and making decisions, an agenda may be particularly important, assuming that you follow it. The most important factor, however, may be the process of interaction that takes place in those meetings. To get a sense of that reality may take some concentrated effort before you attempt specific interventions. A review of the department minutes may help you pinpoint where the dialog goes off track. You can supplement that with your own observations and notes. Any social group that works together regularly is likely to have developed an habitual pattern of dialog. Depending upon the nature of that pattern, groups are either able to make decisions and take action or they become mired in inconclusive debate and endless recycling of issues. If you are able to pinpoint a "diagnosis" you will stand a good chance of being able to intervene at the critical moments when you see that the dialog is about to go off course or become stuck.

A review of the minutes can also help you plot out the business of the department meetings. Are meetings dominated by administrivia? What are the conceptual topics that are debated? How frequently do they appear on the agenda? When administrative questions such as arranging class schedules come up, what criteria are used in decision making? Do members of the department stake out their "preferred" teaching slots, with the most senior members being routinely accommodated? Or does the department discuss the best way to deliver the curriculum within the institutional scheduling system, taking cognizance of student needs? When new courses are proposed, what is the department's role in reviewing and endorsing these before they are submitted to a university curriculum committee? If course proposals are left to the initiative of individual faculty, the chances are that your curriculum does not have a departmentally defined focus. Does your faculty support administrative offices by submitting grades within the allotted time frame? Do they support the work of the admissions department or development office? Does the department have a shared understanding of how students should be advised? To what extent does the faculty share the "grunt work" of teaching? Does everyone share in teaching introductory sections, or is that reserved for novice faculty and part-timers? The answers to such questions can be the foundation for creating a departmental development plan. Once you establish your own clarity on the subject, you can bring the faculty together to help create the "change agenda" for the department's organizational methods.

CONCLUSION

The term "evaluation" has historically been used to refer primarily to the evaluation of faculty teaching as judged through student questionnaires. The term now reflects a much more complex reality. Although the evaluation of individual faculty for retention, tenure, and promotion remains an important chair responsibility, there is more with which to be concerned today. The new frontiers are in developing sound means for measuring and assessing group success and establishing the means for continually enhancing both individual and departmental performance. Although chairs are generally not enthusiastic about being evaluators, the fact is that there are important payoffs for the department that pursues collective assessment, if it carries out that assessment with the goal of perfecting the work of the department. Because this aspect of evaluation is relatively new and since we have a broadening range of methods to apply to the task, there is real latitude in which chairs may work with their departments to create new procedures. The effort is made worthwhile by the promise of the improvements it can bring to the department, which in turn can build the success of that department. However, the greatest benefit to be gained from adopting systematic ongoing assessment of the department may be in the expanded influence it gives the department over its fate. We are all familiar with the saying "knowledge is power." In these times of uncertainty, is there a better justification for a department to support a program of self-assessment, when that holds the promise of giving it a greater measure of control over its own future?

NOTES

1. For example, in 1949-50, of the 498,373 baccalaureates awarded, 252,124 (51 percent) came from private institutions and 246,249 (49 percent) from public institutions. Thirty years later, of the 1,330,244 baccalaureates awarded, 470,111 (35 percent) came from private institutions and 860,133 (65 percent) from public institutions. Although the numbers of students enrolled increased in both sectors, the rate of increase was roughly 85 percent in the private arena, while in the public arena it ran over 300 percent. Figures that measure only the awarding of bachelor's degrees give a very conservative picture of enrollment in the public sector. Total enrollment in the public sector is in fact far larger since the community college sector is almost exclusively the domain of public institutions. The two-year college sector enrolled only 217,572 students in 1950. Thirty years later that enrollment had reached 4,728,000 (ACE 1989, 98, 200).
2. Private communication, University of Technology, Sydney, Australia, 1998.
3. The American Association of Higher Education held its first assessment meeting in 1985. To the association's astonishment, they were deluged with enrollment for the meeting. The result has been that the association now holds an annual meeting on the topic of assessment, providing an invaluable national venue for exchanging information on the continuing evolution of that topic. The topic has become of such generalized interest and the development of new approaches, instruments, and techniques is so rapid that Jossey-Bass now publishes a bimonthly newsletter entitled *Assessment Update*.
4. An example of that kind of legislative pressure being exerted at the state level is South Carolina's law approved by its state legislature "last spring specifying that their appropriations will no longer be based on enrollments and facility needs. Instead, the state is instituting a groundbreaking system under which state appropriations to a public college will be based entirely on how well the institution is judged to perform." It is legislation of this kind that has spawned the movement of "performance indicators." Naturally,

determining what those indicators will be is the locus of strenuous struggle between institutions and legislatures. *The Chronicle of Higher Education*, April 1, 1997, A26.

5. See chapter 2, "Enlarging the Perspective."

REFERENCES

American Council on Education (ACE). 1989. *1989-90 Fact Book on Higher Education*. Division of Policy Analysis and Research, Macmillan Series on Higher Education.

Angelo, Thomas A., and Patricia K. Cross. 1993. *Classroom assessment techniques: A handbook for college teachers*, 2nd ed. San Francisco: Jossey-Bass.

One of the most developed methods of formative evaluation currently in use is that of classroom assessment. Pioneered first by K. Patricia Cross, the movement has developed a battery of techniques. The classic source for identifying those tools is this handbook.

Arreola, Raoul A. 1995. *Developing a comprehensive faculty evaluation system: A handbook for college faculty and administrators on designing and operating a comprehensive faculty evaluation system*. Bolton, Mass.: Anker.

As the title suggests, this is a handbook of evaluation systems, and as such it is an excellent reference for this subject.

Boyer, Ernest L. 1990. *Scholarship reconsidered: Priorities of the professoriate*. Princeton, N.J.: The Carnegie Foundation for the Advancement of Learning.

It is Boyer who has finally raised the question of the suitability of applying the standard that equates scholarship with what he refers to as the "scholarship of discovery." Boyer has pointed out the importance of other forms of scholarship, which he suggests fall into the additional categories of the "scholarship of integration," the "scholarship of application," and the "scholarship of teaching."

Centra, John A. 1993. *Reflective faculty evaluation: Enhancing teaching and determining faculty effectiveness*. San Francisco: Jossey-Bass.

This is a good volume with which to begin examining the process and procedures of faculty evaluation. Centra's discussion includes teaching portfolios, the assessment of research, and service to the institution, as well as legal considerations affecting evaluation.

The Chronicle of Higher Education. 1997a. (4 April): A 26.

The Chronicle of Higher Education. 1997b. (15 August): A23.

The Chronicle of Higher Education. 1997c. International notes (5 September): A74.

On the horizon: The strategic planning resource for education professionals. 1997. 5, no. 5 (September-October): 2.

Seldin, Peter. 1997. *The teaching portfolio: A practical guide to improved performance and promotion/tenure decisions*, 2nd ed. Bolton, Mass.: Anker.

CHAPTER 14

The Chair and External Audiences

INSIDE THE INSTITUTION

This text has sought to probe the changing shape, content, and context of the department chair's complex roles. The extent of change is nowhere more dramatically revealed than in a discussion of external audiences. John Creswell in collaboration with several authors in *The Academic Chairperson's Handbook* (1990) interviewed and surveyed some 200 chairs on 70 campuses. The handbook is a revealing source for anyone wanting to grasp what chairs saw as the focus of their work.

Faculty as Autonomous Individuals

Repeatedly, the Creswell interviews reveal an orientation toward working with faculty as autonomous individuals. For example, we find the following statement on one of the important roles of the chair:

> A need exists for each chairperson to better understand the situation of faculty in his or her department with an eye toward intervening unobtrusively in ways that will facilitate good interpersonal communication with their [sic] staff and enable faculty to grow and develop. (Creswell et al. 1990, 6)

The same orientation is revealed in a discussion of the chair's role in assisting new faculty to integrate into the department. Chairs should first look to supporting new faculty by helping them find the resources they need to pursue their (individual) work. Second, they should help the newcomers develop professional networks; and third, the chair needs to help integrate the novices into existing departmental projects. Two of the three tasks are oriented toward social integration; all interventions look toward the success of the individual.

In discussing the chair's role in improving the teaching performance of faculty, Creswell's subject for chapter 6, his focus is on working with individual faculty to make them better teachers. There is also an underlying assumption that a chair would become interested in this when there are signs—probably through student complaints—that the instructor is not as successful a teacher as hoped. The admonitions advise the use of a consultative model, the need for getting information from multiple sources, identifying the weak spot, and then observing the performance. Once a diagnosis has been made the chair needs to monitor the process of improvement.

The same concern for individual performance is exhibited in the discussion of older faculty. When the chair sees signs of trouble, which are likely to include dissatisfaction, lack of enthusiasm, minimal performance, and "negative attitude," the chair is advised to work with the individual to "explore options." Working together, the objective is to design "a plan for intervention" (Creswell et al. 1990, 84–88). The rationale for focusing on the individual is the fact that individual faculty problems that are not dealt with (by the chair) will spill into the department. Therefore, the chair needs to be prepared to listen to personal problems, act as a temporary buffer when necessary, and know when to seek external help (Creswell et al. 1990, 96–97). The chair's primary agenda needs to be that of supporting individual growth and development—something that can be achieved by understanding the idiosyncrasies of career stages, combined with a grounding in the "institutional and disciplinary context in which this growth occurs" (Creswell et al. 1990, 105–6).

While there is no doubt that chairs do need to work with faculty as individuals, the new challenges are more in the dimension of molding the faculty into a working whole, a subject explored in chapter 7. And it requires connecting faculty as individuals and as a collective department with audiences beyond the department itself. What we want to look at now are those audiences *beyond* individual faculty and beyond even the department, which the chair needs to understand and cultivate. These include "external" groups within the university itself, professional connections in the discipline, and individuals and groups outside the confines of the institution and discipline.

Beyond the Department

It is still not unusual to hear chairs describe as one of their more important duties representing the interests of the department to the upper administration and fighting for the individual and collective interests of the department.

There is no doubt that this is indeed one of the functions of a chair. However, today no one has the luxury of operating in a world of expanding resources. Conservation and efficiency are the new watchwords. An astute chair will not only look at the department's interests, but will see those interests in context with the goals of other chairs. It is particularly important to be aware of the needs of cognate departments, especially those that depend on your department's expertise. Getting the department's "way" may be possible only if those interests intersect with and reinforce the needs of other departments. To present a dean with a decision that clearly involves cutting someone else's resources to support your department's demands will not endear your department to colleagues and may even undermine the standing of the department within the institution. Even clinging to the *status quo* may no longer be possible, because that conservative act may have the effect of choking not only your department's development, but the vigor of related departments. "Business-as-usual" is not a wise option, and, in fact, may not be a possible option.

The following is a specific example that will serve to illustrate the point. Statistics is a branch of mathematics utilized in the research of many other disciplines. Biologists, sociologists, and psychologists regularly use applied statistics. Quantitative historians, economists, and political scientists draw on statistical analyses. A review of college and university catalogs under the rubric of statistics may reveal that the university teaches the subject under a variety of discipline headings beyond the department of mathematics. The rationale given is that the "math people do not teach statistics the way we need it done" in psychology or sociology, or whatever other discipline may draw on statistical methods for analysis. An inquisitive dean who scrutinizes the enrollment numbers, the number of tenure slots, and the unit costs of teaching three or four versions of basic statistics is apt to come to the conclusion that much could be gained through consolidation. Forced from the top, these readjustments are painful and are more likely to create a context of hostility among departments, to say nothing of fueling faculty irritation with a micromanaging dean. The important point is that you do not need to be the "respondent" in this kind of situation. As chair, you can be the initiator of solutions if you can see opportunities for creating linkages that build the expertise of your department in terms both of depth and breadth. For example, a proposal to consolidate statistics courses that is generated through the intervention of the departments affected stands a far better chance of being an effective solution than does a cost-cutting consolidation dictated by a dean. It does not matter whether yours is a department that provides services or consumes them. The chances are, after all, that your department falls into both realms, providing service to some and using the services of others. Remember that you can take the initiative in exploring, proposing, and guiding collaborative solutions to institutional problems. There can be no better manifestation of true leadership than taking such initiatives.

The statistics case provides an obvious example. However, in future the rewards are more likely to come to those chairs who can configure solutions from less obvious situations. For example, whenever there is an opportunity for a new hire, the institutional approvals may come more easily if you have met with appropriate colleagues to discuss how the expertise of the new hire will support the work of related departments. There are even times when a shared hire may be the one means of adding someone to your department. Shared positions are not a popular solution. However, as all institutions face tightening resources, it may be necessary to make such solutions work. The critical leadership for that kind of innovation can come only from departments led by their chairs.

If there are positive benefits to be gained for a department that can build effective collaborative linkages with related departments, there are other benefits to be gained from building good working relationships with the administrative and staff units of the institution. As chair, a useful exercise is to make a list of the administrative offices that your department depends on for particular services. Among these you will certainly find the registrar (assuming this is the institutional office that records student grades and assigns classrooms), the accounting and business office, the head librarian, the admissions office, and the custodial staff. You may find that your department relies on a variety of student services including a learning center, a counseling office, and a career counseling office. If your department has foreign student majors, you may need to know the foreign student advisor. You may call the institutional planning office for departmental data. If you need to hire staff, your department may interact with the human resources office. As fund-raising becomes an ever more pressing activity, you may find yourself talking with the development office. If repairs are needed, you will likely call the physical plant. If you have security concerns, you will be contacting the campus security service.

Once you have identified the staff offices your department relies on to get its work done, ask yourself how well you know the people in those offices. Is there a person in each office with whom you have a good working relationship so that in the midst of a "crisis" you can get help in working out a solution? Do you know something of the challenges the people you are working with face? For example, do you know when the registrar must mail grades to students? Do you know what that office does if a professor has not filed final grades on time? The likelihood is that the registrar will "fill in" the data in some routine manner. It could be with an "incomplete," "deferred grade," or some other established designation. Whatever that may be, remember that it is *your department*, not just the delinquent professor who will be the target of both the student's and the registrar's wrath. For the student, the transcript is a record of his or her performance, and an entry that misrepresents that performance will not be tolerated with grace. For the registrar's office, hand corrections of individual records are not just irritating; they cost time and money. Many annoyances can be avoided and crises thwarted if as chair you develop effective working relations with the myriad offices that keep an institution operating. You can also help your department colleagues understand the methods and limitations of the various offices with which they may need to work. As chair, you can help create an atmosphere of respect for the many people that keep an institution functioning. The faculty may perform the key task of the college or university, namely, teaching and scholarship. However, that work cannot be performed without the effective assistance of many staff offices. A department with good working relations with university staff will have a more pleasant existence than will one embroiled in guerrilla warfare, be it with the physical plant or the accounting office. That department will also be more effective in its own work.

BEYOND THE INSTITUTION

Within the Discipline

One of the tension points in higher education is the tug between loyalty to the discipline and loyalty to the institution. One of the criticisms leveled of late against faculty is that some display greater loyalty to their discipline than to their institution. For faculty heavily involved in research, their intellectual peers are likely to be those working in the same field in other institutions. It is they, not institutional colleagues with their own subspecialties, that are key to the research dialog. Some critics have suggested that institutions have become little more than a platform for individual research and the source of a secure living for individuals who fail to contribute to the daily maintenance of the common enterprise. Parallel complaints are heard about institutions that collect "star" faculty who enhance the institution's reputation, without making much of an on-site contribution to the daily work of the university—the educating of students.

While there may be some justification for these complaints, the fact is that the discipline will (and should) remain an important focus of departmental life. It is not only legitimate but also essential for the chair to encourage faculty to keep active in their discipline organizations (and the chair, should, of course, remain active in his or her discipline, as well). The interest in the discipline, however, needs to be more than individual and personal. There are important departmental interests to be served as well. Remaining current with the new developments in any discipline is vital to maintaining an up-to-date curriculum. If the department is preparing students for graduate work, it is critical that these students be current on new research findings and lines of inquiry in the discipline. Students do not want to look like "country bumpkins" when they arrive in graduate school and your department will not want to build a reputation for being out of touch with the new developments in the field.

Discipline linkages can be national, regional, and local. National linkages are useful in several ways. If your department has the opportunity to add a full-time, tenure track faculty member, active national contacts can help identify and screen applicants. If your department aims to send graduates to graduate schools, national contacts can be immensely helpful. Personal knowledge can help the department give advice to students who will want to know what the strengths of a graduate department may be. Personal contacts can also help you give your graduates some feedback on the strengths, specialties, and style of particular dissertation advisors.

Regional contacts can offer another layer of assistance similar to national connections. Joint faculty research projects may be easier to carry out on a regional than a national level. It may be feasible to place students in summer research internships within the region, as well as accept summer interns from other institutions. The department can draw on regional resources in the discipline for special speakers. In preparing for accreditation reviews, the department may wish to invite informal consultation from colleague experts. Some institutions use outside reviewers for tenure reviews. If that holds true in your institution, regional colleagues may be the people you want to contact for this task.

Local contacts are also important to maintain. Depending on the particular type of institution nearest you, your department may want to encourage research collaboration with your "neighbor." Less formal exchanges are also possible. Students can meet with each other to present or discuss research projects. Internships can be arranged on an exchange basis. When faced with sabbatical vacancies, it may be possible to get assistance from a neighboring institution. Interinstitutional collaborations around hiring and curriculum have even begun to occur. Infrequent at present, we may find this becoming a more accepted practice despite the impediments of differences between types of institutions and their missions. It is also worth remembering that there is an increasing number of Ph.D.s or professionally trained people who are working outside academic institutions. Particularly in applied fields, these people can bring very valuable knowledge and skills to your department.

In maintaining discipline contacts beyond the institution the chair can play an important facilitative role by setting the tone for interaction. If a department is firmly territorial in its orientation, external collaboration will be shut off. It is the chair who can help change such an orientation. Or with a neutrally inclined department, a proactive chair can encourage and foster external collaboration. The extent to which you maintain effective external discipline contacts will have a major effect on your department. Insularity is no longer acceptable economically. It has never been productive intellectually. And pursued at the department level, insularity can threaten the vigor of any department.

Interinstitutional Links

History has created isolation among our educational institutions. Each has tended to work within clearly demarcated boundaries. Schools have been responsible for primary and secondary education. Undergraduate colleges, either stand-alone or within large universities, have educated the baccalaureate candidate. Universities have taken on graduate education. Community colleges were added to fill a niche for those seeking particular kinds of education not addressed by either the precollegiate or collegiate sector. They have also served as a more economical entry point to higher education for those who were either uncertain about pursuing a full undergraduate degree or lacked the means to launch immediately into a four-year course of study. Some of the compartmentalization has been encouraged by the fact that in planning for educational resources, institutional founders always sought to define a local or regional niche for themselves. It was a virtue to assert that they would be serving an unmet need, not duplicating an existing resource. In part through the work of the educational demographer Harold Hodgkinson who coined the phrase "all one system," we have come to realize that all the parts are linked.

Two examples come readily to mind that exemplify this newer approach of emphasizing the connections in the system. One is the movement for school-college/university linkages. The other is the overt creation of smooth transfer mechanisms between community and baccalaureate colleges. School-college cooperation is not a new phenomenon. In fact in 1987 the American Association of Higher Education published the *National Directory of School-College Partnerships: Current Models and Practices.* For any chair who might want to foster a linkage, a review of the diversity of projects in place can be a source of inspiration. The catalog also offers a resource in locating institutions with experience in particular forms of collaboration. The issue of easing transfer from two-year to baccalaureate schools is also a well-worked subject. However, it is coming up with greater urgency today as state legislatures and institutions, seeking to conserve scarce resources, look to developing organized curricular articulation between institutions.

While it is true that building the kinds of connections described in these examples does require policy support from appropriate administrators, effective implementation is impossible without parallel support from departments. While idealistic rhetoric about linkage programs may attract transfer applicants from community colleges, if experience bears minimal resemblance to ideal, students will not hesitate to go elsewhere. Similarly, if schoolteachers feel belittled or find that the expected support is wanting, administrators will find it impossible to continue collaborative school-university programs. The onus rests on department chairs. In that role, it is vital for you to understand the nature and goals of institutional policy. Ideally your department should have played a role in formulating the linkage project in the first place. If your institution is initiating a linkage program, be sure that you play an active and supportive role. Support does not mean blind acquiescence. Effective support includes thoughtful comment with the goal of improving—not derailing—a linkage initiative. If you step in as chair and must oversee an existing linkage program, you do not need to limit yourself to clerical management. Any programmatic effort will be dynamic. There is always room to improve. Sometimes there is the opportunity to expand or reorient. The critical point is to be aware of the changed context of higher education. A life of splendid isolation may still be possible. However, it is fiscally risky and the probability is that it will lead your institution into an intellectual *cul de sac*.

Even more adventurous linkages are emerging. New opportunities are being created, with a range of content and nomenclature. Institutions are looking for ways to increase efficiency in ways that require new dialogs between them. For example, The *Chronicle* (29 November 1996) reported that three independent Pennsylvania colleges were advertising their faculty openings jointly. Because of proximity, it would be easy for academic couples to move together, with each working in a different institution without the burden of resorting to a long-distance commuting life. The agreements necessary for such an arrangement need institutional administrative endorsement. Implementation requires dialog between chairs across institutional (and discipline) lines. In 1996 five independent Boston colleges agreed to work together on a range of issues, including hiring of new faculty following resignations or retirements (*Chronicle* 1 November 1996).

Collaborations are not limited to financially stressed independent institutions. State institutions are also seeking creative ways of working together. Two collaborative degree programs offered through Portland State University are good examples. One program is an international M.B.A. degree offered jointly by the University of Oregon and Portland State University. Students can choose either institution for their diplomas. The courses, which are jointly staffed by the two institutions, are offered in the Portland metro area. Another is a new environmental program that will link the three Oregon universities, University of Oregon, Oregon State University, and Portland State University, in offering a master's degree and possibly a doctorate in environmental studies. Again, approval and support are needed from the administrators of all three institutions. In fact, endorsement by the Oregon Board of Higher Education is also required before such agreements can be implemented. However, at all stages of negotiation the affected departments, through their chairs or administrative program heads, have been involved. When it comes to implementation, the burden will fall primarily on department chairs.

Families and Alumni

One of the potentially more pleasant sides of faculty work can be contact with their own alumni and with students' families. Again, as chair you can influence how these contacts are maintained. Connections with families will be affected by whether your institution is large or small, independent or public. The greatest frequency of contact will take place in a small independent college where families often bring their newly matriculating offspring to college and where the institution may make elaborate preparations for welcoming family and providing programming for them. In a public institution, meaningful contact with families may not occur until the moment of graduation. However, at that point a formidable extended family may appear to cheer the new graduate. Graduation ceremonies can be highly emotional events for families where a parent or grandparent is receiving a long-delayed baccalaureate or where the young recipient is the first in the family to achieve that level of education. Departments have a wonderful opportunity to build familial enthusiasm and support for higher education if they arrange some acknowledgment for the families of the department's students. Taking time for personal contact in a social setting is appreciated by both family and student. And it helps build bonds with alumni.

Alumni contacts are important for the department to maintain. As mentioned in chapter 13, accreditation self-studies may need to draw on alumni data. Departments may need support when the institution is considering program changes. And fund-raising is highly dependent on alumni. Data from 1995-96 on financial support to institutions indicated that 53 percent came from individuals; and that among individuals, alumni constituted 29 percent of the individual givers (*Chronicle* 30 May 1997). Furthermore, a recent study indicates that alumni give because of loyalty to a particular professor (Murphy 1992). Chances are that that professor will have been in the student's major department. Alumni are important contributors in two areas: the institution's annual fund and for special-project gifts. They can also be the source of bequests, which are the form of giving that often brings the largest donations to an institution.

Private institutions have long depended on annual fund drives for a portion of their yearly general fund. To support that, those institutions have historically had well-organized alumni groups and structural systems for solicitation often oriented around the alumni's identity with their graduating classes. State institutions, which are seeing decreases in the percentage of their annual operating budgets covered by state appropriations, are also beginning to create the equivalent of annual alumni fund drives. For them the process is more difficult since they usually lack a well-developed alumni networking system. This is a place where departments have excellent opportunities to participate in development activities, some of which may even be of direct benefit.

Departments are also an important source of information for development offices looking for major donors because they may be in the best position to know about the successes of their graduates—provided departments have mechanisms to follow their students' post-graduate lives. As chair, you can address the topic of an alumni contact system. If one exists, it is wise to review its activities, looking for ways to strengthen it. If none exists, you have the even more important role of opening the topic for discussion and guiding the department toward developing a system of implementation. This is a discussion that can be opened to current majors.

Community Contacts

Applied Education

Another audience of increasing importance to departments, and, therefore, a necessary concern to you as chair, is the public community around your institution. Education has always had an applied aspect as one of its goals. We may think, for example, of England's Oxford and Cambridge Universities (frequently referred to as Oxbridge) as the epitome of elitist, non-applied instruction. In fact, one of the practical roles of Oxbridge, particularly through the middle of the twentieth century, was the training of a cadre of British civil servants. The curriculum may not have included "practical" material that would prepare a graduate to work in and eventually head a government bureau. What it did provide was the entry ticket for consideration for such positions. In fact, it could be the ticket without which you would not even be reviewed for employment within the managerial ranks of the civil service. In the United States we have also had an applied orientation. But even here, through at least World War II, our most prestigious universities often played a role similar to that of Oxbridge, preparing a social cadre for leadership in the professions, government, and business.

The change today is not a fundamental reorientation, but rather a redefinition of our concepts of what exemplifies applied or practical education. There have long been fields where a quasi-apprenticeship has been required. For example, medicine and various health services fields, including nursing, have long had a standard requirement of apprenticeship. Law has filled a similar need with the "law clerk" position that law graduates take immediately after graduation. However, there were two distinct characteristics of this kind of "apprenticeship." First, the applied work took place after the completion of theoretical studies. Thus, young doctors would receive their medical degrees, but still be required to spend a year or more as interns or residents devoting themselves totally to applied work. This kind of training was required before achieving a full license to practice unsupervised. Second, the applied work, though supervised, was not overseen by the institution that granted the degree.

Internships

The move toward internships today has two distinct characteristics. The internships are pursued *during* the basic degree program and they are *overseen by the degree-granting institution.* Teacher education, with its required stint of practice teaching, is a good early example of this new variety of internship. Practice teaching has long been the capstone experience for would-be teachers. Enrollment classically takes place in the student's senior year and active supervision is provided by the degree-granting institution. However, we are still talking about a discipline that by definition prepares students for an applied profession. The important recent change is the concept that institutions need to provide an explicit bridge between school and work. There is, of course, a necessary transition from school (theoretical study) to work (applied knowledge). It is only recently that colleges and universities have accepted responsibility for facilitating that transition. In the expansive 1950s and 1960s the transition was greatly eased by the fact that many would-be employers systematically visited campuses with the objective of hiring new graduates. Institutional responsibility was limited to finding a suitable location for these meetings and notification to students regarding the opportunity to interview. The rest was left to employers and students. The more difficult economy faced by graduates in the 1970s and especially the 1980s encouraged both students and institutions to develop programs that would give students hands-on pregraduation experiences that would contribute to their resumes. Institutions were led in this direction by virtue of the fact that in a "buyers' market" employers were less inclined to conduct campus interviews, especially at the baccalaureate level. For private institutions, the opportunity for applied experience became a marketing device for recruiting undergraduate students. At the extreme edge of this spectrum lies an institution like Antioch College, which has a built-in required alternation between work and study. While this pattern has not been pursued as a general practice in American higher education, many universities now have internship possibilities built into their curricula. Another current example of an institutional effort to bridge study and work is the capstone program at Portland State University where graduating seniors must participate in a community project related to their major.

How do these changes affect the work of a department and its chair? The most obvious alteration is in the concept of the boundaries of departmental responsibility. The assumption that the department terminates its interest in and obligation to the student with the awarding of a particular diploma is eroding. At the department level, the implication is that we must think about what will happen to the student *after* graduation. Will the department have prepared its alumni to function effectively in the work world? The question can appear perplexing in the arts, humanities, and some social science fields.

An important discussion that can be initiated by a chair is what kind of applied experiences should the department encourage for its undergraduate majors? Can (should) the department look to developing a series of internship placements? Or should the department rely on a central university office? If it chooses the latter route, the department still has responsibility for advising and guiding its majors toward enriching applied experiences. The pressures at the graduate level demand even greater attention. By and large academics are most comfortable training future academicians. If that is the department's mission, then it is vital that the department address the issue of appropriate professional pedagogic training beyond the mastery of the discipline itself. For those who do not intend to become professional academics, the department needs to help them prepare for a transition to other work. An important contribution is for members of the department to gain some knowledge and insight into the ways in which the skills mastered in a particular discipline can be transferred to applications in another domain. At the very least, the department can establish a culture that legitimates work outside the university for its graduate students.

The International Dimension

Another "new frontier" for department chairs may well be the international arena. Institutions in the United States have been internationally focused in terms of receiving students since the conclusion of World War II. In fact some disciplines such as engineering and computer science have been known to enroll more foreign than domestic students. The faculty ranks have also been impacted by global change, in this case through the presence of many foreign-born instructors. The flow out of the United States, on the other hand, has been much weaker. Students in the United States have been far less inclined to venture overseas, and this is in part a reflection of curricular orientation within departments. While some disciplines have been internationally oriented historically, foreign languages being the most obvious, the entire swath of fields such as the natural and social sciences have been uninterested or hostile to the thought of their students pursuing a portion of their studies overseas. However, as the work world has broadened, disciplines have found it appropriate to give their curricula an international orientation. In the context of chairs working with external constituencies, a new view of international possibilities opens the overseas world as a potential location for collaborative arrangements. As curriculum is rethought, faculty and departments in parallel disciplines overseas may need to come within the circle of concern for department chairs in the United States.

ACCREDITATION

Whether you become involved in an accreditation visit will depend upon the timing of your tenure as chair. However, since the process of accreditation is lengthy, requiring advance preparation by as much as two years, often followed by implementing change afterwards, the chances are that you will have some involvement in that process. The nature of that involvement will be affected by the character of your department. If you are responsible for a professional discipline, you may face two levels of scrutiny: that of your professional discipline's accrediting body; and the regional accrediting body that gives a general *imprimatur* to your institution. If there are special state bodies involved in institutional accreditation, you will face yet a third level of scrutiny.

The ultimate goal of all program reviews is an objective, factual assessment of conditions under which students are educated. Essentially, such program reviews look at whether the conditions are those normally associated with acceptable quality. If not, the review normally concludes with recommendations for change and improvement. Seldom does an external agency make direct qualitative judgments about an individual program. It usually assesses a set of indicators, and those indicators are customarily associated with quality.

The key to dealing with program reviews and external accrediting bodies is preparation. Procedures vary from one agency to another, and each defines and describes the standards by which it will review the program. Considerable advance notice of such reviews is almost always available. Generally, a department or program will know at least a year in advance when a review team will be visiting. In the case of a regional accreditation, the lead time is almost always longer than that.

Once notice of a review is confirmed, the protocol for preparing the self-study report is generally put in the chair's hands, along with suggested time frames for completing the essential tasks. With a long period of time available before any formal report is due, it may be tempting to procrastinate. However, a valid program review requires good data, and good data takes time to collect. Often this means conducting surveys of alumni, students, and others. It may also require extensive data gathering in departmental files that may be organized differently from the way that accrediting bodies' information needs demand. Waiting until the last minute before organizing or collecting the required data will in itself leave an impression of a poorly administered department, and may even result in having less than complete or accurate data on which to rely. And bear in mind that your department will have to live with the results of the program review for some years.

The second reason to begin work on the self-study promptly is that this is an opportunity to involve faculty and others in a serious and objective review of the status of departmental programs. By involving as many of the key actors as possible, a self-study can heighten awareness and prepare faulty for eventual changes. Furthermore, involving people in the self-study and providing them with the time and resources to do a thorough job will result in an informed and consistent set of interviews when the accrediting team visits and conducts its review.

Sometimes, departments will use the accrediting process as leverage against the dean or the central administration. They will purposely represent their situation as requiring more new resources and a higher level of priority on the dean's or president's agenda. Professional accrediting bodies may be susceptible to such an appeal. But the chair should be aware that deans and presidents receive reports from all accrediting bodies that visit the institution, and that many of the bodies reach the same conclusion. The resulting impression is that *all* accredited fields seem to need more resources and more attention.

It may be good strategy to put one's case in the strongest terms when an accrediting body is available to support the argument. But there are risks, too. If the field looks too weak, it might provoke the central administration to wonder if it can be fixed at any price—and, therefore, if it would be better to discontinue the program. Chairs are well advised to use the accreditation process to conduct nothing more or less than a strictly objective review. They should foster openness and candor in the process, and should work toward getting the best data available. A cooperative attitude and good-faith preparation of the self-study will serve the whole process well..

Accreditation is an episodic scrutiny, which makes it easy to look on as a distraction. More recent demands by state legislatures have drastically altered the climate of scrutiny from episodic to chronic. Many states are demanding not only more data, but also different data. Their demands reflect the public's interest in the results produced by our educational system, by which they mean everything from pre-K through graduate school. The questions directed at universities are asking for things such as completion rates for students and workloads for faculty. The only place where meaningful data can be collected on these matters is from departments. The university planning office or registrar may be the central depository for the information. The point of origin remains the department. In chapter 13 there is a more detailed discussion of data that a department should track. As chair, you bear major responsibility for creating a climate of dialog in the department that will focus attention on critical data concerning the department. You must create an atmosphere in which the discussion will focus on issues and where "turf wars" are not permitted to dominate the agenda.

COLLABORATION

Perhaps the greatest adjustment in attitude is that reflected in the multiplying collaborations among entities. Economic stress has certainly played a role in this evolution. If combining resources can bring benefits to all concerned, there is a willingness to work through the practical problems for the sake of alleviating economic stress. But that is not the sole root of this change in attitude. Although we may not live consciously with the picture of the globe shot through the window of our first tumbling spacecraft, the meaning of that picture is becoming a part of our basic concept of reality. We are moving toward an understanding of the interconnectedness of phenomena, institutions, and individuals. Our physical connections are also being altered by the explosion of the use of e-mail and the Internet. The meaning of time and space are being reorganized. Both the way in which we perceive and think about the world and the way in which we work in it are being dramatically recast. These shifts make it possible for us to think about problems differently and to create linkages that would never have occurred to us to make even 20 years ago. A few news items from *The Chronicle of Higher Education* serve to illustrate the range of collaborative efforts that are taking place in the country:

- "San Jose State University's library is nearly full, and the City of San Jose's main library is bursting at the seams. So the university and city, in an unusual arrangement, want to create a new facility that they can share" (*Chronicle* 1997, A39).
- *Promising Pell Grants to Sixth-Graders:* Representative Chaka Fattah, a Democrat from Pennsylvania... "is the sponsor of a bill that would guarantee low-income sixth-graders the maximum Pell Grant award when they are admitted to college" (Torricone 1997, A26).
- *A Niche for Scientists from Eastern Europe:* "Their broad training makes them valued partners in collaborations with colleagues from the West" (Bollag 1997, A13).
- *25 Colleges Start Joint Effort to Help Students Find Jobs:* "The group plans to begin sharing information about internships as well as jobs, and is designing a common World Wide Web site through which employers could reach seniors on all 25 campuses" (Gose 1997, A38).
- *States Press Their Colleges to Make Transferring Easier:* "In Texas, for example, Governor George W. Bush last month signed a measure that requires every public college to offer an undergraduate core curriculum that can be automatically transferred to any other public institution in the state. .... Alabama, Arizona, Connecticut, Florida, and Ohio have adopted similar measures" (Schmidt 1997, A28).
- *U.S. Plans to Expand Role of Universities in Helping Developing Nations:* "American universities will play a greater role in efforts by the U.S.

Agency for International Development to improve basic education in developing countries, A.I.D. officials announced last week. ....Emphasis would be placed on improving education for girls, early-childhood development, and technology.... A five-year program...[will] involve more historically black colleges and universities in international partnerships" (Selingo 1997, A50).

- *5 Boston Colleges Join Forces to Seek Economics of Scale:* "Without merging, they will coordinate plans on academics, buildings, and student services" (Nicklin 1996, A37).
- *Three Pennsylvania Colleges Say They Want to Make It Easier to Live Under the Same Roof:* "Dickinson, Gettysburg and Franklin and Marshall Colleges have begun jointly advertising faculty opening on their campuses" (*Chronicle* 1996, A12).

Do these moves toward collaboration affect the work of a chair? Absolutely. The San Jose library collaboration will affect the library resources available to departments, and that effect should be to increase available resources, even if it does not directly alter the library budget line controlled by individual departments. If Representative Fattah's proposed legislation is passed, it implies that departments would do well to expand their view of "prospective students" down to the middle school level. The collaboration between East European and western scientists should raise the question of intellectual collaboration or cooperation between any department and selected colleagues overseas. The case studies cited are in the sciences, and one might be tempted to say that in a technical discipline such exchange may be fruitful, but it can hardly be applied usefully in the humanities. This need not be true. For example, exchange over interpretations of the American Revolution among scholars in different countries is likely to produce some new and interesting insights for all concerned.

The collaboration on internships is one that could be readily applied to other institutional groupings. To be useful to students' disciplinary studies, departments will need to become involved in the design of these experiences. The easing of transfer procedures between two- and four-year programs cannot be effected without detailed coordination between parallel departments in both levels of institution. The overseas initiatives being pursued by A.I.D. will not be realized without direct cooperation from specific academic departments. An arrangement such as the five-college Boston collaboration will affect operations on all the campuses, all the way down to the level of academic programs and the hiring of their staffs. The Pennsylvania colleges that agreed to ease the moves of two-career families have agreed to advertise their openings conjointly, a step that requires coordination among different disciplines across institutional lines.

These are but examples that provide a random picture of the variety of collaborative arrangements that are being pursued. The possibilities remain infinite. What is important to keep in mind is that the dimension in which you lead the department should not be limited to concern for the department as a discipline unit or for the department as a stand-alone entity within the university.

CONCLUSION

Departmental horizons need to be broad. It is important to see the discipline linked to cognate intellectual fields. And it is vital to see the department in relationship to the university and not as an embattled fiefdom within the university. Lastly, it is necessary to remain aware of interests beyond the university, for many of these now are having a direct effect on the daily life of departments. The development of the nation and the emergence of public education have gone virtually hand-in-hand. But our educational system is becoming "public" in new ways. No longer content to feed institutional budgets, the public wants to know about the quality of what we produce. This means that higher education institutions are in the public eye in ways heretofore undreamed of. That public dimension has already embraced some chairs and will affect more as time passes. This means that a chair must be adept (and hopefully enjoy) working with a far wider range of audiences than once imagined. No chair can personally manage all these connections. What a chair can do is initiate and lead the dialog within the department so that as a collective body the department faculty can expand its focus, select its course of action, and share the responsibility of implementation.

REFERENCES

American Association of Higher Education (AAHE). 1987. *National directory of school-college partnerships: Current models and practices.* Washington.
    In publishing this directory, AAHE signaled the importance of the practice of partnerships. The variety of arrangements has grown in the intervening years.

Bollag, Burton. 1997. A niche for scientist from Eastern Europe. *The Chronicle of Higher Education* (25 July): A13.

The Chronicle of Higher Education. 1997. (18 April): A39.

The Chronicle of Higher Education. 1996. (25 November): A12.

Creswell, John W., Daniel W. Wheeler, Alan T. Seagren, Nancy J. Egly, and Kirk D. Beyer. 1990. *The academic chairperson's handbook.* Lincoln: University of Nebraska Press.
    The handbook is based on a study of 200 chairs on 70 campuses. The full scope of chair concerns is treated, with much of the material in the form of comments

from working chairs for which the authors provide a theoretical framework. The emphasis does lean toward a concern for the development and interests of faculty viewed from an individual rather than a department/collective position.

Edwards, Richard L., and Elizabeth A.S. Benefield. 1997. *Building a strong foundation: Fundraising for non-profits.* Washington: National Association of Social Workers Press.

Although published by the National Association of Social Workers Press, this slim volume is a good, basic introduction to the subject of fund-raising. It gives background information on the current context of fund-raising in terms of who gives and why; it reviews the actual process of seeking funds and then goes on to discuss several special topics such as planned giving and special events. Its greatest value to a department chair may be that it is written for the non-professional fund-raiser.

Franklin, Wilbur P., and Leo M. Lambert, eds. 1995. *Linking America's schools and colleges: A guide to partnerships and national directory.* Washington: American Association for Higher Education.

This builds on the 1987 AAHE national directory of school- college/university linkages.

Further Education Unit. 1994. *Approaches to partnerships: Who shares wins.* London, England.

The collaborative arrangements described in 14 case studies link British technical colleges with external partners. Some of the linkages would be on the cutting edge in the United States, involving, as they do, sharing resources and engaging in joint program planning. The guidelines for setting up partnerships are worth reviewing.

Gose, Ben. 1997. 25 colleges start joint effort to help students find jobs. *The Chronicle of Higher Education* (20 July): A38.

Kells, H.R. 1995. *Self-study processes: A guide to self-evaluation in higher education.* Phoenix: American Council on Education and Oryx Press.

Accreditation visits rely on departmental self-study exercises, for which this extensive handbook is a useful tool. Aside from practical guidance in the process of self-study, it approaches that task as an exercise primarily useful to the unit itself. The fact that the author works internationally brings an even wider vision to this subject, which has generated concern for tertiary education around the world.

Massy, William F., Andrea K. Wilger, and Carol Colbeck. 1994. Overcoming "hollowed" collegiality. *Change* (July-August):11– 20.

This provocative and insightful article does much to illuminate the phenomena that have eroded collegiality—and, therefore, effective collective activity within departments.

Mercer, Joye. 1997. Private giving to colleges increased 11.8% in 1996, reaching $14.2 billion. *The Chronicle of Higher Education* (30 May): A41.

Murphy, Mary K., ed. 1992. *Building bridges: Fund raising for deans, faculty and development officers.* Washington: Council for the Advancement and Support of Education.

The primary audience for this monograph is institutional deans. However, George H. Jones ("Involving Faculty in Development") and James J. Boyle ("Academic Quality and Resources: Factors Influencing Fund Raising") write from a perspective that is useful to department chairs. A chair who becomes active in the area of fund-raising (beyond the traditionally academic avenue of grant writing) will need to rely on the literature addressed to presidents and chief academic officers.

Nicklin, Julie L. 1996. 5 Boston colleges join forces to seek economies of scale. *The Chronicle of Higher Education* (1 November): A37.

Reaching for College. 1992. Rockville, Md.: Westat.

Volume I reports on 48 school-college collaborations developed in 20 states and the District of Columbia. The approaches are varied. Detailed program summaries are provided. Volume II contains a set of six case studies focused on preparing high school students for college.

Schmidt, Peter. 1997. States press their colleges to make transferring easier. *The Chronicle of Higher Education* (18 July): A28

Selingo, Jeffrey. 1997. U.S. plans to expand role of universities in helping developing nations. *The Chronicle of Higher Education* (25 July): A50.

Torricone, Celeste. 1997. Promising pell grants to sixth graders. *The Chronicle of Higher Education* (11 July): A26.

EPILOGUE

I t has become a cliché to say that higher education is in a state of
fundamental and ongoing change. However, like many a cliché, that
statement has validity. What is emerging with ever greater clarity is the
realization that college and university departments, divisions, or program
units are at the center of the maelstrom. The logical follow-on to that insight
is to understand that the person designated as leader of that unit, be s/he
called chair, head, or any of a series of titles used in our institutions, holds a
position of rare and unusual responsibility. Note: we speak of responsibility
rather than power.

Departments are the heart and soul of our postsecondary institutions. They
serve as the home of disciplinary knowledge and as the intellectual and social
base for faculty. Departments are the organizational units that define, design,
and deliver curricula—the fundamental product of our colleges and universities. Departments are the organizational units that provide the intellectual
substance to students, and only departments can guarantee the quality of that
substance. While students, have responsibility for their learning, departments
are responsible for assisting students in perfecting their capacity to learn and
in guiding them as they select a course of study from a given curriculum. It is
chairs who hold symbolic and practical responsibility for departmental quality,
and it is chairs who are called to account if the department is derelict in its
performance. Thus, like it or not, chairs are designated leaders.

Both chairs and college/university administrators concede that more is
expected of chairs today than 20 years ago. Moreover, the change goes well
beyond the issues of quantity and rising standards of quality. It is the very
nature of the work itself that is in metamorphosis. Insofar as chairs of the

1990s are working in the midst of this unsettling process, their lives are particularly difficult. Earlier patterns of behavior exist while new ones are being defined and instituted. Dearly held beliefs and standards are asserted even when they are no longer appropriate to current reality.

At the end of this journey through the chair's new geography, some concluding definitions are in order. Two changes are redefining the chair's universe. One is the place of departments within institutions, and the other is the balance between individual faculty interests and the collective responsibilities of the faculty. Both changes are redefining the work of chairs.

Twenty years ago chairs could focus almost exclusively on the interests of their departments with limited concern for the activities of other departments. While chairs might keep an eye on the work of their near-discipline neighbors, departments in other schools or disciplinary sectors were rarely a concern. The major work of chairs used to be as advocates of their department's interests. A chair's success could be predicated upon her or his relative success in wresting institutional resources for the use of the department—be those resources money, space, or personnel. Today, chairs still need to be advocates of their departments' interests, but those interests must be pursued under a different banner. The question is, how does the department support/advance the interests on the institution and, ultimately, of society? A chair needs to educate the administrators to whom s/he reports about the discipline, and how it contributes on the institutional and societal mission. When seeking resources, a chair needs to state what the department requires to carry out its responsibilities, but that, too, must be done with an understanding of a broader context.

In advocating for resources, chairs need to be prepared to do several things. At a basic minimum, they need to be prepared to demonstrate how effectively they are using the resources given by the institution and, most importantly, describe the results obtained. This is a type of accountability that was not asked of chairs two decades ago. Another new feature of the landscape is that chairs need to think more broadly about resources than exclusively for *their* department. They need to look for ways to share resources with cognate departments to advance multiple rather than singular interests. This means cultivating contacts with colleague chairs whom they need to see as *colleagues* rather than as rivals. And chairs need to become part of the team that seeks to add resources to the institution rather than just expend them. That search can no longer be limited to grant writing. It may mean making contacts within the community and collaborating with the university development office. In other words, what is needed today from chairs in terms of resource management is accountability for what is used, collaboration in the application of resources, and entrepreneurship in their creation.

The other transformation affecting the work of chairs is the change in the balance between individual faculty interests and the collective responsibilities of the faculty. Twenty years ago department colleagues looked to the chair as the champion of their individual interests and rights. Department faculty expected the chair to plead for travel funds and salary increases. They expected their chair to champion their applications for institutional grants and promotions. Once tenure was gained, department faculty assumed that their chair would mostly support their requests—be it for a preferred time slot to teach a class, relief from teaching introductory freshman sections, the need for a larger library budget, course relief to perform committee work or prepare for a new class, encouragement to develop a course in a favorite area of research without regard for the needs or nature of the student body.

Chairs certainly need to continued to be advocates for individual faculty, but when lending support to individual proposals s/he must see to melding a set of individuals into a functioning group, if not an all-star team. Again, what is changing is the definition of responsibility, and in this case the transformation is fundamental. The core of this shift is embodied in the emphasis on learning as distinguished from teaching. Through the long history of education the emphasis has been on admitting a select group to the mysteries of learning. That meant that the focus of attention was on the process of teaching and on the teacher—and within universities that meant the individual faculty member. In measuring quality, one looked at the performance of faculty as individuals.

As we shift our assumptions from education as a privilege to education as a fundamental necessity, attention moves to the product education and, therefore, to students and their learning. Quality of teaching is measurable only through the results obtained from students. That shift in focus—and it is fundamental—has major implications for the work of departments. It means that we now need to measure success not only in terms of individual faculty performance but also in terms of the collective result obtained by the department. Therefore, we need to look at the quality of curricula and methods of pedagogy as we assess department outcomes.

In the United States we are fascinated by the concept of "leadership." We are always searching for it—even when we have difficulty defining it—and we are swift in dismissing someone as "showing no leadership." At the same time—and academe follows this pattern—we exhibit a propensity to undermine the efforts of anyone who in good faith attempts to exert leadership. Our attitudes toward leadership create a perfect Charles Heller "catch 22"— damned if you do and damned if you don't, with no hope for success. If ambivalence toward leaders is a general social characteristic in the United States, department chairs struggle with this ambivalence in particularly acute form. As one scans the titles assigned to departments, which range from chair, to head, division chair, program head, director, chair and professor, associate professor, and even assistant professor, or professor and chair, one can see the myriad possibilities for defining roles and responsibilities of the persons so designated. The probability that all relevant parties—the chair, department faculty, students, staff, and administrators—produce the same definition of the role for any of these designations is slim indeed. Then all the personal ambiguities and tensions exist between being responsible for a collective of faculty and remaining a faculty member—teacher and researcher—in one's own right. In this landscape of contradiction, what does it mean to be a leader?

In earlier parts of the text we have emphasized the importance of shaping dialog, both its content and atmosphere. Academic departments are capable of developing great skill in chasing trivia, avoiding closure, and delaying decision. Department chairs can exert major influence in transforming those habits when they exist chronically or in defusing them when they emerge episodically. The opportunity for productive discussion is crucially affected by the "rules of dialog" that are established in any group. If innuendo, "put downs," or "nay-saying" become habitual, the issues will not be explored seriously and openly and problems will not find timely solutions. Chairs have immense potential in setting both the tone and content of departmental dialog, and it is that power, as noted earlier in the text, that is perhaps the most potent of a chair's powers. We may fail to recognize this as power because of a penchant to think of power as the capacity to make "the other" blink. We equate power with the capacity to threaten or even to do harm. While that kind of power certainly exists and there may even be occasions when it is appropriate to make use of it, chairs possess very little of that kind of power. On the other hand, when the power of influence is used to create a collectivity that can work through disagreement, join together in vigorous dialog, and take action, the chair has extraordinary power.

We spoke earlier of higher education being caught in a maelstrom of change. Returning to that theme, perhaps the most fundamental of those changes has to do with our concepts of the role of education. In chapter 1 we described the impact of the GI Bill on higher education in the United States. The fact is that from the moment the Republic was established, the United States was launched on a path toward mass education. This is a unique experiment in human history and one that is gradually being imitated with varying pace throughout the globe. Learning began as the exclusive domain of a very small elite. Century by century literacy and numerously has been extended to more and more participants. In the United States we have moved to a point where education, not just at the elementary or secondary level but at the postsecondary and postbaccalaureate level, is open to one and all regardless of age, race, color, creed, or sex. Yes, we acknowledge that the statement is theoretical and that practical limitations exist. Nonetheless, throughout our postsecondary system today retirees are collecting baccalaureates along with recent immigrants and African Americans; and more than half of those baccalaureates are being picked up by women.

A major leadership challenge for chairs is the broadening of vision—their own and those of their colleagues—about the nature of faculty work and the place of the collective department within the university, the community, and society. Certainly 50 years ago, and perhaps even 25 years ago, chairing a department involved working in a cosseted, private, predictable world. Faculty were drawn from similar backgrounds, and students came with broadly the same assumptions and values. Today there is need for the ability to hear different voices and to be able to sustain new conversations, with both students and faculty colleagues. There was a time when chairs could rightfully consider their primary task as being the advocate for their faculty—often for their separate individual interests. Advocacy, individual and collective, is a legitimate activity for any chair. However, advocacy today needs to be balanced with an understanding of how other interests are affected by that advocacy. That means the chair must understand and respect the interests of other departments, the university as an institution, and social bodies beyond the university. The chair has the power to guide the department's reactions to those interests by playing on fear, distrust, and paranoia, or by encouraging listening, sharing, and collaboration.

Chairing a department is perhaps the most complex and ambiguous of leadership positions. The challenges higher education faces today will be met successfully only with the vigorous participation and intelligent support of its departments. And those departments depend in turn on their own internal synergy and the skill, imagination, and daring of their chairs.

INDEX